CREATING PLAYFUL, FUN, AND EFFECTIVE USER

D1002580

# Seductive
## INTERACTION
## DESIGN

*Stephen P. Anderson*

# Seductive Interaction Design:
## Creating Playful, Fun, and Effective User Experiences

Stephen P. Anderson

New Riders
1249 Eighth Street
Berkeley, CA 94710
510/524-2178
510/524-2221 (fax)

Find us on the Web at: www.newriders.com
To report errors, please send a note to errata@peachpit.com
New Riders is an imprint of Peachpit, a division of Pearson Education.

Copyright © 2011 by PoetPainter, LLC.

Editor: Michael J. Nolan
Development Editor: Margaret Anderson/Stellarvisions
Production Editor: Tracey Croom
Copyeditor: Gretchen Dykstra
Indexer: James Minkin
Proofreader: Jan Seymour
Book Designer: Stephen P. Anderson
Compositor: Kim Scott, Bumpy Design
Cover Image:  Richard Cote, courtesy of iStockphoto

## Notice of Rights

All rights reserved. No part of this book may be reproduced or transmitted in any form by any means, electronic, mechanical, photocopying, recording, or otherwise, without the prior written permission of the publisher. For information on getting permission for reprints and excerpts, contact permissions@peachpit.com.

## Notice of Liability

The information in this book is distributed on an "As Is" basis without warranty. While every precaution has been taken in the preparation of the book, neither the author nor Peachpit shall have any liability to any person or entity with respect to any loss or damage caused or alleged to be caused directly or indirectly by the instructions contained in this book or by the computer software and hardware products described in it.

## Trademarks

Many of the designations used by manufacturers and sellers to distinguish their products are claimed as trademarks. Where those designations appear in this book, and Peachpit was aware of a trademark claim, the designations appear as requested by the owner of the trademark. All other product names and services identified throughout this book are used in editorial fashion only and for the benefit of such companies with no intention of infringement of the trademark. No such use, or the use of any trade name, is intended to convey endorsement or other affiliation with this book.

ISBN 13: 978-0-321-72552-3
ISBN 10: 0-321-72552-2

9 8 7 6 5 4 3

Printed and bound in the United States of America

*For Erin, my love…*
*my half of the world belongs to you.*

## ACKNOWLEDGMENTS

Writing a book is a painful process. And then you start the even more painful process of revisions, editing, and layout! But like all things that stretch and challenge us, when you reach the end, you find the pride and joy of accomplishment. For this, I have many people to thank.

In no particular order, my thanks go to...

**Kathy Sierra**, whose writings have been an inspiration to many of us. It was her post on "cognitive seduction" that helped form my initial musings on seductive interactions.

**Matt Jones** and **Matt Biddulph** for bringing Dopplr into the world. This Web app proved, in many different ways, that there is room for delight in the services we use.

**Joshua Porter**. While Joshua is certainly not the first person to talk about design and psychology, his book *Designing for the Social Web* and the many posts on Bokardo have been instrumental in advancing this bridge between the academic and industrial.

**Kevin Cornell**, for contributing his brilliant illustrations. Without them, this book wouldn't be nearly as classy nor as fun.

My friend and mentor **Robert Moore**, whose remarkable approach to design—one that focuses first and foremost on human *insights*—forever changed how I approach design.

**Jesse James Garret**, **Jared Spool**, and **Andy Budd**, for believing in me and giving me a platform to spread this message at their respective events.

**Lou Rosenfeld** and **Michael Nolan**, for seeing that there was a book ready to be written. Also to **Margaret Anderson** and the entire development team at New Riders. I'm certain you're ready to throttle me, after this process. But I think we'd all agree we've created something beautiful to see and read.

**Giles Colborne**, **Trevor van Gorp**, **BJ Fogg**, **Aarron Walter**, **Buster Benson**, **Adam Connor**, **Garrett Dimon**, and **Ruben Gazki** for kindly sharing your thoughts in interviews. While we had cut a lot of content, including several interviews, rest assured, that content will be seen by the world.

**Jared Christensen**, **Christian Bradford**, and **John Gibbard** for stepping in at the last minute to help me get across the finish line.

**Patti's Place**, for offering the most wonderful environment one could possibly dream of for writing a book (not to mention the best soups and hot tea in Dallas).

**Mrs. Zehentmayr** and **Karen Heid-Cooke**, for igniting curious young minds and fanning the flames.

**My family** for, well, everything!

It goes without saying that a book demands a lot of time and energy. Being a parent to four wonderful boys, **Gabriel, Liam, Elijah**, and **Jonas**, demands even more time and energy. Without my wife **Erin**'s support, this book would not have been possible. It's not easy for her to be married to an obsessive personality, and this project only exacerbated my worst tendencies. She's taken on more than anyone should ever ask, and even stepped in to rescue me when things got most difficult. For her enduring support and for being the center to our family during this time, I owe more than I'll every be able to repay. Thank you. I love you.

This is an undertaking I would not have pursued had there not been an overwhelming desire to hear more about this topic. For everyone who attended one of my talks, downloaded my slides on SlideShare, or otherwise indulged my interest in human behavior—I thank you. C.S. Lewis once wrote that "We do not write in order to be understood; we write in order to understand." While this passion for learning is certainly true in my case, the learning has been a whole lot easier with so much interest and support. Thank you all.

And finally, thanks goes to Christina Wodtke, Cennydd Bowles, Richard Dalton, Donna Spencer, Rahul Choudhury, Kelsey Ruger, Kevin Cheng, Nick Finck, Livia Labate, Travis Isaacs, Jeremy Dunck, Jeroen van Geel, Whitney Hess, Chris Pallé, Chris Fahey, Dan Lockton, Dan Brown, Jeremy Johnson, Peter Merholz, Sebastian Deterding, Amy Jo Kim, Luke Wroblewski, Bill Scott, Todd Zaki Warfel, Russ Unger, Jay Morgan, Chris Bernard, Wade Winningham, Paula Thornton, Dave Gray, Alex Bischoff, Dirk Knemeyer, Peter Boersma, Bill DeRouchey, Carolyn Wood, Brandon Schauer, Kaleem, John Moore, Candy Bernhardt, John Weiss, Matt Heard, Aaron Martin, Matt Donovan, Thomas Vander Wal, Andrew Hinton, Matthew Milan, Erica O'Grady, Jay Fichialos, Ken Starzer, Jess McMullin, Matt Donovan, and the dozens of other people I'm certain I'm forgetting. Your work, conversations, and encouragement have truly been a blessing.

## PHOTO/IMAGE CREDITS

Cover, Image courtesy of iStockphoto, © Richard Cote , Image 10745904

Chapter 1, page 10, Increasing Motivation graphic, © Joshua Porter

Section One, page 14, Photo © Kate Tegtmeyer

Chapter 4, page 28, Shell station gas pump, © Sean Munson

Chapter 4,  page 31, Photo courtesy of iStockphoto, © Reuben Schulz, Image 8348251

Chapter 6, page 45, Photo courtesy of iStockphoto, © Faruk Ulay, Image 5642231

Chapter 7, page 49, Photo courtesy of iStockphoto, © poco_bw, Image 9386202

Chapter 7, page 49, Photo courtesy of iStockphoto, © Tom Fullum, Image 12307171

Section Two, page 52, Photo courtesy of iStockphoto, © Linda Kloosterhof, Image 12356048

Chapter 9, page 66, Oh No you broke it image, © Simon Q

Chapter 9, page 67, Wii Help cat photo, © Christian Bradford

Chapter 10, page 74, Photo courtesy of iStockphoto, © Zmeel Photography, Image 8750165

Chapter 10, page 78, Photo courtesy of iStockphoto, © Cindy England, Image 2915742,

Section Three, page 90, Photo courtesy of iStockphoto, © Damir Spanic, Image 7687236

Chapter 13, page 99, Photo courtesy of iStockphoto, © Dan Driedger, Image 7689045

Chapter 18, page 138, Bringing browser to life, © Eirik Helland Urke

Section Four, page 146, Photo courtesy of iStockphoto, © PeskyMonkey, Image 5100704

Chapter 19, page 150, Gamification slide, © Matthew Guy

Chapter 20, page 157, Badges, buttons and stickers shot, © Nan Palmero

Chapter 20, page 158, Photo courtesy of iStockphoto, © stockcam, Image 13216896

Chapter 20, page 167, Photo courtesy of iStockphoto, © Artem Povarov, Image 14028131

Chapter 22, page 182, Target checkout screen, © Dennis Crowley

Chapter 23, page 191, Matrix relating psychology and game mechanics, © Bunchball

Chapter 23, page 197  The Garden images , © Natron Baxter

Chapter 25, page 215,  Motivation Mechanics model, © Sharleen Sy

All Spot Illustrations, throughout text, © Kevin Cornell

# Contents

SECTION TWO
Playful Seduction

## SECTION THREE
## The Subtle Art of Seduction

SECTION FOUR
The Game of Seduction

# Prologue

This book is primarily about principles of human behavior: why people do the things they do, feel the things they feel, and make particular choices.

But there's more to this book.

If trying to understand human behavior was the only goal, I'd have stopped by now and pointed you to dozens of other (much better) books on the subject.

I've spent the last decade trying to design the experiences people have online. I suspect that your own entry into user experience started with an established discipline such as library sciences, visual design, computer science, or education.

I formally entered the design field as a Web and graphics designer for a technology start-up, during the dot-com boom (and subsequent bust). But prior to that, I taught high school English classes.

Like all teachers, my first year was a survival story: getting lesson plans done, photocopying assignments before the morning bell rang, wondering why anyone would put up with ninth graders for such a measly salary! My second year, things began looking up. I cracked the code, and figured out how to motivate students. I had lessons I could improve upon. And I started getting curious—what could the sciences teach me about how we learn? Or how things stick in memory? Most of what I read at that time could be classified as pop psychology—secondhand accounts of "brain science" studies. But, there were interesting nuggets in there. For example, did you know that a steady diet of chocolate actually keeps the brain more engaged? (On that one, we may have violated a few policies on food in the classroom.) One study of particular interest involved our sense of smell and memory. I had been reading Robert Jütte's 2004 book *A History of the Senses* and I stumbled across this interesting remark:

*"Our sense of smell is most directly linked to memory."*

Hmm—smell and memory are linked. I began thinking about how this could be applied to some of our creative writing assignments. What followed was a rather interesting experiment. I collected a bunch of film canisters (this was in the days before digital photography). Inside each small container, I placed a strong smell: spices from the kitchen, a cotton ball soaked in Kool-Aid or Sprite, a squirt of toothpaste. The instructions were simple. Each student was to grab a single canister, open it, smell, and write about the memories that came to mind. I was testing the science I had read about: Would using smell as the trigger for a creative writing assignment result in more vivid writing?

Fast forward to the present.

I no longer teach in the formal sense. The last decade has been spent helping all manner of companies improve their online and offline presence. But this same inquisitiveness pervades everything I do. If I know x, how might I apply that to my current project? If, for example, I read a study about how an energy company added an emoticon to their customers' energy bills, and this influenced the amount of energy used, I want to know if this same psychology might work in other contexts. What effect would adding an emoticon have on online data? We're talking about behavior. While context does have some effect on how we behave, people are people. The things that occur internally when we make a decision should be roughly consistent with the things that frustrate or delight us. When people ask if some of the "playful" ideas I suggest would work for business software, I respond: "Is there a human involved?"

Regardless of context, there are some universal patterns of behavior that, once understood, can help us design better interactions. This book is about some of those ideas—principles of human behavior—and how they might be used to improve the design of interactions. In this book, I try to bridge academic theory with practical Web application. I look at some of the fascinating studies that have been done in behavioral economics or neuroscience and ask, "Can we apply this to an interactive context?" I see my role as connecting theory with practice.

The ideas presented here are precisely that:

ideas. Some of them are my own. Many more of them I've collected as online examples of the psychology I find so fascinating. Some of these have been tested, and proved to positively affect business goals such as conversion, sign-ups, or sharing. Many others are waiting to be tested and proven. The psychology has been demonstrated in other fields. Let's test out these ideas in an online context.

In my early days as a designer, I focused on how things looked. This led to a few years of thinking about larger brand and marketing issues. Then, I learned about making things more usable. My design skills only improved. And then I worked on a project with thousands of pages, forcing me to blueprint the page types and relationships; I began practicing information architecture before I knew that's what it was called.

This led to a "seat at the table" in discussions on product strategy and business goals. I began seeing the much bigger world of concerns: constraints of technology platforms and budgets, the ecosystem of partners and relationships, balancing the needs of current customers while moving ahead, dealing with corporate politics. All this led me back to that same place I arrived in my brief career as an educator: What motivates people? What makes people tick? If I could understand that, I'd be much better at my job, whatever my title or role became.

What I've tried to do in this book is to collect some curious insights into human behavior, and suggest how we might apply those insights to all kinds of interaction design. Understanding human behavior is really the only way to make effective designs. Whether your priority is delighting customers or making a business financially successful, how else can you evaluate the effectiveness of design choices? Even simple things such as an appreciation of visual design (or "aesthetics") have deepened as my focus shifted from beautiful designs to the effect of those designs on people. In writing this book, my hope is that you can share in and experience this same shift in focus.

Enjoy the ride!

*We do not write in order to be understood; we write in order to understand.*

—C. S. LEWIS

# CHAPTER 1

# Why Seductive Interactions?

THE SETTING IS the Odenplan Metro Station in Stockholm, but we could easily be in the subway in New York or the Tube in London. There's an escalator running next to a set of stairs, both leading up into the daylight. Only today something is different. An experiment is taking place. The stairs seemingly have been transformed into piano keys. Not only do they resemble the familiar black-and-white keys of a piano, but through the magic of technology—sensors attached to speakers—every step triggers the resonant sound of a piano key.

We watch as two people start to take the escalator, pause, then place a foot on the first step. A low, loud note rings through the station. They each take a few more steps, caution

transforming into more of a leap in their step. The air is filled with the sound of a musical scale. We see more people approach, just curious at first, but soon they are delighted. For some people the goal is no longer to even exit the station—they step back and forth across the keys to create a melody.

*What's going on here?*

This is an experiment in behavior change: "Can we get more people to choose the stairs by making it fun to do?"

As the video continues, we see that most people choose to abandon the escalator in favor of the makeshift piano key stairs. In fact, on the day this experiment was run, "66 percent more people than normal took the stairs."

This little experiment in human behavior is a good distillation of the kinds of things we'll discuss in this book: ways to influence behavior through fun, playful activities. More specifically, we'll learn how the same tactics we use to attract a mate can apply to interactions between humans and interactive devices.

As our focus is on human behavior, in all kinds of contexts, both physical and digital, let's couple the piano stairs with a second story, this one taking place on a Web site.

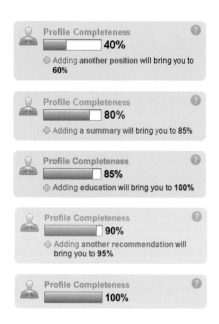

## LINKEDIN AND PROFILE COMPLETENESS

If you were signed up with the professional networking site LinkedIn prior to 2004, then you may remember when they rolled out their Profile Completeness feature (see above). Like many other people, I had a rather anemic profile. I had set up basic account information and added my current employer, but that was about it. Then I got an e-mail about profile completeness. It turns out that my profile completeness was only about 25 percent. But, by adding another position I could be 40 percent complete. That was a simple enough request. So, I added my last employer. Then I got another prompt: "Adding a summary will bring you to 55 percent." So I did that. And so on. Through a series of prompts, eventually my profile was 100 percent complete. My profile now listed past and present employers, my education, a summary, recommendations, and other details you might find on a resume. LinkedIn had somehow managed to pull quite a bit of information out of me. And not just me, but thousands of other users. What's interesting to note is that this little feature wasn't difficult to develop. It didn't require a skilled information architect. It wasn't even a visual design challenge. It was psychology that made this feature so effective. Understanding just a little bit about what motivates people resulted in more people sharing their information and using the LinkedIn service.

The question I like to ask with examples like these is, "Why does this work?" What are the underlying psychological principles that made this an effective feature? In game design, this is an example of *progress dynamic*. And we see this not only in games, with points and levels, but also in other contexts, such as martial arts. Think of the different colored belts you earn while advancing toward a black belt. What would happen if, on the first day of training, the instructor told a young boy, "Stick with it,

work hard, and maybe in ten years you'll be a black belt like me." This goal would seem unattainable. By having different colored belts (and stripes on each belt), you get rewarded and recognized along the path to mastery. These belts are a tangible, achievable goal to work toward, and once acquired, they signal to you and others: look at how far I've progressed!

But this still doesn't answer the question, "Why does this work?" At least not in a way that we can use in another context. And that's what this book is concerned with: why we do the things we do. In the case of colored belts, points, levels, and progress meters, we could look at several ideas from psychology:

- *Sequencing.* We are more likely to take action when complex tasks are broken down into smaller tasks.
- *Appropriate challenges.* We delight in challenges, especially ones that strike a balance between being overwhelming and being boring.
- *Status.* We constantly assess how interactions enhance or diminish our standing relative to others and our personal best.
- *Achievements.* We are more likely to engage in activities in which meaningful achievements are recognized.

This is the perspective I'd like to offer throughout this book—one that looks for the underlying reasons behind the things we do. If we look at examples like piano stairs or percentage completeness, what principles can we take away from them? And how can we apply these principles to our own projects? More specifically, how can we use these principles to help

people to fall in love with our Web sites, applications, and services? This leads us into the idea of seduction.

## WHY SEDUCTION?

With a title like *Seductive Interaction Design*, we'd better start by clarifying what this book is (and is not!) about.

Seduction is defined as:

*"the process of deliberately enticing a person to engage in some sort of behavior, ~~frequently sexual in nature.~~"*

(For our purposes, we'll ignore that last bit.)

Even at that, "seduction" might seem a rather strong (and odd) choice of words, especially if we're talking about things like increasing conversion on an e-commerce site, or getting people to complete their profiles or write a review for your product. Can these kinds of online interactions really be considered seductive?

One negative meaning of the word seduce is "to lead astray." In that sense, you might think of tricking someone into engaging in behavior they might not otherwise pursue. Think of the Sirens from Greek mythology, who lured sailors to their death with their irresistible song, or the famous eighteenth-century womanizer, Casanova.

But seduction can be seen in another way, as a critical part of attraction. To be seductive is to be tempting or attractive.

In this sense, seduction means "to be led along." In nature, seduction is seen when the peacock shows off his plumage to attract a mate, or when humans flirt and play to get to know each other more intimately. Courtroom lawyers are skilled at seducing jurors through carefully chosen words. Great speakers know how to seduce an audience. Even well designed experiences such as Disney World are essentially seductive interactions. And ask any parent: children have to be seduced into doing the right things. We may use other words, like motivate, persuade, or inspire. But in these cases, there is nothing insidious about seduction. It is a necessary and critical game we all play in most areas of our lives. (Whether we're any good at it or not, that's another matter.)

### Why should the things we're building be seductive?

See if this sounds familiar:

You've got a great site (or Web application). People seem to like it. It does fine in usability testing. Maybe you have some outstanding feature requests, but nothing big. In fact, there's nothing particularly wrong with what you've built. But, maybe you've observed some of these problems:

- High bounce rate: people come, but never come back.
- Low adoption: people just aren't using the service. Maybe it's an enterprise app that only 10 percent of employees are using. Maybe it's a startup with few active users.
- Too few registered users: your measure of success is sign-ups or registered users, but people aren't even doing this.
- No differentiation from the competition: you're in a crowded space and the differences between your product and others are too subtle.

- Very few referrals: people just aren't interested in telling their friends about you.
- No clickthroughs on e-mail campaigns.

We could go on, but you get the idea. If your app could speak for itself, it might say: "I'm a great app, if people would just get to know me."

A few years ago, I began observing some of these same problems on two very different projects. One was a media focused software application for a very large electronics retailer. The other was a small technology start-up in the search engine space. In both cases we found that when we walked people through a demo, they generally liked what they saw. But, these applications did a terrible job of selling themselves. Here were two very good applications that people liked and might use—once they got to know them. But that's the problem—outside of a usability lab or the urging of a good friend—few people would take the 5, 10, or 15 minutes needed to get to know these applications. And this is where I began thinking about seductive interactions.

Think of our products as that geeky friend, you know the one—they are the nicest person in the world, or have really great ideas about things. But, they have poor social skills. Maybe they have a difficult time striking up a conversation. Or they need substantial conversational support from friends. Teaching them to be seductive may call for some simple confidence-building exercises. Or maybe a few conversation starters and icebreakers would help. They could also learn to listen and ask interesting questions.

This geeky friend is most of the software and sites we have to interact with. They may be interesting, but we're not going to stick around to find out. Even in corporate environments, industries will spend millions of dollars to roll out some new platform, only to be shocked that no one is using it! Now imagine if that software is an online service. There are no sunk costs to compel you to use the application. Instead, there are billions of Web pages. Free trial accounts. Low monthly subscriptions with no commitments. And there's a new technology start-up launched every day. That's a lot of competition. How can you possibly stand out? We need to learn a bit about seduction—*why* were people seduced by stairs disguised as piano stairs and profile completeness progress bars? We need to learn how to "deliberately entice a person to engage in some sort of behavior."

## THE iLIKE STORY

I mentioned that one of the projects I worked on was a media-focused software application. As part of the design process, I looked at dozens of music and media sites. Many of the sites I looked at were start-ups. And consistent with the problem I described earlier, my first experience with most of these services was so brief or unremarkable that I never came back. With some of these sites I created an account, but they did such a poor job of introducing themselves and letting me know why I should care, that I doubt I'll ever go back. I may even tell others not to bother, possibly for completely wrong reasons.

In contrast, the experience at iLike stood out as positive (as did BLIP.fm). Let's look specifically the iLike *registration* process.

The first few pages of the iLike sign-up process were nice, but unremarkable. They didn't ask for too much information. And they were very clear about why they were asking for the things they did. It's obvious why my e-mail address and a password would be required. But my zip code? They offered very clear (and brief) help text explaining that giving them my zip code would let them notify me whenever my favorite bands were in town. They emphasized that providing this information might benefit *me*. I'm sure they have plenty of business reasons for wanting my personal data—demographics, targeted marketing promotions, and so on—none of which I care about particularly. But their reasons were stated in terms of how it would benefit *me* to provide this information. Think about our dating analogy. At least as far back as Dale Carnegie's 1930s book *How to Win Friends and Influence People*, we've known that we are more interested in people who are interested in us. No one wants to sit and hear someone talk about themselves all night. The same is true in many online interactions.

There were a few other conveniences during the registration process. iLike made it easy to invite more friends by sharing my e-mail information. They also offered the iLike sidebar, an iTunes plug-in that monitors what I'm listening to in order to make better recommendations.

While convenient, none of this was particularly remarkable. It's what came next that got my attention.

In almost every other sign-up process for a music site—or any site that wants to find out your personal favorites—there's a page where you're asked to list your favorite bands. I call it the big, empty text box. It looks something like this:

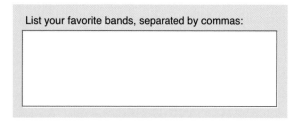

And we dutifully list a handful of favorite bands (or movies, or hobbies, or what have you).

iLike, however, never gave me the chance to *list* my favorite bands. Instead, they showed me a page with 35 artists and simply asked me to "click on your favorite artists." The Beatles. Radiohead. Coldplay. This was fun. I got to the bottom of the page and was presented with an option: I could be done with the registration process or click for more artists. Of course I clicked for more artists! In fact, I continued clicking on more of my favorite bands for nine pages, until "Click for more artists" wasn't an option!

At this point I like to pause and pull out "the money slide." Successful businesses figure out how to join business goals with user goals. We call this *value-centered design*.

In the case of the iLike registration process, I had a great time clicking on bands I like. In turn, iLike gained lots of data about my musical tastes and preferences.

In fact, clicking on bands and artists was a lot more fun than filling out an empty text box. And look what iLike got out of the experience: I shared 35 of my favorite bands with them. Compared to other music sites where, at best, I'd list maybe four or five bands, iLike learned a whole lot more about what I like to listen to. This design of the experience was mutually beneficial.

So why did this work?

- **Feedback loops.** We're engaged by situations in which we see our actions modify subsequent results. iLike made a very small suggestion: "The more artists you rate, the better." They were careful not to spell out when I'd see results; it could have been on the very next page that reloaded or three months down the road after I was an active user. That merely suggested that my actions would tailor my iLike experience.
- **Curiosity.** When teased with a small bit of interesting information, people want to know more. I was curious: how would clicking on the artists I like affect results on the next page? Would I see less of one genre, and more of another? Would the suggestions become more personalized with each new batch of 35 artists?

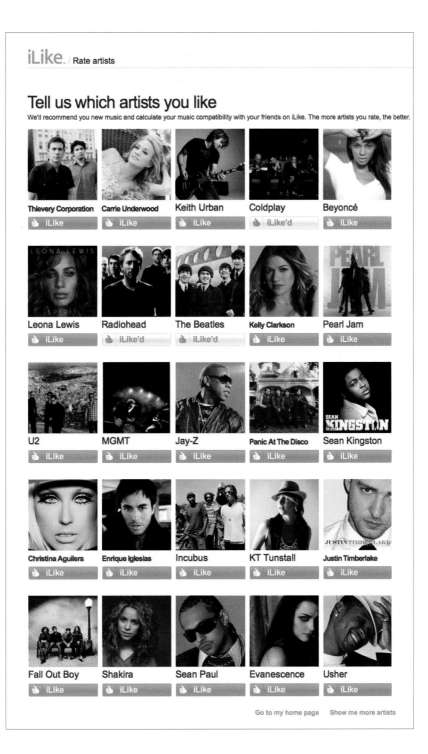

- **Pattern recognition.** Our brains seek ways to organize and simplify complex information, even where there is no pattern. I was looking to see if there was more or less of one type of artist. Also, why these 35 artists? Was there a pattern to the artists I was rating?
- **Visual imagery.** Vision trumps all other senses and is the most direct way to perception. If you think about this page from a technical perspective, it's nothing more than a list of 35 checkbox items. However, by using photographs of the artists, there was a more immediate, visceral reaction. And I had a larger click target.
- **Recognition over recall.** It's easier to recognize things we have previously experienced than it is to recall them from memory. Instead of having to recall bands I liked from memory, this was an easier, passive experience. All I had to do was click on artists I recognized and like. No mental strength was required. More importantly, my hand never left the mouse—it's much easier to click from available options than to type things out by hand.

All in all, this was a remarkable sign-up process. But, my initial iLike experience wasn't over yet.

### The iLike Challenge

About 15 minutes later, I was checking my e-mail. There was a confirmation e-mail to let me know that I had successfully created a profile on iLike. The e-mail suggested what I might do next. I could add a photo to my profile. Not now, thanks. There was another plug for their iTunes plug-in. Meh. Or—and this is the one that piqued my interest—I could "Play the iLike Challenge." I was curious. What was the iLike Challenge?

It turns out that the iLike Challenge is this really addictive game that should be avoided at all costs.

The iLike Challenge presents you with a 30-second sample from a song. The challenge is to identify either the artist who wrote the song or the title of a song. You get points for answering accurately and quickly. For example, the challenge may be "Name this Gorillaz song," and you have four options to choose from. If you answer in the first few seconds, you get ten points. If it takes five or six seconds to answer, you get nine points. The longer you take to answer, the fewer points you get. If it takes you 28 seconds to figure out what the song is, you're only going to get one point! And if you answer incorrectly, you get no points.

This game is fairly addictive in and of itself. It tests your knowledge of popular songs. And, with multiple-choice answers to choose from, you have some chance of guessing correctly.

Here's the part that's particularly evil: visible on the side of the screen is a scoreboard that keeps track of how you're doing.

- Your current rank
- Total points accumulated
- Points to next rank (Remember progress dynamics? Here I only need 48 more points to reach the next level. Hmm. I wonder what's after Music Intern?)
- Questions answered

- Percentage of correct answers
- Average answer time

These are all fun metrics to monitor. But, here's the one that really worked on me: *Best streak*. Best streak is the total number of points based on consecutively correct answers. Even if I did start to tire of the music game, there was another game introduced here, one in which I compete against my own personal best. If my best streak was 47, I had to beat that. And when I did, I'd set goals: can I get above 60? Above

100? All said, I spent over an hour playing this game. And then I shared it with friends and family. That's a *seductive* interaction.

Here's the other interesting thing about the iLike Challenge. As you're playing it, there's an area below the current challenge that gives you all sorts of information about the last song that played. It's very easy, while playing the game, to move your cursor and click "iLike" that song. Think of how nice it'd be if our car radios had a Like button for the songs we enjoy hearing. It'd be an easy way to identify and recall songs we

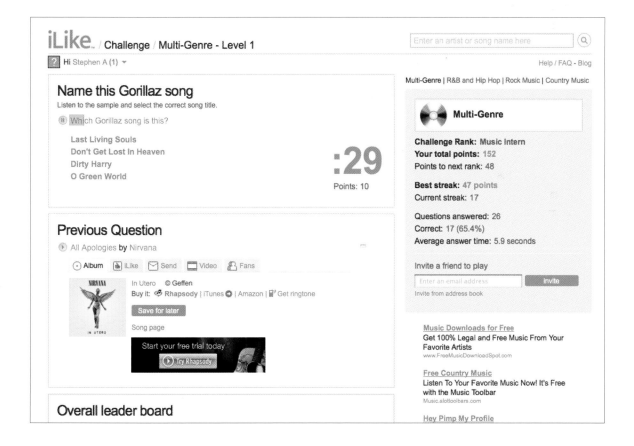

like, especially in cases where we don't know the artist or song title. iLike was providing yet another way for us to share what music we like.

Let's put our business hats on again.

I had a great time playing this game. But what do you think iLike was doing? What are they doing behind the scenes, perhaps? Here's a chance to capture not only more artists and songs I like, but with the right systems in place, the iLike Challenge could be a pretty intelligent system for collecting preferences. If I only get 5 percent of the R&B questions correct, but I answer accurately on just about every indie song they throw at me, that information reveals a lot more about what I listen to. By monitoring my knowledge of different songs, they could learn even more about my musical tastes and preferences. That's clever.

Why did this work? It would be easy to focus on the gaming mechanics: points, levels, a countdown timer. But why do game mechanics work? I devote several chapters of this book to answering that question. Recall four of the ideas you've already seen: *status*, *feedback loops*, *achievements*, and *appropriate challenges*. There is also the *sensory appeal* factor. We're engaged by and more likely to recall things that appeal to multiple senses. Given the constraints of a digital context, it's hard to engage multiple senses, but with the iLike Challenge, you have the artist's visuals, the motion of a timer counting down, the audio input, and the interaction required by a game.

## BEYOND USABILITY

At this point, I'd like to point out something:

*It wasn't a focus on usability that made this a great experience. It was psychology.*

Usability clears the way for a good experience by eliminating troublesome interface distractions, but a great experience stems from something more—an awareness of why people could or do care. The danger is in confusing "ease of use" with actually *desiring* to use something. These are two entirely different things. Both are essential, but simply making something more usable won't guarantee any more clicks or conversions. In this case, it was psychology that made this so engaging. To be clear, if a business approached me tomorrow about making their time-tracking tool fun to use, I'd start by making sure it was first easy to use. Adding "playful" elements on top of a frustrating experience will only complicate things. Fix the basic problems before moving on to the types of things described in this book. However, I've seen cases where the motivation to do something outweighed the usability challenges—the

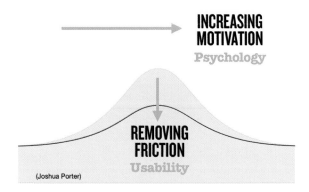

pull outweighed the friction. In one such case, there was a very long form that asked for lots of unnecessary information; but, if you managed to get through the application, your group got listed on a heavily trafficked site. Understanding motivation can be a powerful design tool.

Usability is about removing the roadblocks and obstacles that get in the way of a great experience—there's nearly two decades of excellent literature on this subject; everything I discuss in this book is about increasing motivation.

With this in mind, I'd like to introduce you to a model I developed to help discuss different user experience needs.

## IT'S ALL ABOUT EXPERIENCES

Author and professor Donald Norman once stated, "When technology delivers basic needs, user experience dominates." The mobile phone industry is a great example of this evolution. No one would now consider entering that market with the original Motorola DynaTAC. What made it successful at the time—a phone that doesn't need wires—is now an expectation. Mobile phones have become more reliable and usable and are packed with some useful (and not so useful) features. The introduction of the iPhone and its imitators raised the bar once again—not in terms of more features, but in the way in which people experience information. Now our mobile phones aren't just tools—they're also fun to use! This process of product maturity forms the basis for my *User Experience Hierarchy of Needs* model, in which I propose that most technology product and service experiences go through six levels of maturity,

moving from the bottom to the top, from "Hey, this thing actually works!" to "This is meaningful in my life." However, this model was also my way of resolving a lot of different ideas around what is important to an experience, and the relative priority of those things. This latter idea is seen with a top to bottom focus.

Moving from bottom to top, you have a basic product maturity continuum:

### Functional

Ideas typically start off as *functional* solutions to a problem—something *useful*. Think of the first Motorola cell phone. Sure, it was a brick, but it allowed you to make calls untethered to a fixed spot! Every new technological innovation starts at a functional level.

### Reliable

From there, things have to be *reliable*. This can be reliability of the service (five nines uptime?) as well as integrity of the data. If I purchase tickets on a travel site, the ticket prices need to be current and reliable. If I host with a site, I need to know my data is backed up and accessible at all times. This is reliability. When sites fail at reliability, especially where personal data is involved, little else matters.

### Usable and Convenient

It's not enough to allow me to simply do something—it has to eventually be less awkward to use. This is where the next two levels, *usable* and *convenient*, come into play. I make a distinction between usability and convenience. Both make something easier to use, but in my experience most usability groups focus

SUBJECTIVE / QUALITATIVE

*focused on*
**EXPERIENCES**
(People, Activities, Context)

▼

**MEANINGFUL**
*Has personal significance*

**PLEASURABLE**
*Memorable experience worth sharing*

**_CONVENIENT_** THIS IS THE "CHASM" THAT IS DIFFICULT
*Super easy to use, works like I think* FOR ORGANIZATIONS TO CROSS

**USABLE**
*Can be used without difficulty*

**RELIABLE**
*Is available and accurate*

**FUNCTIONAL (USEFUL)**
*Works as programmed*

▲

*focused on*
**TASKS**
(Products, Features)

OBJECTIVE / QUANTIFIABLE

*User Experience Hierarchy of Needs model. From bottom to top is a basic product maturity continuum: a top to bottom focus starts with the experience you want people to have.*

on fixing known problems—removing the hurdles. A focus on convenience asks, "Is there a more natural way to make this work?" MapQuest and Google Maps are great examples of this contrast. MapQuest was perfectly usable. But Google Maps, with its draggable interface, physics, and other more natural behaviors was a much more convenient way to interact with maps data. Touchscreen interactions, such as those offered by the iPad, are a perfect example of a more convenient interaction. Things work more like they might in the real world.

### Pleasurable

Whereas convenience focuses on cognition, the next level—*pleasurable*—focuses on affect and emotions. How can we make something emotionally engaging (and memorable)? This is typically accomplished using things like friendly language, aesthetics, and humor, and doing things like arousing curiosity, creating flow, leveraging game mechanics, and other similar tactics. Everything described in this book is about creating more pleasurable experiences.

### Meaningful

The highest level is, of course, "meaningful." To be clear, you can't make something meaningful for someone—*meaning* is personal and subjective. But you can design for meaning by focusing on the preceding levels as well as shepherding beliefs and the communities surrounding the product or service experience. Great companies know how to develop a story that people can believe. Disney World is about more than rides. Apple is about more than electronics. Whole Foods is more than a grocer. These brand stories transcend any particular product or service.

Also, whereas the other levels build on each other, a product can be meaningful without any of these levels. For example, I have a 1966 Karmann Ghia that doesn't even run—it doesn't operate at even a functional level; however, the ownership connects me with a group of people in a way that is personally meaningful.

The challenge of this model is this: if you want to truly create a revolutionary product, you have to shift your thinking from a bottom-up *task* focus (which will only get you so far) to a top-down focus that starts with the *experience* you want people to have. By approaching things from this perspective, we see a host of new ideas, not to mention better ways to implement ideas that have been around for a while.

But there's another takeaway: in mature markets, where you have stable, usable products, taking it to the next level means focusing on more experiential things like emotions, clever language, and aesthetics. I present this model as a context for everything in the chapters that follow. The tools and products we build—Web apps, software, mobile apps—have reached a point where we can engage people in meaningful and emotional ways. But let's not forget the basics!

# Aesthetics, Beauty, and Behavior

We're attracted to beautiful people. And we set aside time to make ourselves more attractive. Before going out, we glance in the mirror. Our clothing, hairstyle, jewelry—each choice reflects a personal style. And it's through the visceral—our appearance and body language—that we signal to others the kind of person we'd like to be and be with.

Are there lessons here for designing seductive interactions?

While aesthetics are only one part of the user experience, they are also the most frequently discussed and misunderstood.

On the one hand, we instinctively seem to know that a sense of style is important. Visual designers are constantly arguing for "good design." Business leaders often make snap judgments based solely on appearances. And any good salesperson can rattle off a dozen reasons why it's important to "look your best."

On the other hand, when we get into discussions of utility and usefulness, it's easy to marginalize these visual considerations as decoration. This is especially true of Web and software applications. Consider how designers are asked to "skin" wireframes. Or how the term "eye candy" suggests that visual design is inessential. In traditional software development, "themes" are used to decorate bland GUI elements. Our language constrains visual design to mere styling and separates aesthetics and usability, as if they are distinct considerations.

Lost in these discussions is an understanding of the powerful role aesthetics play in shaping how we come to know, feel, and respond.

If we shift the conversation away from graphical elements and instead focus on aesthetics, or "the science of how things are known via the senses," we learn that this distinction between how something looks and how it works is somewhat artificial.

In this section, we'll look at some recent research to help us discuss aesthetics and interface design with a bit more objectivity.

CHAPTER 2

# Why Aesthetics?

IMAGINE YOU'RE PART of a research study, one that you're told will measure your IQ. You're presented with three objects: A candle, a book of matches, and a box of thumbtacks.

box: you have to see it as a candleholder, rather than a container for holding thumbtacks, and tack it to the wall.

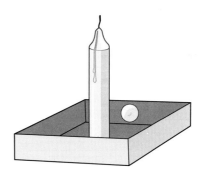

Your challenge is to attach the candle to the wall in such a way that no wax drips onto the table. How would you go about doing this?

A psychologist named Karl Duncker developed this creative challenge—known as the candle problem—in 1945 to measure "the influence of 'functional fixedness' on a participant's problem solving capabilities." Functional fixedness describes a cognitive bias that limits us to using an object only in the way it's traditionally used. We become fixated on the intended used of an object and can't see other uses for it.

Most people end up solving the candle problem after five or ten minutes. Doing so requires that you reconceptualize the function of the

The candle problem has been used in all sorts of behavioral science experiments to test different things that might influence our ability to solve creative challenges. For example:

- Is age a factor?
  Five-year-olds solved the problem more quickly than their adult counterparts.

- Does the way the problem is presented suggest options?
  In 1952, Robert Adamson found that research participants were twice as likely to solve the problem when presented with an empty tack box next to the tacks. Using the phrase "thumbtacks in a box" also gave subjects a hint as to the solution.

- Do incentives help?

  In 1966, when Sam Glucksberg offered participants a cash prize for solving the problem faster than the average person taking the test, they took an average of three-and-a-half minutes longer! Dan Pink popularized this version of the study in his 2010 book *Drive: The Surprising Truth About What Motivates Us.*

- Does affect influence success?

  In one of the best-known experiments, subjects were induced into a bad or good mood and then asked to solve the problem. One group was shown a positive movie and given a small gift while another group was shown a negative movie. The findings? Subjects who were first put into a good mood were "significantly more successful at solving this problem." We'll talk more about this finding in Section Two.

## WHAT'S THE CONNECTION?

While all of this is interesting, it may seem odd to begin a chapter on "looking your best" with a study that appears to have nothing to do with the topic. After all, what does the ability to solve a creative challenge have to do with choosing a typeface or selecting a color palette?

Everything.

Choosing a particular shade of lipstick or getting a new haircut is as much about personal style as it is about eliciting a response from others. The same goes for visual design. How do you choose between different visual design options? While there's certainly some amount of artistic expression involved (what we commonly refer to as style), our eyes should be on the resulting behaviors.

As you'll soon see, design choices influence perceptions, elicit different responses, and affect a person's ability to complete a task. When we talk about a button or a typeface, the focus should be on the *effect* of these objects, not the objects themselves. This is the domain of *aesthetics*.

## WHY AESTHETICS?

For starters, aesthetics include everything that appeals to the senses—not just what we see, but also what we hear, smell, taste, and feel. As user experience designers, we must consider every stimulus that might influence user interaction. In the digital realm, this includes visual design, motion, sound, and even haptic (tactile) responses.

Perhaps more importantly, "aesthetics examines our response to an object or phenomenon" (according to Wikipedia). In other words, aesthetics aren't just about the artistic merit of Web buttons or other visual effects, but about how people respond to these elements. The question becomes: How do aesthetic design choices influence understanding and emotions, and how do understanding and emotions influence behavior?

In the the remaining chapters of this section, we'll look at how aesthetics influences *cognition*, *affect*, and *associations*.

# CHAPTER 3

# Are You Easily Understood?

COGNITION IS THE PROCESS of knowing. Based on patterns and experiences, we learn how to understand the world around us: What happens if I push that? What does this color suggest? Cognitive science studies how people know things, and aesthetics play a critical role in cognitive processing.

Which of the two examples below is clearly a button? And why?

Here, aesthetics communicate function. The example on the right resembles a physical button. The beveled edges and gradient shading remove any doubt about its purpose. These are *perceived affordances*—cues that communicate how a user can, and should, interact with an object. Translation: if it looks like a button, it must be a button.

Similarly, there's a reason good confirmation screens have a check mark and are likely to involve some shade of green. Green is good. Red is bad. Yellow is something to think about. When designing, we must consider how the brain interprets the meaning of color, shadow,

and shading. We rarely notice these aesthetic choices, except when people get them wrong:

*In this example, the visual language conflicts with the intent of the message.*

What we're discussing here is how the brain interprets color, shadow, shading, and other natural occurrences. Just pick up a piece of paper and watch how the shadow changes as you bring the page closer to you. Now consider the two examples at the top of the following page.

How are you able you tell which box is closer to you? We infer meaning from cues like the size and opacity of the drop shadow or the apparent overlap. We observe these kinds of natural occurrences every day in the real world. When we use these cues on a screen, they carry the same real-world properties with them.

*In each of these examples, one window is closer to you. How do you know?*

The tricky part is when we start referencing real-world patterns without obeying the rules governing those patterns. For example, consider the simple "drawer" pattern shown below:

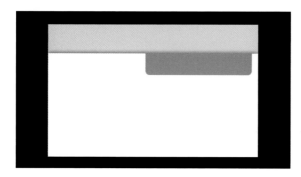

This seems alright until you show a drawer sliding down–but from where?

By simply flipping the direction of the shadow, the design makes much more sense:

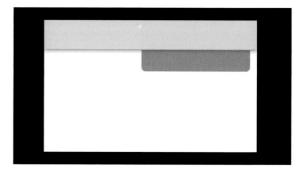

Whatever the natural reference is—shadows, reflections, lighting, bevels—I like to ask designers, "Could you build a physical model of this page?" If you can't, then the viewer will likely be disturbed, as something feels not quite right.

## GESTALT PSYCHOLOGY AND A DRINKING GAME

In addition to referencing real-world properties, aesthetic choices may also suggest relationships between different objects. Gestalt psychology suggests several laws to explain perceptual organization, or how smaller objects are grouped to form larger ones. For example, the law of *proximity* explains that if I place two or more items in a cluster together, you'll assume they are related.

If one object has different characteristics from other objects, we perceive it as being different. This is known as *contrast* (an idea we'll explore in greater detail in Chapter 15).

Additionally, elements connected by uniform visual properties are perceived as being more related than elements that are not connected. This is known as *uniform connectedness*.

## LIGHT ABUSES

Think about the natural rules for reflections:

- Things must be seated on a plane to suggest perspective and scale.
- The surface must be of a reflective material.
- The object being reflected must touch the surface and be oriented (or stand) in a certain way.

Given these properties, can you spot the problems in these examples?

*Hint: What kinds of surfaces are reflective?*

*Hint: Think about the function of photo corners.*

Let's look at a few more examples of how aesthetics help us to understand the functional space in which we interact:

*The "genie effect" animation communicates where a file is being stored, for easy retrieval later.*

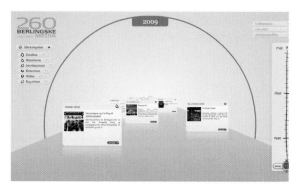

*260.dk uses 3D depth to simulate going back in time.*

*In this screen from Blinksale, paper torn from a spiral notepad is a visual cue that this is an estimate.*

*When invoices have been sent, this top bar suggests the invoice is "in the mail," (or will be when you move this out of draft mode).*

# SHOWING RELATIONSHOPS WITH SIFTER*

With the bug tracker Sifter—and almost any bug tracker for that matter—bug and issue statuses are one of the key attributes, and they generally follow a progression as they are fixed and reviewed for quality. Unfortunately, it's not always immediately obvious what step should be next. Creating a visual relationship between the options helps overcome that challenge and makes it clearer which step is next.

The statuses could be listed in a traditional list of radio buttons, or they could be listed in a drop down, but in both cases, the context isn't really there. By arranging the statuses horizontally with relevant arrows in between, we're communicating a progression, or in some cases, a regression.

By using radio buttons, all available states are always visible, as opposed to being hidden in a drop down. This helps provide a clear context and communicates the relationship between the different statuses. By arranging them horizontally, they almost begin to feel like a status bar. When an issue is in a

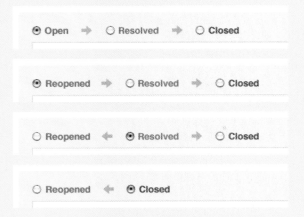

resolved or closed state, the arrows combined with moving right-to-left instead of the natural left-to-right reinforce that reopening the issue is taking a step backwards.

–Garrett Dimon, Sifter creator

| Measure | | Prior Period | Week 1 | Week 2 | Week 3 | Week 4 | Period to Date | Year to Date |
|---|---|---|---|---|---|---|---|---|
| Sales at Cost | $ | 3,333,826 | 756,779 | 0 | 0 | 0 | 756,779 | 18,757,608 |
| | %PY | 108.7 | 108.1 | 0.0 | 0.0 | 0.0 | 108.1 | 107.0 |
| | $ PLan | 3,253,893 | 804,559 | 0 | 0 | 0 | 804,559 | 18,674,197 |
| | % PLan | 102.1 | 95.2 | 0.0 | 0.0 | 0.0 | 95.2 | 100.4 |
| | +/- Plan | 69,933 | -38,780 | 0 | 0 | 0 | -38,780 | 83,4111 |
| Gross Sales | $ | 3,362,244 | 771,932 | 0 | 0 | 0 | 771,932 | 18,930,091 |
| | %PY | 108.7 | 108.1 | 0.0 | 0.0 | 0.0 | 108.1 | 107.1 |
| Net Sales | $ | 2,992,176 | 700,687 | 0 | 0 | 0 | 700,687 | 16,989,426 |
| | %PY | 107.1 | 107.1 | 0.0 | 0.0 | 0.0 | 107.1 | 105.8 |

*The nested layers in this spreadsheet indicate that these numbers "roll up" into a greater number.*

* excerpted from my conversation with Garrett Dimon, visit www.sixdbook.com to read full interview

Much more could be said about these natural laws. We could discuss more laws from Gestalt psychology. We could discuss color theory. We could explore why things like following a grid or using the golden ration in our layouts create a natural rhythm. But these kinds of aesthetic decisions, while not always appreciated, are rarely challenged. They make sense. As with our button example, there's a rational argument for these visual design choices.

However, there's more to aesthetics than just communicating function, and more to styling than mere enjoyment. Since there are several excellent books devoted entirely to visual perception and how we understand things by way of our senses, let's move on to the much trickier subject of emotions.

## MORE READING

For specific training on how to make more effective aesthetic decisions, here are some brilliant books that offer a scientific perspective:

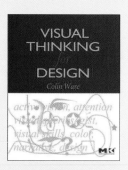

*Visual Thinking: for Design*
by Colin Ware

*Watches Tell More Than Time: Product Design, Information, and the Quest for Elegance*
by Del Coates

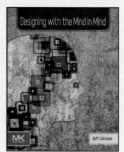

*Designing with the Mind in Mind*
by Jeff Johnson

*Understanding Comics: The Invisible Art*
by Scott Mccloud

# CHAPTER 4

# Are You Attractive?

WHEN WE TALK ABOUT *affect*, we're talking about feelings and emotions. In marketing, feelings are often reduced to "I feel positive about your brand." Here, however, we consider the ways in which feelings and emotions can influence perceived and actual usability. Let's revisit our button example, with a slight change:

Cognitively speaking, both of these are obviously buttons. Neither button is "wrong" as in our earlier example. However, research into attention, persuasion, choice, happiness, learning, and other similar topics suggests that the more attractive button is likely to be more usable by most people. To get an idea of where this perspective might come from, consider this comment on emotions from neurobiologist Antonio Damasio:

*"Emotion is not a luxury: it is an expression of basic mechanisms of life regulation developed in evolution, and is indispensable for survival. It plays a critical role in virtually all aspects of learning, reasoning, and creativity. Somewhat surprisingly, it may play a role in the construction of consciousness."*\*

That our emotions govern our thinking is a theme we'll develop throughout this book.

In many design conversations, there is a belief that applications are made enjoyable because we make them easy to use and efficient. (Whether it's stated or not, these conversations value the role of aesthetics in cognition.) However, when we talk about how emotions influence interactions, it's closer to the truth to say things that are enjoyable will be perceived as easy to use and efficient. Allow me to explain.

Since the effects of our emotions may be one step removed from actual use, let's consider the things emotion (or affect) influences directly.

*Contrary to popular opinion, things that are enjoyable will be perceived as easy to use and efficient.*

---

\*Damasio, Antonio. "Emotions and Feelings: a Neurobiological Perspective." *Feelings and Emotions, The Amsterdam Symposium*. 2004.

## YOU REMIND ME OF...

Product *personality* influences our perceptions. Think about how quickly we form expectations about someone simply based on how they dress or present themselves. This is something the automobile industry has known for years, as they spend money to create products that express a specific personality that customers might identify with. Why does a Dodge Ram seem more durable? What makes a Mini Cooper seem zippy and fun? While there are certainly performance features to support these mental claims, we can also see these attributes expressed in each car's form.

Similarly, the user interface design decisions we make affect the perceived personality of our applications. In the examples below, which window is friendlier? Which one looks more professional?

To be clear, it's not that either of them is necessarily right or wrong. Each user interface has a distinct personality appropriate for the content, the context, and the audience. The example on the left has the "pro" look and its sophistication may actually appeal to that intended audience. The example on the right was a simple widget designed to track points in a rewards program. So, in each case, the personality is tailored to the intended purpose.

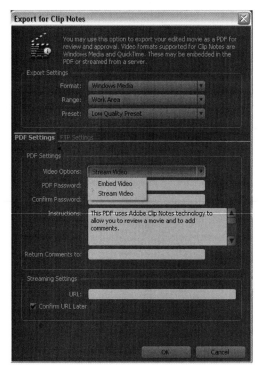

*Notice how each of these user interfaces has a unique personality.*

If this robot was an adult butler that responded to only half our requests and frequently did something other than what we asked, we'd consider it broken and useless. But as a puppy, we find its behaviors "cute." Puppies aren't known for following directions. And when the robot puppy does succeed, we are delighted. "Look, it rolled over!" What a great way to enter the robotics market.

Consider what kind of personality you're creating with your application, and what expectations that personality brings with it.

Products have a personality. Why should we care? Consider this:

- People identify with (or avoid) certain personalities.
- Trust is related to personality.
- Perception and expectations are linked with personality.
- Consumers choose products that are an extension of themselves.
- We treat sufficiently advanced technology as though it were human.

By making intentional, conscious decisions about the personality of your product, you can shape positive or negative affect responses. Take a look at Sony and how they applied this knowledge in the Sony AIBO. Let's consider why they made this robot resemble a puppy (above).

Here, you have a robotic device that isn't perfect. It won't understand most of what you say. It may or may not follow the commands it does understand. And it doesn't really do all that much.

## CAN YOU TRUST ME ON THIS?

Can you guess the most frequently cited factor for evaluating the credibility of a Web site?

According to a 2002 study out of Stanford University, it is the "appeal of the overall visual design of a site, including layout, typography, font size, and color schemes," (Fogg, et al., 2002). The look and feel of a site influenced judgments about credibility far more than other factors like structure, usefulness of the information, tone of the content, and name recognition!

| | Percent (of 2,440 comments) | Comment Topics (addressing specific credibility issue) |
|---|---|---|
| 1. | 46.1% | Design Look |
| 2. | 28.5% | Information Design/Structure |
| 3. | 25.1% | Information Focus |
| 4. | 15.5% | Company Motive |
| 5. | 14.8% | Information Usefulness |
| 6. | 14.3% | Information Accuracy |
| 7. | 14.1% | Name Recognition and Reputation |
| 8. | 13.8% | Advertising |
| 9. | 11.6% | Information Bias |

A different study found that "Web users form first impressions of Web pages in as little as 50 milliseconds (1/20th of a second)." What's more, these initial attractiveness evaluations based on just a brief exposure "were very highly correlated with attractiveness evaluations of the same pages under unlimited exposure.*"

These findings make sense. Think of how quickly we form judgments about people in the first few moments after we meet them. Conversely, think about how our personal appearance (our personal aesthetic) affects the way people perceive us; or how product packaging influences our perception of the product inside. We may know better, but we continue to judge a book by its cover.

Below left is a gas pump near my house. Contrast that with the station shown on the right.

I've stopped filling up at the gas station on the left, even though it's closer to where I live. Why? This kind of maintenance (or lack of maintenance) leaves me unwilling to trust them with my credit card information. Clearly, appearance does affect trust.

So, how do we create trust in our application interfaces, aside from providing the basics, such as reliable information and uptime? Be attentive to visual design, for one thing. Attention to design details implies that the same care and attention has been spent on the other (less visible) parts of the product, which implies that this is a trustworthy product.

I've seen many great design comps get butchered during development. Things such as inconsistent fonts, odd padding, line heights, and over-compressed images plagued the final release. While this may never come out during functional testing, how might these sloppy UI details affect perceptions of your product?

*Which gas station would you trust to safely process your credit card information?*

*Gitte Lindgaard, Gary Fernandes, Cathy Dudek and J. Brown, "Attention web designers" in *Behaviour & Information Technology*, 2006.

*The sloppy lack of attention to UI details in the lower, implemented version will negatively affect user perceptions.*

## PERCEPTIONS OF TIME

If you've ever been to a Disney theme park, then you've experienced firsthand the magic of Disney—not just in the shows and rides, but in how lines are handled. Disney's "imagineers" have perfected ways to make a long wait seem shorter, with some lines so elaborately designed that it's hard to tell where the line ends and the ride begins. Through distractions and illusions, the experience of waiting in long lines may not seem so bad.

Along the same lines (no pun intended), consider preloaders and progress bars. Given that a download will take the same amount of time in all cases, are there different preloaders that would seem to take less time?

The magazine *New Scientist* ran an experiment in which at least nine variations on the progress bar used to monitor Web downloads were tested. It was found that:

- Pulses that become more frequent as the bar progresses create the illusion that it's moving faster.
- Bars filled with ripples heading left make a progress bar appear to move faster.

The magazine found that "by using an effective illusion, it can seem like a file is downloading 11 percent quicker than it really is."

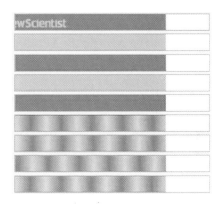

I've observed a similar illusion with different kinds of preloaders. Our brains tend to count cycles, not seconds. Consider two preloaders that involve a clear, cyclic routine. I believe that a slower cycle would make time appear to pass faster. Why? It might only make it through two complete cycles in a five-second period. Contrast that with a much faster spinner that we tire of much sooner because it's faster.

We know that speed is in the eye of the beholder. While engineers toil away shaving off two milliseconds from a load time, what might we gain by creating preloaders that buy us more time?

*"...something that takes longer but that is perceived to be efficient is superior to something that is shorter but perceived differently."*

–Donald Norman

## PUT IT ALL TOGETHER

So perceived time, personality, trust—certainly these are important. But these are just perceptions, right? How much should we really care about shaping perceptions? Well, our experiences (and to some extent our reality) are based on perceptions. But our evaluation of a system's performance is surely based on something more substantial, right?

Consider these findings from research presented at the human-interaction conference CHI 2007. Users were asked to "judge the relevancy of identical search results from different search engines." The only difference in the studies was the branding attached to the results. The search results were identical in all cases. Were people rational? Did they focus on the relevancy of the results? Nope. "Participants in the study indicated that the results from Google and Yahoo were superior to identical results found through Windows Live or a generic search engine."

What is a brand but perceptions? In this study, functionally identical results were perceived as better due to brand attributes such as trust, personality, and perception. I'd say that our own perceived experiences might be more important than a measurable reality.

We should be very concerned with how aesthetics shape perceptions, especially given the extent to which perceptions shape judgment, influence behavior, and shape our memories.

## "ATTRACTIVE THINGS WORK BETTER"

Okay, so maybe perceptions are important to product design. But what about "real" usability concerns such as lower task completion times or fewer difficulties? Do attractive products actually work better?

One of the most widely cited studies associated with the "attractive things work better" argument is cited in the opening chapter of Donald Norman's 2003 book *Emotional Design*.

Researchers in Japan set up two ATMs that were identical in function, the number of buttons, and how they worked. The only difference was that one machine's buttons and screens were arranged more attractively. In both Japan and Israel (where this study was repeated to test for cultural differences), researchers observed that subjects encountered fewer difficulties with the more attractive machine. A point of clarification: if you read the original studies, you'll see that people *perceived* that the attractive machine actually worked better. This is a slight difference, and a small detail that in no way diminishes Norman's argument that attractive things work better.*

The explanation Norman offers cites evolutionary biology and what we know about how our brains work. Basically, when we are relaxed, our brains are more flexible and more likely to find workarounds for difficult problems. In contrast, when we're frustrated and tense, our brains get a sort of tunnel vision where we only see the problem in front of us. Sound like the the candle problem (see Chapter 2)? It should. How many times, in a fit of frustration, have you tried the same thing over and over again, hoping it would somehow work the seventeenth time around?

Norman offers another explanation: we want those things that we find pleasing to succeed.

We're more tolerant of problems in things that we find attractive. How many of us have tolerated faults in a person due to their attractiveness? You don't have to answer that question.

Following these ATM studies, a number of other researchers have explored connections between visual aesthetics and usability. While many of these have proven a correlation between attractiveness and perceived usability, a few recent studies are finding more direct correlations between visual aesthetics and actual performance.

In one study, described in the article "A Blessing, Not a Curse: Experimental Evidence for Beneficial Effects of Visual Aesthetics on Performance" (Moshagen, 2009), volunteers completed a series of search tasks on a site that provided health-related information. "Four versions of a website were created by manipulating visual aesthetics (high vs. low) and usability (good vs. poor)." The results? Good visual aesthetics *did* compensate for poor usability, improving task completion time, and reducing errors.

Another study, "The Influence of Design Aesthetics in Usability Testing: Effects on User Performance and Perceived Usability," (Sonderegger and Sauer, 2009), presented adolescents with one of two mobile phones, an attractive one, and one less so. The conclusion? "The visual appearance of the phone had a positive effect on performance, leading to reduced task completion times for the attractive model."

Not only do aesthetics affect *perceived* usability, they also influence *actual* performance. However, more studies under different circumstances are needed to clarify these findings.

*Kurosu and Kashimura, 1995; *Noam Tractinsky*, 1997.

## STITCHING IT ALL TOGETHER

For simplicity, I've presented two separate arguments for the value of aesthetics: one focused on cognitive benefits, the other citing how aesthetics influence affect.

But there's another bit of information I saved for last.

Recent studies of emotions are finding that we can't actually separate cognition from affect. Separate studies in economics and in neuroscience are proving that:

*"affect, which is inexplicably linked to attitudes, expectations and motivations, plays a significant role in the cognition of product interaction...the perception that affect and cognition are independent, separate information processing systems is flawed."** 

In other words, how we think cannot be separated from how we feel. At all times, we are *evaluating* (affect) and *interpreting* (cognition) the world around us.

This raises some interesting questions—especially in the area of decision making. In short, our rational choices aren't so rational (something we'll talk about in Section Three). From studies on choice to first impressions, neuroscience is exploring how the brain works—and it's kind of scary. We're not as in charge of our decisions as we'd like to believe.

Consider what you're doing with your interfaces to speak to people's emotions. Industrial product design, automobile manufacturing, and other more mature industries get this—with tools such as Kano modeling that have been used for decades (see Chapter 24). But user interface development is still catching up on what these other disciplines already know: the most direct way to influence a decision or perception is through the emotions.

So, is "pretty design" important?

When you consider application design and development, how do you think of visual design? Is it a skin that adds some value—a layer on top of the core functionality? Or is this beauty something more?

In the early 1900s, "form follows function" became the mantra of modern architecture. Frank Lloyd Wright changed this phrase to "form and function should be one, joined in a spiritual union," using nature as the best example of this integration.

The more we learn about people, and how our brains process information, the more we see the truth of that phrase: form and function aren't separate. If form exists independently of function, and we can treat aesthetics and function as two separate elements, then we ignore the evidence that beauty is much more than decoration. Our brains can't help but agree.

*Frank Spillers. "Emotion as a Cognitive Artifact and the Design Implications for Products That Are Perceived As Pleasurable." Design and Emotion. 2004.

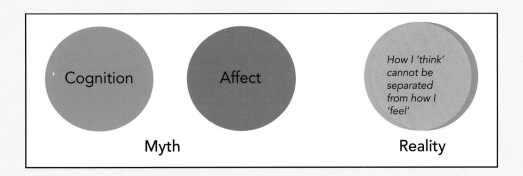

Myth

Reality

"Do users want applications that work, or applications that can wrap themselves into funny shapes? I'm sure it looks really whizzy in demos, but come on, we're just trying to give users applications that help them do their jobs."

"It doesn't matter how pretty your site is or how many bells and whistles you have. While a high-quality site is important, the majority of people today value usability more than good looks or fanciness."

"The beauty of the Web lies in its function, not its form, and I would rather that my sites attract attention because they are widely useful and usable than because they are pretty."

"The site doesn't need to look good, it just needs to be easy to use."

While sentiments like these may be accurate, they're inconsistent with the way humans respond to visual stimuli. The distinction between how something looks and how it works is somewhat artificial.

# REALITY CHECK!

This chapter was largely an argument for visual aesthetics in interactive environments. However, none of this should be taken as an argument against basic usability and usefulness. The most attractive site in the world will fail if it doesn't deliver on basic promises or is too difficult to use.

If adding more images adds significantly to the load time, this will detract from the overall experience. If a fancy-looking title bar confuses people into thinking it's clickable, that's a problem. If a really nice layout means your content will be difficult to read on a mobile device, that's a serious consideration.

As interaction designers, we make things people use. We have to consider the people, the activities, and the context of these interactions. And while there are certainly plenty of patterns and conventions we can fall back on, every project presents new and unique challenges. There is rarely a clear-cut way of doing things (and I'd be wary of anyone saying otherwise). What works in one situation may fail miserably in another, and we often have to prioritize one thing at the expense of another. Agencies tend to value branding and identity over all else. IT departments often see visual design as an afterthought. Usability tests focus on functionality, efficiency, and task completion, but rarely measure whether or not the experience was actually enjoyable.

Design, in a general sense, is largely about making difficult decisions. "If we do x, will it detract from y?" Sometimes it's about finding the delicate balance. Sometimes it's about a trade-off. Other times it's a prioritization. The key is to be clear about the end goals of the project, and then make decisions accordingly.

My aim with this section is to elevate the role of aesthetics in our functional conversations, to provide an objective way to balance aesthetic considerations and traditional (functional) considerations. In doing so, I'm hoping people can make more informed and less-biased judgments. Aesthetics are but one aspect of the overall user experience. But they should be taken as seriously as reliability, uptime, or speed. By shifting the conversation to perceptions, judgments, and behavior, we can make informed design decisions, whether for or against a particular choice.

Since entering the field of user experience design (UX) more than a decade ago, I've witnessed the constant tension between usability engineers, development teams, designers (with different levels of experience), business folks, marketing groups, and others. Each has something quite valuable to add to the equation. But, it's frustrating when we don't value one another's contributions or understand how to orchestrate these different interests to work together to create value for both business *and* customers.

Aesthetics are only one consideration. However, much is lost by isolating them as an afterthought or a separate consideration. I think it's more accurate to think of aesthetics as a key ingredient in a recipe, as opposed to the icing on the cake.

# CHAPTER 5

# Who Do You Remind People Of?

THERE'S A THIRD, and final, dimension to consider when evaluating the effect of aesthetic choices: *associations*. In truth, we make cognitive as well as emotional associations with just about everything processed by our brain. But, there's enough to be said specifically about aesthetic associations that we should discuss this dimension separately from cognition and affect. Let's revisit two versions of our familiar our button example one last time. First we we have:

Pretty standard, right? Let's examine the choices presented to us: Cancel (do nothing) or Delete Everything. The latter is a pretty serious option—and one that should be treated with a little more gravitas. Consider how you'd react if this button were presented in a way that's a bit more evocative:

Yikes! That button looks like something we don't want to touch—a sticker burr, or perhaps a stick of dynamite going off. But this image is consistent with the action we'd be performing by clicking that button. The sharp and explosive shape says, in a cognitive and affective way, "Watch out, this is a dangerous option!"

I use this example to demonstrate a point, but aesthetic associations are rarely this obvious. In fact, we may not even be conscious of many of the associations we make, until they are pointed out to us.*

---

* Example, "Delete Everything on your HD?" from Keith Lang, used by permission.

## AESTHETICS, ASSOCIATIONS, AND APPLE

In a 2005 essay on design and perceptions, Luke Williams recounts how another designer discovered why so many people think of the iPod as a "clean" device. Apparently, this designer had been sitting on the toilet (where all great ideas happen!) when it occurred to him that the iPod references the same materials used in a bathroom, "the shiny white porcelain of the bathtub and the reflective chrome of the faucet on the wash basin." This might sound laughable, until you factor in that Jonathan Ives, Apple's senior vice president of Design, once worked for an agency that designed—you guessed it—bathroom appliances.

Coincidence? Perhaps. What's important is that "consciously or unconsciously, the iPod materials reference a convention of 'cleanliness' that everybody interacts with every day—a bathroom."

We're talking about human perception, and the system of conventions that shapes our perceptions. Perception is essential to the process of design.

These aesthetic associations are evident in other Apple products. If you own an Apple laptop, you may have noticed the soothing sleep-light indicator that's visible when your computer is "sleeping." The rate at which this light fades in and out is comparable to that of the average respiratory rate for adults, about 12 to 20 breaths per minute. Coincidence? Apple owns the patent for a Breathing Status LED Indicator (US 6,658,577 B2), which "mimics the rhythm of breathing which is psychologically appealing."

One final example: when Apple launched the original iPod shuffle, they compared it directly to a pack of gum, due to the equivalent sizes of the two products. This is a great example of a conceptual metaphor, in which we make sense of new information by associating it with something we're already familiar with.

This was a brilliant metaphor, as size was a key market differentiator for the shuffle, and everyone is familiar with the approximate size of a pack of gum. Moreover, if you want to launch your low-cost, entry-level music player and break away from the premium associations established by the iPod and iPod nano, what better connotation than a pack of gum? Gum is cheap, small, and disposable. We might think twice about jogging with a $400 music player. But a pack of gum? No problem.

Apple even made a little joke about this association: In the fine print, they added the line "Do not chew iPod shuffle."

But this association extended to something else that, to my knowledge, no one else has commented on: the packaging. Do the arrows and shades of green bring to mind a particular brand of gum?

Wrigley's Doublemint is probably the most universally recognized brand of gum. And what are its two distinctive visual traits? Arrows and shades of green. Another association reinforced by an aesthetic choice.

## ADVERTISING AND CODED ICONIC MESSAGES

The idea of aesthetic associations is nothing new to advertisers. In 1964, the French philosopher Roland Barthes published his paper "Rhetoric of the Image," which deconstructs an ad into three messages: the linguistic message, the coded iconic message, and the noncoded iconic message. What we're talking about here are the *coded iconic messages* associated with specific images, that is, those things suggested or associated with the literal objects pictured. In Barthes's example, he discusses how the decision to show beautiful, fresh vegetables (and a box of pasta displaying a brand name) in a mesh grocery bag suggests freshness, plenty, and even "Italianicity" (in the yellow, green, and red of the tomato and peppers). A certain still-life aesthetic is also suggested. All in all, these are very positive brand associations.

How might thinking about these associations help us design better interactions?

*The layout and photography used by Groupon bring to mind high-end catalogs.*

## POSITIVE AND NEGATIVE ASSOCIATIONS

Groupon is a Web site that offers "one ridiculously huge coupon each day, on the best things to eat, see, do, and buy in [your city]." I've purchased gift cards for everything from a favorite Thai restaurant to an artisan cheese shop. The daily deals are typically on the classier side—think salons, fancier restaurants, and shopping. These are not closeout deals like you'd find on other "deal" sites. In fact, I believe Groupon wants to avoid any suggestion of a *cheap* deal. Consider the photography and layouts used in their daily deals. The photography is usually top notch. And the layout style brings to mind high-end catalogs (see above).

That's an example of positive associative priming. But here's an interesting discovery I made while researching the site: in earlier versions of the site, Groupon used the familiar dotted line or scissor-clipping element to border their deals, a design choice that has since been dropped for a simpler, solid border.

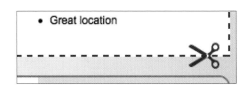

Why did they lose the scissors and the association with coupon clipping? I suspect this goes back to communicating a "value" message versus one that suggests cheap clearance. This would be an example of avoiding what for Groupon would be a negative (cheap) association.

## LANGUAGE AND ASSOCIATIONS

We construct mental associations via aesthetic suggestions. This is true in what we see as well as what we hear. Consider the Bouba-Kiki Effect, which highlights the connection between shapes and the sounds we make.

If I were to tell you that one of these shapes is called "bouba" and the other "kiki," which would be which? This study has been repeated in different cultures with the same results: almost everyone (95 to 98 percent of respondents) labels the shapes with the same names.

We all guess the rounded shape is probably "bouba" and the angular shape is "kiki." Why? Consider the shape of your mouth and the sounds you make as you utter each word.

There are obvious limits to these kinds of connections—much of language is borrowed or built on top of other languages. But, studies reveal the universal aesthetic associations we make that go beyond cultural or social norms.

## APPLICATIONS

Thinking about the associations that all people make, every moment, can significantly improve your designs. If we were to review our examples of product personality, we could identify each visual element that contributed to our perceptions: the harsh or smooth corners, bold or sophisticated color choices, contrast in type size, and so on. By understanding the *associations* suggested by different aesthetic cues, we can shape how people respond to our designs.

This leads us to a final, and perhaps controversial, topic: making aesthetic choices that aren't about beauty.

# A FRAMEWORK FOR EVALUATING VISUAL AESTHETICS ON WEB SITES

I've now presented three dimensions to consider when evaluating aesthetic choices: cognition, affect, and associations. We've explored the effects of each of these dimensions on behavior. But is there something more tactical we can apply to evaluate Web sites and applications? Inspired in part by Jared Spool's 2009 article "Deciding When Graphics Will Help (and When They Won't)," I've identified four groups of visual elements we can use to focus our conversations. These are:

- Basic design elements of color, typography, and white space are always present. Even word processing programs offer users their choice of line spacing, text choice, and text color.
- Iconic elements, such as icons, buttons, and navigation elements, communicate a message or action. The field of semiotics is devoted to visual representations like these.
- Content includes words as well as images, whether they are big pictures of a travel destination or product shots. Content is what users seek out.
- Texture and decoration include everything from wallpapers and ornamentation to line separators and the smiling lady staring at you on a homepage. These are not typically considered essential to the interaction.

Every visual element on a Web page should fit into one of those four buckets. But here's where problems enter into the conversation. If we stick with a flat list of these four kinds of visuals, it's easy to make judgment calls about their relative value: the value of basic design elements is debatable, iconic elements and content are critical, and decorative elements are fluff. However, as you've no doubt seen in the previous chapters, visual aesthetics may influence cognition, affect, and associations. With this in mind, I combined these two sets to form a matrix (see following page).

By understanding different types of graphic elements, and considering how each element might affect understanding (cognition), emotion (affect), or associations, we can have a more structured conversation. The model is intended as an evaluative tool. You can use it to look at a proposed or existing design. Simply break apart and map every design element to some square on this matrix. This will help determine the function of a given graphic element and evaluate its role in your design. From this perspective, if an element isn't defensible, then perhaps it should be cut.

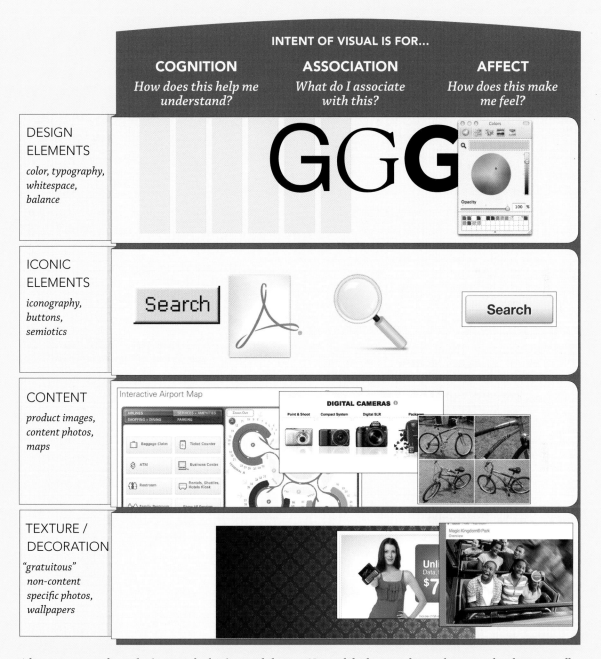

*A better way to evaluate the functional role of a visual element. Note, while the examples are shown are placed intentionally in this matrix, most visual images do play several functional roles. For example, with the digital camera example, these images serve both as content and as iconic elements, influencing cognition (camera type) and affect ("Ooh, I like the looks of that one!").*

# CHAPTER 6

# When Aesthetics Aren't Attractive

TO BE CLEAR, I love beautiful things. And I love the idea that a skilled designer can make the world a more beautiful place, one ligature or pleasing color palette at a time. But I need to clarify something.

Up until this point, I've used the words aesthetics and attractiveness interchangeably. However, aesthetics encompass more than just beauty or any of beauty's siblings: good, pleasant, pretty, or nice. Recall that aesthetics are concerned with how we perceive and interpret the world through our senses. In this regard, aesthetics are as much about our response to a beautiful woman as our response to an ugly duckling. Aesthetics are concerned with those things that elicit a response, even if that response is disgust.

Let's explore the implications of this.

## CURIOUS IMPLICATION 1: THE GOOD, THE BAD, AND THE UGLY

In the early days of SlideShare, a site for sharing presentation slides, co-founder Rashmi Sinha made an interesting statement: "Underinvest in visual design." She was commenting on designing for social interactions, and felt that having an unpolished look, as SlideShare did, actually let users feel ownership of the site. If you've ever heard someone negatively describe something as "too slick and polished," you'll understand the point Sinha was trying to make. The designers of SlideShare made a conscious choice to leave some details "undesigned" in order to make users feel a certain way about the site. They made a conscious, aesthetic choice to influence perceptions, judgment, and behavior.

As a side note, Craigslist might be following this undesigned aesthetic, though I think there's far more going on in this case. For many people, Craigslist is about a story that goes beyond the actual service. Right or wrong, people have come to associate Craigslist with a certain visual aesthetic. Changing the site, even in minor ways, might communicate a shift in values or a change in the story.

On a similar note, think about most donut shops. Intentionally or not, most non-chain donut shops look uniformly generic. Signs are typically in uppercase yellow or red letters and simply state "DONUTS" (even if the name is Lucky Donuts or Family Donuts). Most designers would love to create an identity for their local donut store. But think about these identities for a second:

The logo on the bottom promises something unique: a different donut, maybe nicer decor. There's something *distinctive* about it. But look at the sign on the top. We could be in any city in the U.S. and we'd all react to that sign in much the same way. Even before entering the store, we can be fairly certain that the donuts will be of a certain variety, and there will be the same somewhat generic and dated decor. The donut box will be the same white box sold to all donut shops. We could even predict the kind of napkins they'll be using! In many ways, this *undesigned* aesthetic is almost a brand unto itself. What kind of harm might a well-designed identity do to a donut store that benefits from being generic? Might people turn away, thinking that prices might be a bit higher? If you want to pay more, you go to an established brand like Krispy Kreme, or Dunkin Donuts, right?

Whether you care about visual design or not, aesthetic judgments are a reality. Even an undesigned site can be made more effective, depending on your intentions. A good designer might go so far as to intentionally make low-brow visual aesthetic choices to accomplish an objective—just don't make your system difficult to use in the process.

### CURIOUS IMPLICATION 2: WHEN UTILITY IS BEAUTIFUL

Remember, we make design decisions in support of a particular behavioral goal. While there's a natural desire to make the world a prettier place, this may not always be in the best interest of the project. Take road signs as an example.

It might be fun to design a prettier stop sign. But would this be appropriate? Given the behavioral objective—making people aware that they need to stop—how would your makeover look?

Would this design be an improvement over the familiar stop sign? No. In this case, the aesthetic choices should get your attention, speak clearly, and use as few words as possible. I might even venture to say that our current road sign is aesthetically pleasing, given the functional context.

This naturally leads into issues of context.

Let's revisit our gas station example from Chapter 4. You'll recall that the poorly maintained appearance of one gas station resulted in a lack of trust—and business. I turned instead to the more attractive (and presumably trustworthy) Shell station. My context for this example was living in a fairly well-off suburb where this kind of inattention sends a terrible message. What happens if we change the context? Suppose we're on a dusty desert drive across the U.S. The inferior gas pump might be part of a good narrative we can share with others later on. The Shell station in this context would suggest a dull, predictable experience. Safe, perhaps. But certainly not the stuff of stories.*

What is attractive in this case depends on the context.

To some extent, we make contextual judgments online based on the industry or the size of the company. Think of the peculiarities of different industries: luxury brands will likely have an all-Flash site, heavy on photography and gratuitous animation. Despite accessibility and search engine optimization (SEO) issues, these choices signal a certain kind of company. A Web site for enterprise software applications is likely to have text that is overly verbose, riddled with jargon, and set at a point size that is difficult to read. There won't be any screenshots and if there is a demo, it'll be mostly aspirational with heavy use of stock photography.

Contrast this with the Web 2.0 aesthetic that favors large type, clear and succinct explanations, and actual screenshots of the tool. While I love the clarity of this latter example, you have to wonder what happens when a software app that costs six figures is designed in the same style as a popular hosted Web app that has a monthly cost only slightly more than that of a few lattes. While we can argue for good and bad design, the *context* in which we're designing should influence the final visual aesthetic.

This leads us into the issue of personal preferences.

## CURIOUS IMPLICATION 4:
## IS BEAUTY SUBJECTIVE?

I mentioned SlideShare and Craigslist as having undesigned aesthetics. But what about a site like Quora compared to one like Gowalla (see top of following page)?

Both of these sites are beautiful. Much thought has been put into the visual aesthetics of both user interfaces. In terms of classical aesthetics, both sites make nice use of contrast, in both size and color. The fonts are legible. Appropriate padding, spacing, and line height have all been considered. Yet, when we think of design awards and what someone might put in their portfolio, we typically think of a site like Gowalla. Due to its *expressive* qualities, it looks like something that was touched by a visual designer.

*This perspective from a comment by Mads Bøkder on my April, 2009 posting at alistapart.com, "In Defense of Eye Candy."

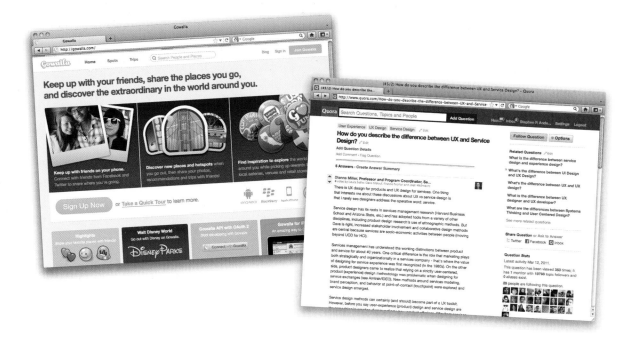

This brings us to the subjective nature of aesthetics. You may have a strong preference for one of these designs. But to say that beauty is in the eye of the beholder isn't entirely accurate. Just think of who we find attractive. While everyone has their own actor or actress they find attractive, we do, as a culture tend to agree on some characteristics that make one person attractive and another person ugly.

### Three modes of beauty?

Designer Cennydd Bowles proposes on his blog that there are three modes of beauty: universal, sociocultural, and subjective.

1.  *Universal beauty* is concerned with fundamental aesthetic principles of design, such as symmetry, harmony, the rule of thirds, and the golden ratio. These are the classical underpinnings of attractive design. A good deal of psychology and evolutionary biology offers explanations for these universal principles. Our visual system is tuned to organize information and find patterns and order in things.

2.  *Sociocultural beauty* is what we find attractive as a culture at a particular point in time. Marilyn Monroe was one of the most celebrated figures in the world. Yet, if she were alive today, it's doubtful she would be considered as a model of beauty. On the Web, think of the different stylistic trends that have been popular among different groups at different times.

3.  *Subjective beauty* is what you personally find attractive. This is where your personal tastes and preferences enter the picture. You may find the spartan aesthetic of Quora very pleasing or you may find it rather dull.

Bowles goes on to suggest that these three modes are hierarchical: subjective beauty overrides sociocultural beauty, which in turn outweighs universal beauty.

### Most Advanced, Yet Acceptable (MAYA) aesthetic

Another theory about beauty, this one proposed by Raymond Loewy in 1951, suggests that we prefer the Most Advanced, Yet Acceptable (MAYA) aesthetic. This approach balances the delight we find in new stimulus with the security we find in familiar things.

According to Paul Hekkert, who researches emotional design and aesthetics, "Designers need to find a balance between innovation and novelty (advanced) and a certain amount of typicality (acceptable)." His 2003 study offered "a strict empirical test" for the MAYA theory in support of "attractive designs."

While this is a brilliant model for evaluating aesthetics, how might it be helpful? In Hekkert's study, participants rated objects such as telephones and tea kettles on these three dimensions of novelty, typicality, and aesthetic pleasure. Could we do the same for our audiences? As we design for a particular audience, we need to think about what is novel and what is typical for that group. It's easy to design the tool we'd like to use. But if the audience is different from us, we may design something unappealing to them if they have different aesthetics. If you eat, sleep, and breathe startup applications, your aesthetic preferences will be quite different from someone who lives in the world of enterprise software applications, for example. It's not that preferences can't change over time—they do. We just need to be aware of our audiences' existing aesthetic preferences. Nowhere is this clearer than in how we decorate our homes or choose our clothes.

What I like about Bowles's modes of beauty and the MAYA approach is that these explanations recognize universal as well as personal aesthetics. Beauty isn't purely in the eye of the beholder.

## CLOSING

While most of us do enjoy attractive things, the point of all this is to think about the intended effect of our aesthetic choices. Once you understand the effects of different aesthetic choices, you'll see that it's entirely possible to make intentional design choices that may seem to lack any sense of style—if you believe that will accomplish a particular behavior goal.

At a fundamental level, our brains are trained to make associations. This is a basic way that we learn and acquire knowledge, leveraging what we already know to make sense of new information. Just as specific words or phrases can trigger an association, so can images.

Visual comprehension can be summarized as "what you see depends on what you look at and what you know." When we're talking about associations, we're focusing on what we know, whether from past experiences or from some universal wellspring that influences our judgments and behavior.

What is being suggested by the aesthetics details in your Web app or services?

# CHAPTER 7

# The Power of Faces

GIVEN THAT THIS SECTION is devoted to aesthetics and beauty, it's worth noting the unique benefits of introducing faces, even in as simple a form as avatars, into our online interactions.

Interface designer Joshua Porter made a curious statement on his blog: "The mere presence of others dramatically changes our behavior." Deciding to explore this statement, and have a bit of fun in the process, I created the images at the bottom of this page. Perhaps more than any other visual element, faces carry with them associations (some positive and some negative) and can influence our perceptions and behavior in interesting ways.

For example, we tend to look where other people are looking. So, in the next column, we look where the smiling woman is looking: back at this text.

In this example then, the "decorative" image of the woman plays a *functional* role in guiding our eyes to a specific area of the page.

Faces can also be used to reinforce social proof. Rather than simply listing a number of supporters, I've come across a few advocacy sites that display the avatars of everyone who has tweeted about their cause. The resulting wall of faces is fairly persuasive.

*"The mere presence of others dramatically changes our behavior."*

*"The mere presence of others dramatically changes our behavior."*

*"The mere presence of others dramatically changes our behavior."*

*How does your perception of the quote change simply by swapping out different faces?*

With one of my own projects, I needed to indicate how many people had attended a meeting. I initially used a group icon and a number count. While looking at icon variations to associate with different group sizes, it occurred to me to ditch the icon and use avatars instead. I replaced the icon with a string of very small, 20×20 pixel avatars, one for each person who had attended the meeting. You can now see not only how many people are in the meeting (by the length of the bar formed by faces), but also who was in a meeting—the actual faces of the people who attended. And this higher fidelity of information in less space is much more useful, especially when searching for a meeting you had a few weeks ago with a particular group of people.

In this same tool, we wanted people to follow through on commitments or promises they had made. One small nudge we added was showing the face of the person making the request.

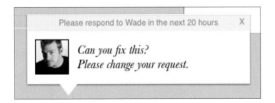

So, now you have to look at someone asking you about some task you committed to do. Just the presence of that face makes it seem more personal, like something you need to follow through on.

## LEAVING YOUR FRIENDS

Does adding a face make a difference? We don't yet have the statistical data to prove this one way or another, but I can share how adding faces to the deactivation screen worked wonders for Facebook.

The original Facebook deactivation page was pretty boring. It simply stated: "We're sorry you're leaving. Tell us why Facebook was not useful." One of the designers suggested that closing your account be "more like leaving summer camp (you know, a place that has all your friends and you don't want to leave.)"

Inspired by this concept, the design team created a new deactivation page that pulls faces from a few of your friends' profiles, along with the message that asks, "Are you sure you want to deactivate your account? Your 498 friends will no longer be able to keep in touch with you." Has this made a difference? According to Julie Zhuo, design manager at Facebook, this has reduced the deactivation rate by 7 percent. At least a million fewer users have deactivated their accounts!

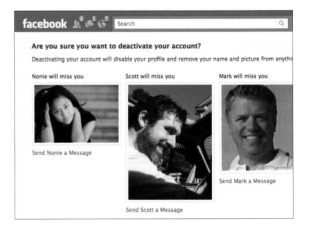

Aside from being aware of aesthetic choices, how can you make use of everything presented in this section? I've tried to speak to the value of aesthetics, and some deeper considerations that are often overlooked., That said, here are a few suggestions for making visual aesthetic choices.

## SUMMARY

### Don't

- Violate aesthetic suggestions. It's easy to get caught up in popular design memes without fully understanding the associated messages. Remember, if you were asked to build a physical model of what is shown on screen, could you?
- Break Gestalt laws of perception. In the abstract, Gestalt laws make perfect sense. Yet, I frequently see the most basic ideas violated on the Web.
- Dismiss non-functional design elements as gratuitous before evaluating possible emotional and associative (or noninstrumental) value.
- Prioritize visual design over other considerations. As much as this section is an argument for aesthetics, remember that good design is about making holistic, evaluative decisions.
- Treat visual design as decoration, added in at the end of a project. Enough has been said about this approach.

### Do

- Consider the meta-narrative that is constructed through visual associations. Every aesthetic element suggests associations—consider these associations carefully.
- Look for opportunities to reinforce or replace text with visuals. I often evaluate designs by asking, "Could a five-year-old understand this?" Changing perspectives like this is a great way to evaluate a page with fresh eyes.
- Explain difficult concepts with visual metaphors or models. I've used or referenced a number of models throughout this book. Complex ideas can be made much simpler through just a bit of visual thinking. For more on this, check out Dan Roam's 2008 book *The Back of the Napkin*.
- Obsess over basic design details. Regardless of your visual style, basic design principles like white space can make a big difference in how people perceive the experience or your content.
- Make aesthetic choices appropriate to your audience and the goals of your business.

# Playful Seduction

In the context of dating, we use playful behaviors to connect with others. We tease each other with little tidbits of information about ourselves. We serve up flirtatious smiles at just the right moment. We ask silly questions or make humorous propositions. We "accidentally" brush a hand against the other person's skin. Assuming there's some mutual interest, these signals say, "Hang out with me and you'll have a good time."

So what about Web sites?

Unfortunately, most Web sites and applications—especially software applications—care very little about making things fun. Conversations about users tend to focus on task completion and efficiency. Instead of a "hang out with me and you'll have a good time" message, we get something quite different:

Check. Move on. Next please. The message is clear, but also a bit boring. There's also an implied message: Leave your smiles at the door. It's time to get down to some serious business.

But wait! Aren't we supposed to be designing systems that are easy to use, efficient, and get out of people's way? While there's an argument to be made for utilitarian experiences, a tool that works isn't necessarily a tool that people will use.

In dating terms, it's easy to think, "People will like me for who I am." The truth is people have to be interested just enough to get to know you (your app) in the first place. What we're talking about in this chapter are ways to design interactions that are more interesting and playful—interactions that engage people in both intellectually and emotionally. This leads to experiences that do more than merely work, they delight people.

# CHAPTER 8

# Are You Fun To Be Around?

CONSIDER THESE two signs:

Both signs communicate the same message: *Do not park here*. However, only one engages us in an emotional way.

Southwest Airlines is famous for adding humor to their in-flight messages (I've included a few here to the right). Are these messages a bit irreverent? Yes. But most travelers seem to enjoy a bit of humor added to otherwise routine messages.

What's noteworthy in both of these cases is that the message is clearly communicated—it's never obscured by the humor. But, the language is much more natural and human (and something we'll remember later).

*In the event of a sudden loss of cabin pressure, oxygen masks will descend from the ceiling. Stop screaming, grab the mask, and pull it over your face. If you have a small child traveling with you, secure your mask before assisting with theirs. If you are traveling with two small children, decide now which one you love more.*

*Ladies and gentlemen, if you wish to smoke, the smoking section on this airplane is on the wing and if you can light 'em, you can smoke 'em.*

*There may be 50 ways to leave your lover, but there are only four ways out of this aircraft.*

**SOUTHWEST.COM**®

This raises an interesting question: Is this same kind of humor appropriate in a Web context? Surprisingly, this has actually been a matter of debate, and for valid reasons.

For example, humor doesn't always translate well across cultures. Or even within cultures for that matter! Given the global context of Web sites, you're never sure who you might be speaking to. Also, without contextual clues like facial expressions and other signals, attempts at humor might be taken seriously and offend or confuse; hence, the use of emoticons to indicate irony, humor, sarcasm, and other emotions.

That said, these are good arguments for the *careful* use of humor. But these are not reasons to avoid adding humor to our interactions. Sure, if there are doubts, it's much easier to *avoid* taking the risk of humor. However, you also risk publishing content that fails to engage people in a meaningful or memorable way. Adding a bit of humor will not only make you interaction more human, it can also add levity to an otherwise stressful situation, leading to any number of beneficial physiological effects (more on this in a moment).

Perhaps a more honest reason for avoiding humor is this: The use of humorous elements forces you to *know* your audience—something that is extraordinarily difficult for most businesses, as businesses often try to appeal to as many people as possible. In Chapter 25 I'll speak a bit more about establishing a clear identity and attracting the right people.

## USE HUMOR, WHEN APPROPRIATE

I often encounter people who say, "I work in [such and such an industry]. Do you think humor is appropriate?" My simple answer? If it's appropriate in a real-world interaction, why not online as well? Are we suddenly transformed into emotionless automatons when we sit in front of a screen? No.

If I walked into a bank to report that I'd been a victim of identity theft, it would be quite inappropriate to make light of the situation. I'd be comforted by a different emotion—sympathy. Humor would not be welcome. However, if I were opening a bank account, an entirely different activity, would it be okay for some humor from the teller opening my account? Yes.

Humor is appropriate (or inappropriate) based on the situation, not the industry.

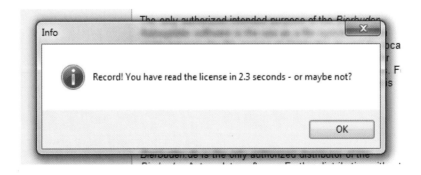

## A CASE FOR HUMOR: MAILCHIMP

One site that excels at making its customers smile is MailChimp. MailChimp is a service for managing e-mail campaigns. Whether your business needs to send out 500 e-mails or 500,000, MailChimp is an excellent choice, but not just for the business of managing e-mail campaigns. Early on, the owners made a conscious decision to focus on the *emotional* experience they were creating.

The first thing you'll notice is their mascot: a chimp named Freddie. He's always present in the site header, and he's always exclaiming rather interesting phrases, like:

*I kissed a chimp and I liked it.*

*How much mail would a mail chimp mail if a mail chimp could chimp mail?*

*My weapon of choice in any battle? The bacon lance. ["Bacon lance" links to a video on another site.]*

In fact, the very first time I used MailChimp, the image below greeted me at the top of the page. *Who would win in a death match between Bruce Lee and Iron Man?* What does this have to do with the chore of managing e-mail campaigns?

Of course I clicked on the link (wouldn't you?), which opened a new window, sending me to a YouTube video where someone has created a stop-motion fight between Iron Man and

Bruce Lee action figures. (If you want to know who wins, you'll need to find the video.)

MailChimp delights in other ways as well. The site is stocked with plenty of funny sayings. More curious YouTube videos. Hidden "Easter eggs," like popping the monkey's arm out if you create an e-mail larger than the recommended 600 pixels. A fake DOS screen preloader with plenty of humor in the text. Check boxes with text like "Enable evil pop-up mode."

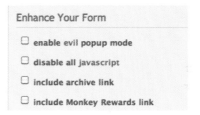

You might be wondering what all of this has to do with the business of managing e-mail campaigns. I think this quote from a MailChimp customer sums it up rather well:

*"Oh MailChimp monkey. Just as I get frustrated with wrangling e-mail addresses, you're there with your little witticisms to cheer me up."*

As frivolous as all these details may seem, there's solid thinking behind every decision. I had the chance to interview Aarron Walter, one of the creative minds behind this mischief.

# MAILCHIMP : A CASE FOR HUMOR

*Interview with Aarron Walter*

*One of the things I love about MailChimp is how you engage people emotionally in little ways, across different interactions. Did the company begin with the idea of making e-mail management fun, or was this a change along the way?*

The humor and personality of MailChimp is really just a natural channeling of who we are as a company. People don't want to interact with a corporate edifice if they don't have to. We've found that by letting our personality shine through in the application we can make mundane work feel kind of fun. The emotional engagement we layer into the app is designed to enhance the experience, and never impede the workflow. The little jokes that Freddie, our chimp mascot, cracks at the top of a page set a tone for the relationship people have with the app.

We've found that just as visual design can improve the perception of the usability of an interface, emotional design can have a similar effect. Customers have commented that the humorous greetings spur them on through task flows. When people are in a good mood, they're more creative about problem solving, and they can work through points of confusion more effectively. When people contact our support team, they crack jokes because of the application's personality—which I know our support team enjoys. It's a lot easier to help a happy person than a cranky one. We've found that designing for emotion isn't just fun, it makes good business sense too.

*MailChimp is essentially a business application. How have people responded to humor in a business tool?*

In general, people love our sense of humor, but as is true in the real world, when you let your personality come through you're bound to discover some people who just don't like you. We've heard from some users who want the app to be more buttoned up and "professional." We actually created a special mode in the app called "party pooper mode" that people can turn on to satisfy the frumpiest of bosses. As it turns out, only 0.007 percent of our users turn it on.

*What's one of your favorite MailChimp interactions?*

People love the e-mail preview Easter egg. Freddie stretches his arm out to show you how wide your e-mail will be in e-mail clients. If you stretch the preview window too wide, his arm pops off and spurts blood out of the socket. It's a bit macabre, but it seems to appeal to the British sense of humor.

Strong Bad, the famous luchador character from homestarrunner.com, made a guest appearance a while back. By pressing *T* on your keyboard as the app loaded, Strong Bad appeared in front of a computer monitor with an old school green screen terminal saying something wry about MailChimp. That was by far the coolest Easter egg we've ever implemented.

If people discover these little gems, great. We see lots of tweets reporting how a small surprise just made someone's day. But many people miss them, and that is just fine by us. Moments of delight lose their luster if they are imposed rather than discovered.

*Is there science behind your monkey business?*

Our emotional design techniques employ a common psychology concept called priming. Each emotional design interaction point shapes a user's perception of the MailChimp brand, and, if well executed, slowly builds good will and trust. The limbic system in our brains handles both emotion and long-term memory so we can easily recall things that are good for us or bad for us. By employing emotional design in our app, we're consciously shaping positive memories of our brand that not only encourage users to stick around, but also turn them into evangelists for a product they love.

*For companies wanting to add humor to their service, what advice would you offer? Are there lessons you've learned about what not to do?*

Humor isn't right for every situation. Personality is really what people should be thinking about in their websites. It's the thing that can make an interface feel more human. But if you construct a fake personality that isn't true to your company, you're going to come across as disingenuous. People can smell bull a mile away.

*There's a tendency for people to mimic things without understanding the process that led to those things. What would you say to the businesses that are looking at MailChimp and saying, "Let's make our business fun like them."*

Our approach to design isn't right for every business. Letting your personality shine through can help you connect with your audience. You'd never mimic another person's personality, so why do it with a brand? Companies should carefully consider who they are and create a design persona that reflects that.

*Are there any efforts at humor that have backfired, or weren't understood?*

The great thing about the funny greetings from Freddie in the header of the app is that they make our customers feel like a real human being is speaking to them through the interface. Nine point nine times out of ten, that works to our advantage to create a fun, human experience. But every once in a while a customer will misread one of those little jokes as a personal slight.

We had one greeting that read "Does this hat make my bum look big?" It's kind of funny because Freddie wears a tiny little hat and he's a big ape. A few people contacted our support team and were pretty mad that we were making fun of how big their butt was. The greeting said nothing about the user (we would never dream of insulting customers), but because the human mind can be primed to read a situation based on their previous experiences, the message they received was totally different than we intended. We've since learned to scrutinize each greeting more closely to consider the various ways people may interpret it.*

*Visit www.sixdbook.com to read full interview.

WHY BOTHER MAKING SOMEONE SMILE?

Thanks to a number of psychology studies going back to the 1940s, and more recent studies from neuroscience, we're starting to understand how positive and negative *affect* (a more accurate term for discussing mood and emotions) influences other things like our ability to solve creative problems, recall memories, make decisions, or help others.

For example, when subjects are made to feel happy (by being offered food or a small gift), they perform a complex task more efficiently than the control subjects. In one study, participants were asked to decide which of six cars they might purchase. The people in the positive affect group (who were told they'd performed above-average on a task of perceptual-motor skills) reached a decision much more quickly: 11 minutes versus the 19 minutes for those in the control group. Being in a good mood allowed people to "eliminate unimportant information and find useful heuristics to solve the problem" (Isen and Means, 1983).

Positive affect has also been shown to help us with creative problem-solving skills. We saw this in Chapter 2 with the candle problem. In another study on the effects of humor, college students were asked to solve puzzles involving word associations. The students who first watched a short stand-up routine by comedian and actor Robin Williams fared much better: they solved more of the puzzles (and "significantly more by sudden insight") compared to the students who watched a scary or boring video beforehand. But what is the thinking process that leads to these breakthroughs?

One study shows that our mental approach to sorting and rating information—how we categorize things—changes in response to our affect: when we're in a good mood, we see more associations (Isen and Daubman, 1984). This was extended to another study involving free associations from a list of words; the participants who were happy gave "more unusual and more diverse associations" (Isen et al., 1985). We know that having broader mental categories

---

**Business Model Generation Waiting List**

\* Required

**Your Name**
You can make it up if you want

Stephen P. Anderson

**Email** \*
Don't make this one up, we want to let you know when its available

stephen@poetpainter.com

*The microcopy beneath each of these form fields adds a bit of delight to an otherwise boring task.*

for things—more keywords if you like—helps with memory. Positive affect enables us to recall specific things we might otherwise forget.

On a chemical level, we can also talk about what goes on in the brain to make us respond in different ways. When we're anxious, the neural transmitter *norepinephrine* is released into the brain. Norepinephrine is the brain equivalent of adrenaline, and it creates a rush of fear or anxiety. During these anxious moments we are more alert and focused. In situations where focus is needed, such as editing a paper for grammatical errors, a bit of anxiety-induced norepinephrine might be just the right thing.

Contrast this with what happens when we're in a positive state: *dopamine*, a chemical associated with rewards and pleasure, is released into the brain. Where norepinephrine makes us alert, dopamine makes us interested. Good levels of both chemicals are needed for arousal; but each plays a different role. It's this latter kind of arousal, resulting from a release of dopamine, that not only excites us but also in a sense puts us out of our minds. It's in this state, also associated with happiness, that it becomes difficult to focus or shut out distractions. In his book *Emotional Design*, Donald Norman describes these states as "depth-first" (focused) and "breadth-first." It's in this latter state that we are more likely to make the unusual and diverse associations needed for creative thinking.

## ARE JAZZ MUSICIANS OUT OF THEIR MIND?

We're only now beginning to understand the functions of different regions within the brain. One area, the prefrontal cortex, is largely concerned with executive functioning, planning, and coordinating other areas of the brain. Without it, we'd be unable control our impulses, make decisions, or solve problems. When we make conscious choices, it's the prefrontal cortex that negotiates the memories and impulses offered up by other areas of the brain. So what happens when we're making the kinds of free associations involved with creative problem solving?

In a rather interesting study, jazz musicians were hooked up to an fMRI scanner and asked to play scales and do a bit of improvisation. The results? Scientists discovered that "activity in the dorsolateral prefrontal cortex [a large chunk of the frontal lobes associated with planned actions and self-censoring] reduces during jazz improvisation." In a sense, jazz musicians are out of their rational minds (without inhibitions) while improvising.

*Even mildly positive affective states profoundly affect the flexibility and efficiency of thinking and problem solving.*

—SCOTT BRAVE AND CLIFF NASS, "EMOTION IN HUMAN-COMPUTER INTERACTION" (2002)

# CHAPTER 9

# Are You Unpredictable?

URBANSPOON CREATED an interesting twist on choosing a restaurant. Taking a cue from slot machines, it turns deciding where to eat into a playful experience. You simply shake your phone (the app was one of the first to take advantage of the iPhone's accelerometer) and three slots for cuisine, price, and location are randomly selected. Don't like your choice? Shake again. While you can "lock" any of these slots, and the service does offer restaurant reviews, it's this simple playfulness that sets Urbanspoon apart from other restaurant review apps. And of course, this is the kind of thing people like to share with one another. The app is fun and (when it was released) it showed off a cool new feature of the phone.

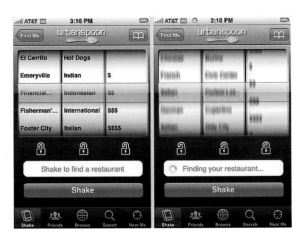

## Surprise taken to the extreme

Chatroulette offers a similar unpredictable experience. It's a live video chat site, but not one involving a list of friends or any intentional conversations. Instead, you're randomly paired with a stranger, at least until one of you clicks Next and is paired with someone else. The completely random nature of this system attracted a lot of curious—mostly younger—users and created an opportunity for some rather odd forms of expression. Impersonators, performers, curious onlookers, and yes, exhibitionists have all flocked to the site. Advertisers used the site to promote a remake of *The Exorcist* (users were paired with a teenage girl who suddenly appeared to become a demon possessed). Musician Ben Folds used the site to do piano improv live onstage. There have even been interesting social experiments, like being paired with a handwritten message stating, "Tilt your head and I win." (Most people tend to comply, at which point a hand appears to add another tally mark to the sheet of paper.)

Unfortunately, the complete lack of identity—you simply click Play to join in—encourages voyeurism and exhibitionism. Despite efforts to clean up Chatroulette, it has become associated with men flashing their privates. Still, there's something more than novelty going on here. In a world where most connections are based on a shared interest or history, there's something refreshing about a service based on serendipity.

Shervin Pishevar, an advisor to Chatroulette, notes, "Most of us have connected with the vast majority of our old friends, colleagues, and acquaintances by now," thanks to social networks like Facebook. "The venues to meet people *randomly* are increasingly limited." In the wake of Chatroulette, dozens of new services with business models based on serendipity have begun to emerge, including a dating site, a site for designers to get feedback on their work, and numerous Chatroulette clones that are trying to avoid the trolls by requiring authentication methods, such as Facebook Connect.

### Our brains are aroused by the unexpected

While stability and a sense of control are no doubt critical user interface principles, there's something exciting about the unexpected. Not knowing what to expect heightens our anxiety, and our curiosity.

*Our brains are aroused by new and unexpected discoveries within our normal routines.*

From a neuroscience perspective, being surprised releases a cascade of dopamine, a reward chemical. We actually get a brief high from this momentary surprise. In the case of Chatroulette, this surprise (and the anxiety preceding each new turn) is heightened by the social aspect of the experience. This is the antithesis of predictable and boring.

Note, in both of these experiences, control is never taken away from the users. I can pass to the next person in Chatroulette, or in the case of Urbanspoon, control the outcome by locking one or more slots. These random experiences never seize control of the experience—they enhance it.

In each of these cases, *surprise* is central to the experience. However, surprise could also be some small change. Consider a confirmation message that is different every time: "Got it!" or "Your data is safe with me!" or "Home run!" Or an image that changes on a frequently visited page. These little changes make the interaction seem more human. Do you want to work with an automaton or a feeling human? Surprise can be a very minor change that adds flavor and variety to an otherwise routine experience.

Surprise can also be external to the experience you've created. In advertising, there's the idea of zigging when everyone else zags (and vice versa). If everyone else is doing something one way, you'll get noticed if you go against the grain. How you can get people's attention by deviating from expected patterns set by other sites or experiences external to your site? Certainly design patterns and tested usability principles should be followed, but there's always room to do or present things differently. *Are there any small surprises in the experience you've designed?*

## MIXING SURPRISE WITH REWARDS

Surprises may also come in the form of variable rewards. Slot machines are a sinister example

of *variable rewards*. Just when you're ready to give up, you win a little bit. This win, however small, suggests that there is more to be had—if you just keep playing. The rewards may seem random, but in fact they're calculated to keep you feeding the machine. Too many rewards and you come to expect wins, and will be likely to quit when they don't come. Too few rewards and you'll give up. This technique is commonly used by dog trainers and parents alike to reinforce a desired behavior.

Gowalla is a mobile check-in service that uses variable rewards. Part of the game of playing Gowalla is collecting and trading virtual stickers. How do you get stickers? By checking into places. Imagine you're grabbing a peppermint mocha from the café around the corner. You pull out your phone, check in, and see, "Congratulations! You've found a virtual soundboard." You've been given something for this activity. Chances are good that you'll check in again at the next location you visit. But here's the catch: you're more likely to repeat this behavior if the reward of finding a sticker occurs at variable intervals.

If you were rewarded every time you performed the activity, you'd come to expect it. By randomizing the reward schedule, you become addicted (for better or worse).

Some variable rewards are calculated. Others are naturally occurring. Consider Twitter. If I'm following someone for a particular purpose, such as staying up on the latest tech news, these useful tweets are often mixed in with other kinds of expression, say, what the person is having for lunch. All it takes is one or two really useful links shared by some folks for me to be engaged again, looking for even more. This is part of the addictiveness of this service (and why it can be so disruptive to normal routines). If I don't follow the stream, I may miss out on something useful! The variable reward of something really useful or personally relevant makes it difficult to turn away from the never-ending stream of tweets.

*Gowalla's random reward notification.*

## DELIGHTERS

Another kind of surprise comes in the form of *delighters*. Like variable rewards, these occur at unpredictable times. They're unexpected. However, their intent is not to reinforce a particular behavior, but to simply bring joy—delight—to the user.

The term delighters comes from the hospitality industry and is used to refer to little things added to an experience that create delight and joy. Think of chocolates on your pillow. A plush towel. Free movies. Maybe a hot cup of tea when you're checking in.

I was on a trip to New York scouting locations for a workshop. As I walked up the stairs to exit the basement of the Ace Hotel, something caught my eye. A message had been written on one of the steps:

I smiled. *Everything is going to be alright.*

I've never seen anyone use a staircase in this way. And the message made me grin. Everything is going to be all right.

This is a perfect example of a delighter: it was *unexpected*—who thought of using that space? It was *unnecessary*—it wasn't critical to the act of getting up and down the stairs. It was also *pleasant*.

While different from a gift in that nothing was given to me, this very minor, creative addition to the hotel staircase offered the same effect as a gift: making people feel good. There is no functional justification for adding the text to the staircase, but it does engage people emotionally.

It was an unnecessary, unexpected, but altogether delightful surprise.

A good date is full of delightful moments—some planned, some not—that make the overall experience memorable and pleasant. What does my wife remember from our first date? Among other fond memories, it rained and we got our shoes stuck in the mud!

Think of an unexpected pleasure. A free dessert after your meal. A hidden level in your favorite video game. The Google logo changing to celebrate a holiday or a person.

Opening the MOO.com sticker packaging in a way you're not supposed to reveals a hidden message:

On rare occasions, a simple Google search will reveal a hidden surprise:

If you own a Nintendo Wii, you may have discovered the Wii Help Cat. It's a cat that wanders on the screen after some period of inactivity. If you move your cursor quickly to grab the cat, he runs away. But if you move carefully, you can sneak up on the cat and grab him (your cursor becomes a hand). Once you've grabbed the cat, you unlock a secret tip about how to use the Wii dashboard.

This is certainly not an efficient or easy way to present help text. But it does create engagement by reframing these tips as challenges to grab (literally). It also works because these tips are not essential to use the Wii, but are instead undocumented, secret features.

The notion of delighters first came to my attention in a post written by Matt Jones, co-founder of the travel site Dopplr. The site had recently rolled out a new feature: Personal Velocity, your total distance traveled divided out over a twelve-month period. By itself, the number isn't all that interesting. Who cares that my personal velocity is 6.47 km/hr? What's interesting is what they added to this metric: an avatar from the animal kingdom whose average speed is about the same as my personal velocity. (It turns out that 6.47 km/hr is about the same speed as a duck.) This small addition turned a boring metric into a playful and fun design element, and one that was well received by many Dopplr users.

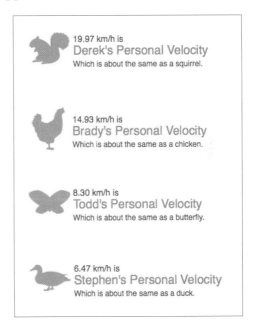

This leads me into one final kind of surprise: *gifting*.

## MY PERSONAL ANNUAL TRAVEL REPORT

In late 2008, I received an interesting e-mail from the travel site Dopplr:

*"We'll be sending you your personal annual report in January. To make sure your data is accurate in Dopplr, be sure to add any past trips in 2008 that you might have missed."*

Dopplr is a service where you can track your travel itineraries and share them with other people. It was built by a group of frequent travelers to increase the likelihood of chance meet-ups during travel.

The e-mail went on to show a sample of what to expect. I logged into my account, added the two or three trips I had forgotten to log, and then waited patiently for my personal annual report. Two weeks later, my poster shown below, arrived as promised. It was a gorgeous, personalized poster, delivered as a PDF file. And it was, quite simply, a delightful experience, one that exceeded my expectations of the service.

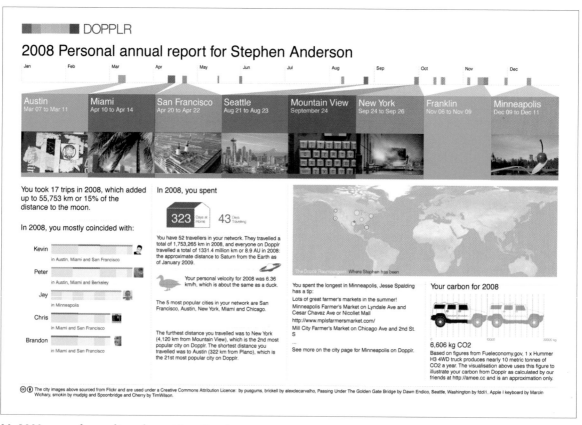

*My 2008 personal annual travel report from Dopplr.*

Brandon Schauer, consultant for Adaptive Path, speaks frequently about "the long wow" moment, when companies plan a string of thoughtful and delightful experiences that go well beyond the initial sign-up or purchase. He had this to say about Dopplr:

*This month Dopplr delightfully surprised me, supplying me with something I didn't know I needed. The result: I'm now a more loyal Dopplr user. It's a great example of a long wow moment.*

*What's remarkable is how much it delighted me and caused me to change my relationship with Dopplr. It delighted me because it was perhaps the best-designed statement I've ever received. I pine for the day that a bank or a phone company delivers a statement to me that provides insight about my behavior and makes me want to hang it on my refrigerator. But it also made me change my behavior:*

- *I immediately added my other trips that were missing from 2008 into Dopplr.*

- *I searched around to see if my most desired Dopplr feature existed yet. It does!*

- *And now I'm paying more attention to my update e-mails from Dopplr and spending more time with it. In all, I've reinvested in Dopplr all because they delivered something I wasn't expecting.*

So what's going on here? While we could certainly discuss any number of things (delighters, self-expression, humor effect, feedback loops, set completion), I'd like to focus on the idea of gifting, also known as *reciprocity*.

Reciprocity states that we are all bound—even driven—to repay debts of all kinds. When someone does something for you, you feel obligated to repay. Social scientists say it's an almost automatic reaction.

So what about online interactions? Is there some gift you can give away to your customers?

Unfortunately, when the idea of a gift is suggested, we go straight for gift cards, expensive prizes, or cheap trinkets branded with the company logo. (Hint: a good gift isn't about you.) Giving something away sends us straight to "it'll cost us money." Fortunately, as interaction designers, most of us deal in a digital currency of ones and zeros that has no hard physical costs: information and virtual gifts.

We're fortunate to work in a time and profession where information of all kinds is valued. But first, let's talk about what makes a good gift.

# WHAT MAKES A GOOD GIFT?

Remember the Saturday Night Live skit "Pumping Up with Hans and Franz" and the characters' catch phrase: "We're gonna pump you up!" Well, forget bulging biceps and Austrian accents. A good gift is one that pumps up the recipient.

# P.

### PERSONAL

Seriously, how many more pens with a stamped company logo does the world need? Unless you're Harley Davidson, Apple, or Whole Foods, you might think about something a bit less self-centered. Writer Dr. Robert Cialdini recalls checking into the Mandarin Oriental Hotel in Hong Kong. When he went to grab some stationery from the desk, he found his name embossed on it! Not the hotel's branding—his own name. He now recommends that hotel more than any other he has ever visited.

*The Dopplr travel journal was a report about me. Not the cities I visited. Not about Dopplr's users. It was about me. My travels. My friends. My carbon footprint (for better or worse).*

# U.

### UNEXPECTED

This one is easy enough. The more unexpected a gift is, the more pleasant it will be. Companies fall into the trap of copying one another's unique ideas. And guess what? Pretty soon that unique idea isn't so unique. I'm sure the first time a company gave away some stationery it was a nice thing. Now, it's cliché.

*The idea of a personal travel report had never occurred to me. I might have expected a few stats presented online, like Web site analytics are presented, but not a nicely designed, printable personal travel report.*

# M.

## MEANINGFUL (USEFUL, NOT GENERIC)

In the late 1990s, Red Sky Interactive had a knack for creating meaningful promotions. How? They promoted brands by giving customers something they could actually use—something meaningful. For Sutter Home, America's leading producer of premium varietal wine, they created the Mood Maker, an app combining animated, user-customizable blends of wine country sights and sounds.

Some of the best promotional items I've held onto were useful to me in some way. The "It's Miller Time" campaign (for Miller beer) was extended through a Miller branded instant-messaging client. Colorado-based EffectiveUI recently gave away a dot grid sketchpad and a stencil set for sketching wireframes. How much better might the swag given away at a conference be if companies started with the premise that their logo would not be making an appearance?

*My Dopplr travel report was something I could print out and put on a wall. It was an artifact of my travels and held a mirror up to such things as the number of days I was on the road and my carbon footprint (as measured in Hummers).*

# P.

## PLEASANTLY PACKAGED

A friend of mine who designs packaging for such brands as Maui Jim, Tag Heuer, and Zales jewelers talks frequently about the "point of gifting," how the presentation of something is critical to shaping the perception that something is a nice gift to be cherished.

*Essentially, Dopplr gave away information. But the information was packaged as an attractively designed poster. It was fun to look at and share with others.*

Other than personal informatics like the Dopplr report, what are some other kinds of information you can give away? Information could also be exclusive research, or an unpublished or personally relevant article. Perhaps a podcast or a music download. Some authors provide notes or slides to go along with their books. For Web apps, maybe it's a free month (just for being a customer) or access to a locked or not-yet-released feature. Information could be expert knowledge and advice, experiences, stories, links, PDF files, photographs, humorous videos, recipes, tips, free online seminars, white papers, code, plug-ins, wallpapers, screensavers, audio files, transcripts, or online tools. There's no shortage of things we can reproduce and share—publicly or privately—online.

If you've succeeded in creating your own online community, or if you operate inside an existing online community, virtual gifts such as stickers, avatars, and badges are also highly esteemed within an active social group. A powerful game mechanic behind the explosive growth of the game FarmVille was the idea of social gifting, where you need to give away seeds and items to other players to advance in the game.

Also, look beyond your own domain. How can you work with other services to provide a unique gift? Partner with a service like Gowalla to create a unique badge. Gift someone in the form of a public compliment or post.

I prefer to stay away from monetary gifts for a reason other than cost. In his 2008 book *Predictably Irrational*, Dan Ariely distinguishes between "social exchanges" and "monetary exchanges." People might gladly do something as a favor, but feel insulted when they

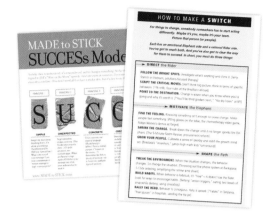

To promote their books, speaking, and training, brothers Dan and Chip Heath give away one-page crib notes, podcasts, and other goodies—in exchange for your e-mail address.

are offered compensation. You wouldn't get up from the table after a wonderful meal at someone's house and ask your host how much you owe them for dinner—that would be insulting. Similarly, many lawyers would rather do a small amount of volunteer work than offer their services at a reduced rate.

When negotiating new consulting opportunities, I make it a habit to share articles and links that the prospective client will find relevant to their business. This shows that I'm listening to their needs and that I am interested in the topic. While I have no expectations associated with passing on this information—it is given freely—I do hope this small gesture is reciprocated by a continued dialogue, hopefully leading to work. But there are no strings attached.

Remember, reciprocity is about gifts being given with no expectation of getting something in return. Some sites push this principle a bit further and suggest ways to return the favor. While suggesting actions is certainly okay, especially if it's something small such as liking

*Scribd, a social reading and publishing site, suggests you "give back" to the community—transaction or gift?*

a page or sharing it with other people, this can come off as pushy if handled poorly. Think about the dating analogy: "I paid for dinner, now it's your turn to put out." You don't want your Web app to be like that creep.

Also, a bit of real-world relationship advice: Gifts given freely, with no expectations, tend to pay off more than *quid pro quo* transactions masquerading as gifts. The whole "I'll do this for you, if you'll do this in exchange" idea cheapens otherwise nice gestures. If you're in love with someone, you want to do things for them. You want to make them happy. And here's the irony: when you give with no expectation of return, the favor is often returned in some meaningful way. But this isn't an exchange of services. These are acts of caring.

In the case of Dopplr, they didn't ask for anything in return for sending my personal annual report, but I told people about Dopplr. I mentioned them in my presentations. I invited my friends. Even as more of my friends began using

Dopplr's primary competitor, TripIt, I remained loyal for several years.

A word of caution: today's gift may be tomorrow's commodity. If other companies or similar services are giving away the same thing, it's not a gift anymore—it's an expectation. For example, if everyone offers a free sample chapter from their book, that becomes the new expectation. It is no longer a gift.

Case in point: a classic gifting study involves the inclusion of personalized mailing address labels. When a nonprofit site included personalized mailing labels in their solicitation letter, donations nearly doubled, from 18% to 35%. Here's the problem: how many solicitations have you received that include personalized mailing labels? At one point, I would save and use these. Now, they go straight to the recycling bin. What was once a unique and meaningful gift is no more.

Gifts can also include the joy of discovery, something that you'll see in the next chapter.

# CHAPTER 10

# Are You Stimulating?

LOOK AT THE IMAGE on the opposite page. See the anything interesting?

If you stare long enough, no doubt you'll find several patterns. But there isn't one, at least not intentionally. The brain naturally seeks ways to organize and simplify complex information, even when there is no pattern.

And when we find a pattern, we are delighted. It's akin to solving the Rubik's Cube, or aligning jewels in Bejeweled. We delight in bringing order to chaos. In fact, our brains actually get a brief "high" from solving difficult problems.

If you use the movie rental service Netflix, you've no doubt experienced the delight of this pattern recognition. All new members see a fairly random assortment of movies; the site knows nothing about you. Your idea of movie night could be a chick flick or a bad sci-fi film. The site simply doesn't know anything about your preferences. But, there's a game involved. There are no points or levels—instead, the game is built entirely on feedback loops and pattern recognition. Users are urged to rate movies they've seen. It's simple, the more movies you rate, the better the recommendations. And so you give three stars to one movie, five stars to another—and you notice something. The recommendations seem to be getting better. And, you notice more movies you want to see, and fewer from the genres you don't care for.

This happens in everything from puzzles to basic shape identification. What makes the letter A an A? We can set it in dozens of different typefaces, but we still recognize it as the first letter of the alphabet. But the ability to recognize patterns goes beyond shape and puzzles—it's fundamental to learning. In fact, neuroscientists have argued that "pattern recognition represents the key to understanding cognition in humans." In every new situation, we learn by recognizing patterns and associating this stimulus with things we've encountered before. This is true of recognizing objects such as letters and faces. It's also true of concepts, being able to recognize how a new idea relates to your existing mental model of the world.

You can hack people's ability to recognize patterns. Turn the page for an example:

# CAN YOU FIND THE SEVEN DIFFERENCES BETWEEN THE TWO IMAGES?

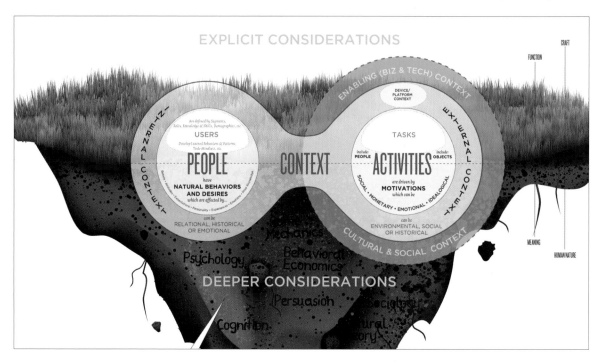

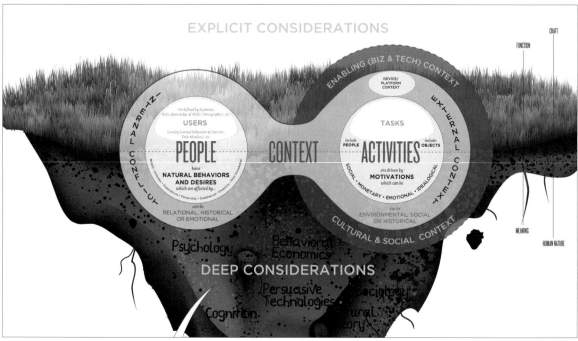

So what's going on here? Did you find the seven differences between the two concept models? If you were diligent, you might have, but that was not really the goal. My behavioral goal was to get you to spend more time with the content. Did it work?

Okay, that was fun. But let's not stray too far away from practical applications of this idea.

What information can you display in a way that arouses curiosity and encourages pattern-seeking behavior? Patterns can be found within a single page (a list of albums, for example) or spread throughout a site (a curious icon set or color coding that make sense once the pattern is discovered). Also consider playful ways to enable users to organize or label information, such as making a game of arranging things.

Here are a few examples.

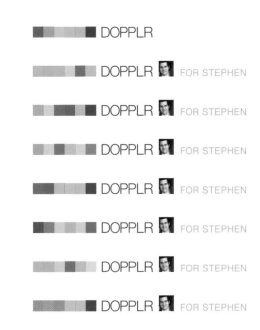

## WILL THE REAL DOPPLR LOGO PLEASE STAND UP?

When I first started using Dopplr, something odd caught my attention: the logo seemed to change all the time. It was always six colored blocks. But the colors shifted in subtle ways over time. The changes were never random—there were always remnants of the colors I had seen previously. But what was the pattern? To make things more interesting, everyone else seemed to have a wildly different version of the logo—six completely different colored blocks. Since the changes were obviously not random, I had to figure out the pattern, or rule, governing these changes. This was a puzzle to be solved!

Dopplr's visual aesthetic is largely grayscale. Color is used only in association with a city (first clue). After a bit of digging, I found a blog post that explained how the site assigned colors.

Dopplr's co-founder Matt Biddulph says he arrived at a simple formula to assign every city in the world a unique color: "Take the MD5 digest of the city's name, convert it to hex, and take the first six characters as a CSS RGB value."

Once I understood this, I could see that the color changes reflected my own travels. This small string of six colored blocks would change as I added new trips. Accordingly, everyone else would have a different set of blocks, except where our trips overlapped.

Dopplr's Matt Jones notes, "As well as the aesthetic delights we believe that city colours bring to the service, we're using them as visual affordances—ways to create implicit meaning and usefulness in the user-interface. When you look at a list of your fellow travellers, you'll see a coloured border around their icon, which correlates to their current location—allowing you to spot coincidences visually."

Puzzle solved.

On a similar note, I was working on a project that used a curious set of icons to indicate the status of a request.

The question came up as to whether we should make the icons more explicit by adding labels or all tags. While you could certainly argue the need to offer clear visual cues, I felt that the icons reinforced what the text already stated. And once you learned the pattern language, it made complete sense. In the end, I decided that the user's delight in deciphering this visual cue on her own would create a better overall experience.

What information can you display in a way that arouses curiosity and encourages pattern-seeking behavior?

> look at the inbox me
>
> modify (add nail) to
>
> respond to Matt Dev
>
> find out why email v
>
> talk to Matt Heard a
>
> follow up with Keith
>
> roundup some featu
>
> contact Jakub abou
>
> follow up with Jacol

## PATTERN RECOGNITION AND...QUILTING?

My wife called me while I was on the road.

"My mom and I went to a quilting exhibit. We took the boys."

"Oh no," was my response. You can probably guess the image that came to my mind. Children, especially boys under the age of six, aren't known for their patience. Take four wild boys. Put them in a room full of quilters and ladies going on about different fabric patterns. You can imagine what would follow.

It turns out, however, that the disaster was averted. Upon entrance to the exhibit, each of my boys was given a crayon and a sheet of paper with 20 quilting patterns to look out for. As mom and grandma meandered through the exhibit, the boys had a game to play—find all the quilting patterns. Some genius had created a game that combined pattern recognition with set completion.

# CHAPTER 11

# Are You Mysterious?

IN THE PREVIOUS CHAPTER, we looked at how people delight in the puzzle-solving aspect of pattern recognition. Now, let's go a bit deeper and explore what drives this pattern seeking behavior: *curiosity*.

Great storytellers know how to turn an ordinary event—say, a trip to the grocer—into a suspenseful one by withholding information. In new relationships, flirtation often involves some element of playful teasing, whether through conversation or more sensual revelations. And newsrooms have made a science out of crafting irresistible headlines: "Your PC might be infected!" or "Are you prepared for the tax law changes?"

We are captivated by unanswered questions.

## CURIOUS MARKETING

In recent years, Hot Wheels has begun including a "mystery car" in their store shipments. While the other cars are encased in clear plastic, the mystery car is shielded by opaque black plastic. You have no idea what kind of car is in there.

With two or three dozen Hot Wheels to choose from, guess which one the kids go for? In my experience, the one that gets attention (and allowances) is the mystery car—the one that is unknown.

Crazy? Perhaps it is. But this exact same bit of psychology also works on grown-ups.

Here's a rather interesting promotion from California Pizza Kitchen. At the end of my dinner, I was given the bill and a CPK "Don't Open It" Thank You Card.

It's a coupon with an interesting twist: you bring this card with you the next time you come to CPK. You've already won something, from a free appetizer up to $50 dollars (or more). But you won't know what you've won until your *next* visit. The instructions are pretty clear: whatever you do, do not open the card or your prize is null and void! A manager has to open the card for you when you return. You are guaranteed to get *something* worthwhile—and this is a critical part of arousing curiosity. Coupons are too explicit: "Here is your 20% off." Scratch-offs and lottery tickets are most likely to reveal that you've won nothing. With the CPK coupon, the fine print teases you with a list of the possible prizes. Now I'm curious: *which prize have I won?* This is a mystery that needs solving.

So are there ways that we—as interaction designers—can leverage curiosity in our designs?

## VENTURING INTO THE UNKNOWN

I've been thinking about two kinds of information: "known" and "unknown."

As user experience professionals, we excel at making things known. If it's unknown, it's unclear and likely to be confusing. A puzzling button label? Make it clear. A confusing process? Make it more familiar. For good reasons, we value things like user control, clarity, and consistency. We remove uncertainty in interfaces.

But once we've removed all the usability potholes from a particular path, how can we reintroduce the simple thrill of driving? How can interactions be made more effective—and fun—by introducing a bit of controlled uncertainty?

Let's go back to our Hot Wheels and CPK examples. Did you notice these things?

- Some tiny bit of information makes us aware of something that is unknown. Black plastic packaging hides a toy inside, or we are presented with a mysterious card.
- Context provides some relevance. These are kids shopping for a toy. I'm eating at a restaurant that I presumably like.
- Enough clues are given to help us make a judgment about the personal value of that unknown information. Kids can infer that the mystery car will be similar to other Hot Wheels. The fine print on the back of the CPK card explains the range of possible prizes. Value can come in many forms: the winning lottery ticket, the satisfaction of solving a puzzle, being entertained by a story.

Information can be presented in a manner that is straightforward or curious. If we opt for the latter, we are guaranteed not only attention, but probably higher engagement as well—curiosity demands that we know more! What was known information (another toy car or a simple coupon) that might have been ignored has been converted into something unknown, something mysterious, something that demands resolution.

## THE INFORMATION GAP THEORY

When we become aware that information is missing—when something changes from being known (or so we thought) to an unknown state—we become curious. This is the explanation of curiosity posed by behavioral economist George Loewenstein in his information gap theory. Loewenstein says, "Curiosity happens when we feel a gap in our knowledge."

The feeling we get from these information gaps is best described as deprivation, which is critical to understanding why we are motivated by curiosity. To "eliminate the feeling of deprivation," we seek out the missing information. This is ironic, of course, considering that we routinely seek out puzzles, mystery novels, and other curious situations that create this sense of deprivation. However, it's important to note that many researchers once viewed curiosity as something aversive; a decision-theoretic view

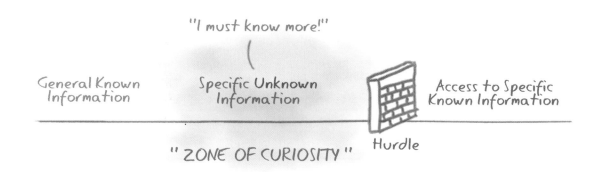

suggests that we should only want to know something if it helps us make more informed decisions. Why would we be attracted to something that offers no extrinsic benefit? Many other debates have surrounded curiosity: Is curiosity internally or externally stimulated? Is curiosity a primary drive, like hunger or fear? Is curiosity a state or trait? And this one: "If people like positive levels of curiosity, why do they attempt to resolve the curiosity?"

In his 1994 paper "The Psychology of Curiosity," Loewenstein surveys the body of curiosity research, much of which was done in the early 1960s and 1970s. In doing so, he provides a backdrop by which to understand his own research and how it resolves many of the debates surrounding curiosity. Simply stated: I'm curious because there's a gap between "what I know and what I want to know." Two notable implications come from this perspective:

- The *intensity* of curiosity correlates to the likelihood of certain information to resolve the information gap. Loewenstein's own tests confirmed that subjects were more curious when given parts of a greater whole—the need to complete enough of a picture puzzle to determine what it was (a picture of an animal) resulted in more interaction than a scenario where each block was a discrete picture.
- Curiosity correlates with our own understanding of a particular domain. The more we know about some topic, the more likely we are to focus on our own information gaps. If I know eight of ten items, I'm more curious about the remaining two than if I only know two of ten things.

## BUSINESS APPLICATION?

Given that curiosity reflects a desire to close information gaps, how can we apply this to interaction design?

### *LinkedIn*

Let's illustrate this gap in knowledge with a look at the professional networking site LinkedIn. One of the site's business goals is to sell paid accounts. Like most businesses, LinkedIn has a generic description of the benefits you receive with a paid account. Think of this as generally known information. While this information could certainly be compelling, there's a population for whom the cost may not be worth the perceived value.

Of course, those customers with paid memberships have access to specific known information.

This is how most businesses run: *"Cross the [registration/paid account/personal information] threshold and you can have all this!"* Unfortunately, this generic description of benefits is often not enough for many people.

LinkedIn gives you a *personalized* glimpse of what could be known, essentially teasing you with relevant information such as, "Someone at [company name] viewed your profile." The site moves you into an unknown state by sharing bits of knowledge that can only be fully known as a paid member. Nothing has been given away for free—I still don't know who looked at my profile, but I'm aware of some partial knowledge that might be worthwhile to know in full (see the top screen on the following page). As one friend said, "If someone from Apple has been looking at my profile, you can bet I want to know who!"

If this partial information proves relevant and valuable, you'll want to know more, right? In essence, they've created a "zone of curiosity" between two previously known states.

Your profile has been viewed by 11 people in the last **2 weeks**, including:

Someone at **Team One Advertising**
**Principal** in the design industry
**Owner** in the internet industry
Someone at **Pcms**
Someone at **Nhs**

To see **6 more people**, **upgrade your account**

*LinkedIn teases you with partial information about who has viewed your profile.*

*On the Quantcast site, the text barely showing beneath the sticker is intriguing.*

### Quantcast

Quantcast does something similar, only they've created a much larger zone of curiosity. With nothing required on your part, you can get a ton of free and quite useful site metrics: traffic stats, demographic information, lists of similar sites, and so on. The value to a site owner is obvious. But there's a bit of information withheld: to get business activity data, you must "Get Quantified."

What's nice about this version of Quantcast's call to action is what our brains see: something being hidden from us (see screens below). You can almost see through the sticker covering some data! Obviously, this is a static image—there is no live data there beneath a sticker. But we think in images and this visual affordance registers as, "Here's a sticker. We need to know what's underneath it. We can't allow this knowledge to remain unknown!"

### Netflix

Netflix leverages these same ideas when returning a movie rental. For Netflix, the data from your movie rental preferences is gold. Rating a movie not only improves your recommendations, but collectively improves the entire recommendation system. Consequently, the site is built around the idea of rating movies. Why then would the site ask you, "Rate your recent return to reveal two movies you'll love?"

(click the stars)

There is immediacy to this request—we see the empty slots where two movies will be revealed. Sure, I can rate movies and get recommendations all over the site, but there's something more immediate and novel about how this is presented.

As with Quantcast, I see the thing I want to take action on. I'm presented with two unknowns. For the "cost" of rating this movie, I can reveal two more (hopefully interesting) movies. I can make the unknown known. Even using a word like "reveal" suggests that there are already two movies waiting for my response.

## SPECIFIC MOTIVATION

It's human to be curious. And it's human to pursue a mystery until it's resolved. If teased with a bit of interesting information, we want to know more. But to be clear, what we're talking about here is a very specific kind of curiosity.

In the early 1950s, D. E. Berlyne identified two dimensions of curiosity: one extending between perceptual and epistemic curiosity, the other spanning specific and diverse curiosity. I've plotted these at the top of the following page with a few of examples based on my understanding of his research.

Although Berlyne's concept of curiosity has been challenged, it remains the backdrop against which many subsequent curiosity studies have defined their research. I've found this model useful for thinking about different kinds of curiosity and for clarifying which type is most easily applied to interaction design.

In the context of this book, I'm referring to perceptual-specific curiosity, one in which we confront people with very specific gaps in their knowledge in a novel manner or context. While you can certainly create gaps in knowledge in a variety of ways, the examples in this chapter are more concerned with a variety of curiosity akin to teasing. After all, this book is about seductive interaction design.

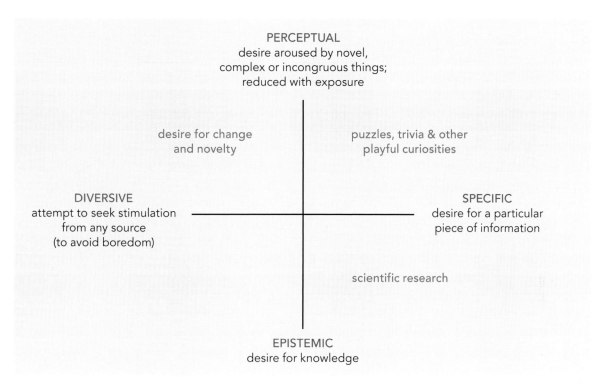

PERCEPTUAL
desire aroused by novel,
complex or incongruous things;
reduced with exposure

desire for change
and novelty

puzzles, trivia & other
playful curiosities

DIVERSIVE
attempt to seek stimulation
from any source
(to avoid boredom)

SPECIFIC
desire for a particular
piece of information

scientific research

EPISTEMIC
desire for knowledge

*This matrix presents the different dimensions of curiosity originally proposed by D.E. Berlyne in the early 1950s.*

## NOW WHAT?

If you want to make someone curious, make them aware of something they don't know. Find information you can use to tease people. Chances are, you're either withholding all the specific information or giving it all away. To get attention and engage the senses, look for ways to turn these direct messages into a quest. A few tips:

- Make your tease interesting, or at least proportionate in appeal to the cost.

- Strive to make the information personally relevant to the user.
- Offer the promise of something worthwhile—what will it cost?
- Establish trust through previous experiences and context clues.
- Use visuals to suggest or create the immediate perception of mystery.
- Don't try to lure users with something that is given away freely elsewhere.

# ANXIETY AND DELIGHT

## Interview with Giles Colborne

*When creating delightful experiences, we focus on making things pleasant, removing points of frustration, maybe adding playful elements. You have a different perspective.*

Yes. When I ask people about experiences they've found delightful, their stories involve unpleasant situations or where playfulness would be inappropriate, like online banking. When I ask them about playful experiences, they seem underwhelmed and far from delighted.

Themes of anxiety and disappointment run through people's stories of delightful experiences. The passenger ringing his airline to complain is anxious. He is delighted when the anxiety is unexpectedly removed. I think that *anxiety*, present or vividly remembered, is an important part of experiencing delight. The contrast makes the delight intense and memorable.

*Are you saying anxiety needs to be present to create a delightful experience? What about simple forms of delight like play or humor?*

Anxiety was a common thread in the stories. You could take that two ways: either anxiety needs to be present, or the heightened emotion led people to remember the events more vividly. Personally, I think you need contrasts when you're designing emotion—as you need them to design a page layout.

However, the stories did not always include an immediate source of anxiety. One person—a young father—told me about his delightful moment coming across a device for feeding babies without mess. The anxiety was remembered.

Out of the thirty people I spoke to about delightful experiences, none of them mentioned play or humor. I was asking them specifically about companies or services, but still no one mentioned 'paint balling' or 'comedy club.' They seemed to separate delight from play. They were much more keen to tell me about their mobile phones or vacuum cleaners.

But play and humor also need contrasts between the positive and negative feelings. Play provides safe rules for exploring situations like conflict (think: team sports) or for exceeding normal social bounds (think: using dolls to play 'grown-ups'). Humor also is a safe way of exploring negative situations—often relying on shock or on setting the audience off balance in some way.

*How might you apply this? Can we design for anxiety? Can the experiences we design be solutions—heroes, if you will—to anxieties? Conversely, would you advocate creating a service experience that manufactures anxiety?*

Absolutely. As designers, we should seek out anxiety. We should ask users: tell me about the times you felt anxious. Fix the problems that users remember and fear the most. If you can, you'll delight your users.

To take it to the next level, you could try to create anxiety, in order to release it. But you'd need to be very careful about doing that. It's appropriate in playful situations—people understand play as a safe way of experimenting with anxiety, often it's expected. Enhancing anxiety in a credit card transaction is not such a good idea.*

*Visit www.sixdbook.com to read full interview.

# CHAPTER 12

# Can People Express Themselves Around You?

HAVE I MENTIONED that I was in a video with the rap artist 50 Cent? I was. And so was my wife, a few of her friends, and some of my friends—and anyone else who visits the Myspace Fan Video page.

Here's how it works: by connecting with Facebook Connect, the site is able to access your profile photo, which is then inserted (through the magic of technology) into a music video. There are actually several videos to choose from: 50 Cent, Alicia Keys, N-Dubz, David Guetta, Pixie Lott, Florence and the Machine, Lostprophets, and Chipmunk.

It's a fun little site to play with, and in all cases, I've found myself sharing the videos with other people. It's amazing how such a small thing—seeing your picture in these music videos—can bring so much delight. In a very small way, we've personalized something that is normally beyond our control.

And this leads us into the final principle for this section: *self-expression*.

People want to leave their personal mark on something, to say, "I was here," "I made this," or, "This is who I am." From vanity plates to tattoos to laptops decorated with stickers, we love opportunities for self-expression. We seek out ways to express our personality, feelings, and ideas.

But self-expression isn't only limited to the expressive variety, such as we'd normally associate with art. Self-expression is evident any time we tailor something to reflect our personality or personal preferences. Both Myspace and Facebook offer examples of self-expression.

It's easy to say that Myspace allows self-expression, given the ability to customize the *appearance* of your page. Facebook allows self-expression, too, only of a different sort: by adding apps to your profile, playing games, or joining groups, you're expressing yourself. These associations form the *online identity* that you project to other people.

I first became aware of just how strong this need for self-expression is while doing qualitative testing on a potential media application. We had designed a page where the retailer could push new music releases, recommend artists you might like, and other kinds of marketing. We were testing the visual metaphor of a shelf, much like what the iBook uses now.

However, the fidelity of the page was just low enough that testers assumed the shelf was for them to display *their* media collection. As one person said, "Oh, cool, is this a page where I can put my favorite artists and movies? Can I share this with my friends?" We took note the first time this happened. And the second time. And the third. While the sessions were all one on one, this became a theme throughout the day of testing. In fact, people were more excited by this one mistaken assumption than anything else we showed them. Needless to say, we

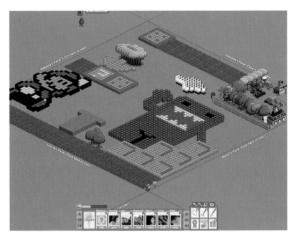

*Players in FarmVille can get very creative when planting their crops.*

made a personal media shelf in the next design iteration.

The need for self-expression shows up in just about any area where people are allowed to control something, especially where this control is tied to an identity. The most obvious place for this is games, especially ones where the player has an avatar to dress and decorate. (It's interesting to note that these avatars are most often *idealized* versions of the person in real life.) While the game FarmVille doesn't have avatars to customize, the player's farm becomes an artistic canvas. Most players start off by simply thinking about an organized way to plant crops; more ambitious players use their farms to create some rather interesting works of art.

But self-expression isn't limited to games. In the productivity application Mindbloom, you plant a tree that represents the different areas you want to improve: health, career, spirituality, leisure, lifestyle, finances, relationships, and so on. You start by picking three areas that matter to you. The selection of these three areas is a subtle form of self-expression; the virtual tree that's planted for you starts with three branches and can be shared with friends. A more overt form of self-expression comes next: you're allowed to choose images that inspire you for each area. For example, if your spirituality is better represented by a crucifix than candles, you can change that image. The tree and associated images become a personal expression of you and, over time, your personal growth as you work on each area (adding leaves) and add new areas (represented by the branches) in which to grow (see screen below).

Opportunities for self-expression can also attach themselves to mundane activities, such as printing a recipe. While most recipe sites allow you to select the final print size (3×5, 4×6, 8.5×11), CDKitchen takes this a step further, allowing you to select the font and a decorative border.

The restaurant review site Yelp encourages self-expression by providing a structured way to give compliments. Rather than simply giving you an empty form field, Yelp suggests a dozen specific compliments you can give another user: Thank you!, cute pic, good writer, write more, you're funny, among others.

At the most basic level, simply opening up your site to allow comments and reviews is a way to allow self-expression. As long as these comments are linked back to a person's profile, these are opportunities for the user to express themselves online. Even familiar conventions, such as letting users select widgets, choose content to follow or share, use emoticons, and customize the aesthetics of a page, are all ways to enable self-expression.

How can people express themselves on your site? Look for opportunities to surface and celebrate your customers' unique voices.

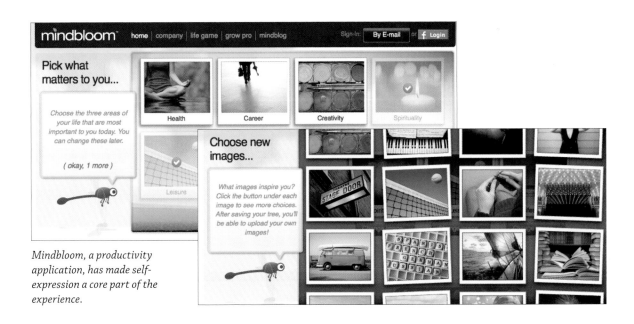

*Mindbloom, a productivity application, has made self-expression a core part of the experience.*

# The Subtle Art of Seduction

The art of seduction is a subtle and enticing game. We put people at ease with thoughtful questions. Our gestures and glances direct attention. Our words are chosen carefully, to invite favor and avoid offense. We know when to make decisions and how to present choices. Even serendipitous moments occur within the safety of a planned experience. So how might Web sites practice some of this subtlety?

In the previous section, we discussed playful forms of seduction. We talked about turning the steps into a piano, seducing people into making a healthy choice. We saw how LinkedIn's Profile Completion feature entices people to complete their profiles. We learned how MailChimp uses humor effectively in the business of e-mail campaigns. Our focus was on things that make for a fun and engaging interaction.

In this section, we'll talk about the really small details: the subtleties that make an experience more or less engaging. Part of the reason for doing this is to respond to a concern I've heard from some of the established businesses I work with. For a variety of reasons, pushing through some of the more playful ideas can be challenging. I'm often asked, "Are there some really small things we can do—things we can implement right away?"

What follows are suggestions for minor interface changes that can make a big difference, based on some fascinating studies from the field of behavioral economics. Given the curious nature of some of these suggestions, I've tried to reference actual research as much as possible. Will these ideas work for you? I invite you to try them out and share the results and then share—through posts or presentations—the results. In this way, we can all learn from each other.

# CHAPTER 13

# Small First Steps

LET'S BEGIN WITH a famous study that was done at Yale University in the 1960s. Social scientist Howard Leventhal wanted to see if he could persuade a group of college seniors to get a tetanus shot. He brought in a group of about 120 seniors, and had them sit through a lecture on the importance of getting the tetanus shot (and the dangers of not doing so). The students were then instructed to go to the campus health center to get a free tetanus shot. One month after this lecture, only 3 percent of the students had actually gone to get their shots.

Leventhal then repeated the test with a different group of students. They sat through the same presentation and were cautioned about the same dangers of not getting a tetanus shot. Everything was the same as with the first group, with two minor additions:

- Students were given a map of the campus with the health center circled. Keep in mind, this was almost certainly not new information; these were seniors who would have already known the location of the health center.
- Students were asked to think about when they would actually get the tetanus shot, and then write this information down. They weren't signing up—this wasn't registration.

This was purely for personal reference (and to force students to think about when they'd get the shot).

These are two very small changes. But did they make a difference? In the second study, 28 percent of the students got their free tetanus shot. That's nearly ten times as many students as in the first study!

## SHAPING THE PATH

When I first came across this study, I had to pause to consider the possibilities suggested here. We've all heard about the power of suggestion (we'll talk more about this later), but what's going on here? Where *arguments* for doing something had failed, the introduction of some minor situational details made a big difference.

The psychologist Kurt Lewin coined the phrase *channel factors** to describe these minor additions that have a major impact on behaviors. More recently, in their book *Switch*, Chip Heath and Dan Heath refer to the introduction of these external influences as *shaping the path*.

Whenever you can put something into simpler terms, you increase the odds that people will actually do that thing. Suggest a particular course of action, nudge people to take a first step, set up defaults, get a small initial commitment—these are the kinds of little details that can shape the path and change behavior.

How was the path shaped in the Leventhal study? First, students were given a *trigger* in the form of the map. Think of how often we need a small reminder to follow through on something. (Take business cards, for example. Aside from providing contact information, they are a trigger to remind people to follow through on a conversation.) Second, by thinking about when they would get their shot, students were taking a first step from an abstract idea (*I should get a shot*) to an action (*When am I going to do this?*). Let's look more closely at small first steps.

## MAKING A COMMITMENT

In the Leventhal study, thinking about when to get the tetanus shot was a small first step. It was also a very subtle example of *commitment and consistency*—we desire to act in a manner consistent with our stated beliefs and prior actions. When we make a statement, whether it's public or just to ourselves, we tend to want to be consistent with this statement. While the decision to get the shot was never publicly stated (unless you count being asked to write down a time for personal reference later), being asked to think about when to get this shot forced students to make a decision: *Am I going to get this shot or not?* That was the small first step.

There have been studies where researchers asked people to make small commitments and then, over time, those commitments were raised to a ridiculous level. In the end, people ended up doing extreme things they would have never done had they been asked outright. Why? The participants wanted to honor their prior commitment.

## SHARING PLACES

A few years ago, I worked on a start-up mobile photo-sharing service where people were asked to go out and photograph their favorite places, be it their favorite restaurant or their best view of the city skyline—whatever it was, the service wanted people to share those things. We also knew this was a behavior change: we were asking people to do things that might not be part of their normal routine. While thinking of ways to encourage this behavior, one idea that came up was to ask people to list a few of their favorite places during the sign-up process. We gave the list a bit of structure by asking some specific questions:

*What are three of your favorite places to eat?*

*Your ideal evening would include a trip to...*

*What's the most interesting place to shop in your city?*

*When you want to feel cultured, you go to...*

---

*Channels in this case refers not to media channels, but to geography—the natural or human-made deeper courses we create to channel shallow bodies of water.

# DEEPER READING

Suppose I wanted to place a public-service billboard on your front lawn. Would you allow it? The message is harmless enough—DRIVE SAFELY—but after seeing a photo of the large billboard obscuring an otherwise beautiful house, your suspicions are confirmed—this is a preposterous request. This is what researchers Jonathan Freedman and Scott Fraser asked homeowners in California. As you'd expect, most homeowners, 83 percent to be exact, refused.

However, in the follow-up experiment, the results were reversed—76 percent agreed to place the billboard on their lawns. What had changed? Two weeks prior, residents had been asked to display a small 3"×3" sticker—in either their car or their house window—stating BE A SAFE DRIVER. It was a trivial request that most people agreed to (who wouldn't?). However, when researchers made the more daunting request of placing the billboard, the group felt compelled to accept, having already agreed to display the small sign. This is the power of commitment and consistency.

For more information about this study and more like it, please see Freeman and Fraser's remarkable paper "Compliance without pressure: The foot-in-the-door technique."

*Freedman, Jonathan L. and Scott C. Fraser. 1966. "Compliance without pressure: The foot-in-the-door technique." Journal of Personality and Social Psychology 4: 195–202.

But that's it, just a simple list. We felt this was a harmless addition to the registration form—most people love making lists. (For more on why making lists has such broad appeal, see "Self Expression" in Chapter 12.) Here was our strategy: once you made your list, you were given your first personalized photo assignment. When you opened the mobile app for the first time, instead of just saying, "Now, go photograph your favorite places," the app would say, "Hey, you said Jasper's was one of your favorite restaurants. Why not go there and photograph the place? Or, photograph your favorite dish?" We now had a list of suggestions that you, as the user of this system, had created. And it was a completely personalized list! This was one way to motivate people to begin shooting and submitting at least ten photos. We broke down a big request by helping people take the first small step of deciding *what* to photograph.

## PICKING UP ITEMS PLACED ON HOLD

Here's another way to encourage people to take small first steps. My team and I worked with a retail chain that has 2,000 locations. The company doesn't do e-commerce yet, but wanted to let customers browse the online catalog, then call on the phone and place something on hold for in-store pickup. But here's the problem: our research found that most people who call and place something on hold never come in to the store and pick it up. In fact, one store we spoke to in a major city said this happened 90 percent of the time. Imagine how much easier it is to place something on hold when you don't even have that personal connection of a phone call! This is a very big business problem, and one we didn't want to exacerbate. With this concern in mind, our team recommended a very minor addition to the Hold Request form:

*This recommended Hold Request form asks users to think about when they will pick up the item.*

We added a question to the required contact information: "What time do you think you'll pick this up?" The extra field was optional—customers didn't have to fill it in. But, we hoped that the same psychology that played out in the Leventhal study would work here. By encouraging people to decide when they were going to drive to the store, we hoped more would actually pick up their on-hold items. We recommended that the design team A/B test this minor change to validate that the results are consistent with our expectations.

**Welcome to Checkout**

Secure Shopping Guarantee

| Existing Customers | New Customers |
|---|---|
| **My Account** | **Checkout** |
| | Create an account or checkout as a guest |
| Sign in for faster checkout | |
| ✳ Email Address (used to sign into your account) | ● Proceed to checkout |
| | |
| ✳ Password | |

**Create My Account Password**

Register for an My Account with Dell and save time during your next checkout

Password                    Confirm Password

Password must be at least 6 characters long and contain at least one letter and

*A typical checkout process. Users are invited to create an account during checkout.*

## COMPLETING A TRAVEL BOOKING

Here's another example of small first steps. Imagine you're working on a travel site. To date, you've just let people book, but you've never let them set up profiles. You're now rolling out profiles for the first time. When and how should you ask someone to set up an account? Typically an e-commerce site, such as the Dell example in the above screen, has two columns, one labeled My Account for returning customers and another labeled Checkout for new customers.

If you're a new customer, at some point during the checkout process, the site will normally ask if you'd like to add an e-mail address to create an account. There's a good argument to be made for the convenience of this approach; you're asked to provide just one more piece of information (a password) to save your information for future purchases.

As I was researching the really small changes we can make to change behavior, I came across a site that approached the whole returning customer/new customer fork in rather novel way. If you look very closely at the booking process on Hotels.com, you'll notice some subtle but noteworthy user interface decisions.

After selecting a hotel, you see the screen shown on the next page. Notice how the screen defaults to "I want to create an account." Returning customers can switch to "I want to sign in

| Step 1 | Step 2 | Step 3 |
| Get Started | Rooms & Guest Details | Payment |

**welcome rewards.** | **Sign in or create an account** to get 1 free night for every 10 nights you book. ℹ️

\* Indicates Required Fields

⦿ **I want to create an account**

◯ **I want to sign in for faster booking**

Email address\* [                    ]

Password\* [                    ]

Password must be 6 to 20 characters and/or numbers

Forgot your password?

◯ **I want to continue without creating an account**

[ Next ]

*The first page of the Hotels.com checkout process.*

for faster booking" or, as is more often the case, a browser cookie will default to this option, with your account information prefilled.

There is of course a third option: "I want to continue without creating an account." Let's think about this for a second. You've already selected your hotel, so all you have to do to continue is click the Next button to continue checking out. With one click, you implicitly state, "Yeah, I want to create an account." That's a very subtle commitment, but would it make a difference? Consider the extra effort required to click the radio button option that states "I want to continue without creating an account." We're only going from one mouse click to two mouse clicks. This may sound ridiculous, but in

my experience, it's exactly these little details that add up and make a difference in how people respond. Every extra bit of effort results in lower completion rates. By taking the most convenient path, you've also made a very small commitment to create an account. (We'll discuss the power of default options in a few pages).

Let's continue with our new customer scenario. You click Next. Not only have you made the small commitment to creating an account, but notice this next very minor detail: you're now on Step 2. All you did was click one button and you're already on Step 2 in the process! If you look at e-commerce checkout processes, Step 1 is generally where you do all the hard stuff—filling out your address and account

| Step 1 | Step 2 | Step 3 |
| Get Started | Rooms & Guest Details | Payment |

**Guest Names and Room Preferences**

* Ind

**Room 1**

First Name*

Last Name*

Bedding Preference   King Bed ▾

Smoking Preference   Non Smoking ▾

Accessibility Requests   ▸ Select accessibility requests for this room

Bedding and smoking preferences are not guar

**Confirmation Preferences**

*Step 2 of the Hotels.com checkout process.*

information. With Hotels.com, this all happens at Step 2. You might wonder whether it really makes a difference. Well, let's turn our attention to another study that that demonstrates the power of perceived progress.

## ENDOWED PROGRESS EFFECT

Your car is kind of dirty, so you decide to take it to the car wash. With your wash, you receive a special loyalty card: each future visit earns another stamp on the card. When you get eight stamps, you earn a free car wash.

Sounds simple enough, right?

Research by Joseph Nunes and Xavier Drèze found that there's actually a catch. In their experiment, two different types of cards were handed out to customers. The first type of card was fairly straightforward: eight stamps earned the customer a free car wash. The second type

of card required ten stamps to earn a free car wash, but the first two stamps had already been filled in.

Both scenarios require eight stamps to earn a free car wash. The difference is how the program is framed: are you starting with 0 percent or 20 percent completion? Nunes and Drèze set up this experiment to find out if being given a head start in a loyalty program would encourage participation.

Did the two-stamp artificial head start make a difference in the response?

In the months that followed, 19 percent of the customers with the eight-stamp card earned their free car wash. And what of the ten-stamp cards? Thirty-four percent of the ten-stamp people (who had been given a two-stamp head start) followed through and filled up the stamp card. In fact, this latter group filled up their cards in a shorter time—four days sooner than the eight-stamp group. By framing the task as one that has already been undertaken, nearly twice as many people completed their cards. Nunes and Drèze described this as the *empowered progress effect*.

Let's also not forget commitment and consistency—how many people felt compelled to complete the loyalty card once the task was started for them? This simple head start helped people to be consistent with their intention of earning a free car wash. And I suspect that as people came closer to collecting all of the required stamps, the urge to complete the task became even stronger. This is called *set completion*, an idea we'll discuss in the next section on gaming.

So, go back to the Hotels.com example. Does it make a difference to be on Step 2 versus Step 1? Based on the logic of the endowed progress effect, it probably does make a difference. Are there ways you can create the *perception* of progress in your application?

## SEQUENCING

Closely related to the endowed progress effect is a principle called *sequencing*—if you want to motivate people to do something, break the task down into small steps.

Parents are very familiar with this idea. Asking a toddler to "get ready for bed" doesn't work. Instead, you have to break down your request into a series of much smaller tasks: *Get your jammies on. Brush your teeth. Use the potty. Get in your bed.* Small first steps are about setting people on the path. Sequencing is laying out that path.

Think about tasks such as setting up a bank account or writing to a member of Congress. If these were routine, the process would probably make sense. For most of us though, the infrequency of these tasks makes every step seem

extraordinarily complex. How does one go about writing to their government representative? Where do you start? How do you identify the representative for your district? What information is needed to identify your local representative? (My zip code has two representatives!) Should I contact my representative directly? If I'm concerned about a specific issue, is it better to join together with a group of people to insure my voice is heard? If so, which groups are legitimate? Are there formalities to consider? What information will I need to identify myself? The list of questions goes on. No wonder people give up before they ever start! By breaking potentially complex (and even simple) activities into smaller tasks, you make it more likely that people will advance through the process.

Unfortunately, most software from larger organizations does a terrible job of sequencing. How many times have you clicked on a highly targeted keyword ad, only to land on a generic homepage that had very little to do with your initial interest? Or how often has a site linked to a separate system that had little or no awareness of where you came from and the task you were trying to complete? (To find out who my local representative is, the government site handed me off to a different site to look up my nine-digit zip code). This is, sadly enough, the state of much software. Why? Because these different systems are built to solve discrete problems. Reframing the design of this software from the myriad of possible user scenarios requires the *experience-first perspective* described in Chapter 1. This is also a noticeable element of well-designed services. Rather than just delivering a set of features, customer-focused companies think through the *experience* of using the services they've provided.

In most of my personal and professional interactions, I've stopped making big requests of people. My e-mails are direct and to the point, and I clearly state the next intended action. I've also stopped making multiple requests in a single e-mail, unless they are all closely related. Based on what I've learned about attention spans, interest, and motivation, if getting people to actually *do* something is the goal, you have to make the process as simple as possible!

Sequencing doesn't just apply to complex processes. Think of scenarios where there are multiple nonsequential things to be done. While being able to choose the next task is nice, I'd argue that having someone direct us is probably more effective at getting people to actually complete something. Left to our own devices, we're terrible at prioritizing where to spend our time.

Let's apply this to the two screens below:

The screen on the left shows LinkedIn's Profile Completeness bar. The one on the right is from Shelfari, a site where you can talk about books you're reading. The difference here is that LinkedIn asks you to do one thing next, while Shelfari lists all the things you have done and the things you haven't. Which of these options is more likely to influence a response? Which one would actually encourage people to click through to complete 100 percent? You might say the Shelfari list is preferable, because it shows you everything outstanding. However, based on what we know about sequencing and choice, I'll bet the LinkedIn one works better because it only asks you to do one thing next, and after you complete that task it tells you the next thing to do after that.

Sequencing can be used to break down a complex set of questions into a series of simpler

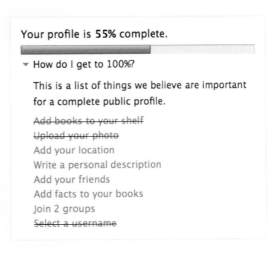

*Two different strategies to encourage people to complete their profiles. LinkedIn's Profile Completeness bar (left) only shows you one option at a time, while Shelfari's list (right) shows you everything outstanding.*

ones. Luke Wroblewski describes an approach to form design called *inline contextual actions*. Instead of presenting people with four options, you present them with two. If the person hovers over the Not Interested option, it's only then that three additional clarifying options appear. You've taking a potentially overwhelming set of choices and reduced them to a simple choice, potentially followed by an additional question. Like a choose-your-own-adventure book, you're sequencing the conversation (see the screen to the right).

This idea of sequencing is very powerful, not just in raising kids but in games. You don't start a game with all the abilities and all the powers. Instead you slowly work up to more advanced challenges. This leads us into the final small first steps concept—shaping.

## SHAPING

Whereas sequencing breaks down a complex task into simple steps, shaping is used to reinforce a desired habit. Think about training a dog or teaching someone to ride a bike. To teach something new, you start with the simplest form of the behavior, and build on that, to reinforce increasingly accurate approximations of the desired (final) behavior.

Video games use shaping to help players succeed at increasing challenges. All players start at the simplest level, with trivial challenges designed to introduce basic gameplay skills. Once these basic skills are mastered, players advance to the next level, where they must learn new skills that build on what was previously learned (sounds kind of like our educational

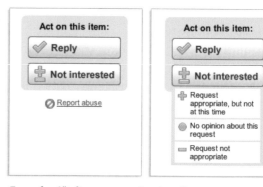

*Example of "inline contextual actions."*

system!). This continues as players progress throughout the game, with each new level reinforcing increasingly complex skills, until a level of mastery is achieved and the game is no longer interesting.

Contrast this with desktop software, where users are expected to read a manual or go through training before they can use that application. Could complex systems like these benefit from shaping? Rather than immerse someone in your application, why not start with a small set of features and reveal more with use?

*"With the right baby steps you can get almost anybody to do anything."*

—B. J. FOGG

Another option might be to offer rewards for mastery of a subject or increasing proficiency. Identify the desired behavior, list the steps necessary to reach that behavior, reward completion of a step until mastered, and then add in the next step as a prerequisite for receiving the reward. Ribbon Hero, a plug-in for Microsoft Office, does just this. While pitched as making a game out of using products like Word or Excel, it's really a simple training program designed to help people take advantage of all the features offered by these products. Sure, there are points and rewards for doing things like formatting text or adding margins, and you can challenge your friends on Facebook, but Ribbon Hero is really a series of challenges designed to help you be more proficient at the Microsoft Office suite of tools (see the screens below).

If the idea of "shaping" a behavior sounds familiar, it's probably because it has much in common with classical conditioning: the punishment and rewards approach to behavior change that dominated behavioral psychology for most of the 20th century. In the next section on gaming, we'll discuss newer ideas about how to motivate people.

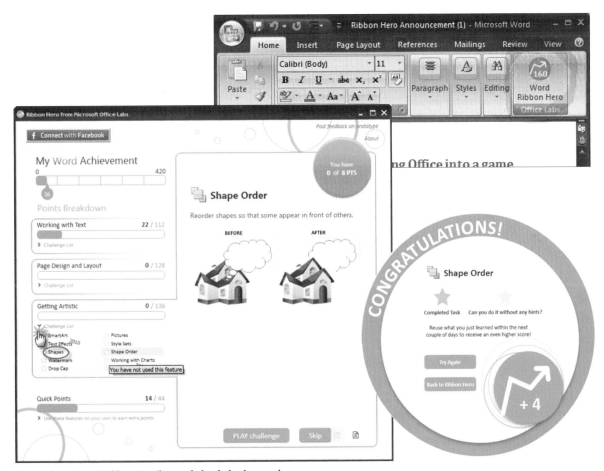

*Screenshots from "Ribbon Hero" intended to help the user become more proficient in the Microsoft Office suite.*

## CHAPTER 14

# Coming on Too Strong (and how not to!)

IN THIS CHAPTER, let's look at some different ways to make our interfaces a little less intense.

## FEWER OPTIONS

Does limiting the number of available choices make a difference? Numerous researchers have found that when presented with more options, we're far less likely to take any action at all.

The most famous of these studies looked at how shoppers reacted when many different flavors of jams were made available to them.* Some shoppers had only six jams to choose from; others could select from 24 varieties. While shoppers certainly preferred more choices, the data revealed something different: when there were fewer options (only six flavors), ten times as many people made a purchase!

This same research topic has been tested in other ways; one study looked at the effect of introducing more investment fund options from which employees could choose. As with the jam study, fewer people even signed up when more options were introduced.

People are more likely to take action, purchase, or do whatever it is you'd like them to do when you limit their choices. How does this play out in a user interface? Whether in drop-down menus or search results, I'm frequently asked, "How many options should we present to users?" Unfortunately, with online interactions, the correct response to this question can be tricky, as part of the appeal of going online (for some people) is the infinite selection, accompanied by filters with which to narrow down the options.

For example, travelers want to see all available flight and hotel options—they hate the idea that there is an option available that isn't shown. In cases like these, I suggest looking for ways to simplify the choices presented based on other data (like preferences or past booking history, for example), or finding ways to cluster the selections into buckets that get the users closer to their intended match.

*Sheena S. Iyengar and Mark R. Lepper, in Menlo Park, California, in 2000.

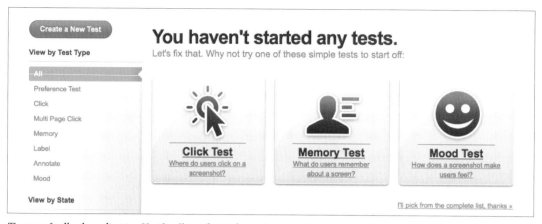

*The user feedback application Verify offers a limited set of tests to first time users.*

Sometimes, this idea of limited choice is easier to apply. Verify, a user feedback application, has tackled this potential overload issue in a rather elegant way. Verify offers eight (at the time of this writing) different ways to collect user feedback. However, you can see here they're offering only three options when the user first logs in: a Click Test, a Memory Test, and a Mood Test (see the screen above).

Notice, however, the designers haven't taken away choice or control. To access the additional five tests, you still have the option to "Pick from the complete list, thank you." For a first-time user, I'm guessing they probably handpicked the three tests that best represent their service, with the option to pick from the complete list. Based on the psychology studies, I'd predict first-time users are more likely to actually try out one of these tests when there are fewer options to choose from. I could easily imagine scenarios where new users, impressed (and overwhelmed) by the number of available tests, don't actually test any of them!

In technology, we rarely see this kind of restraint. That's why images like this are so humorous:

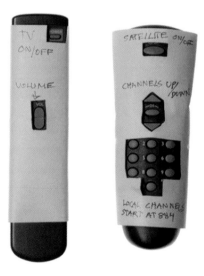

Apparently, someone masked most of the buttons on the remotes to make them usable when their parents come over to babysit. All of the options that don't apply have been covered up, thereby limiting choice and confusion for the user. For more on ways to simplify your interface, I recommend Giles Colborne's book *Simple and Usable Web, Mobile, and Interaction Design.* (He even uses a remote to demonstrate four different approaches to simplifying an interaction.)

What's the opposite of limited choice? You can see in the image below. A few years back, I was trying to order a pizza online. Normally, with a well-designed form, you direct people to the primary action, usually the one big button.

In this pizza order form, one button is a bit bigger than the others, but look at how many

other distractions have been placed in the ordering path: seven different buttons are all screaming, "Click me!" This is the opposite of limited choice, and something to be avoided.

## LESS TEXT

Since this chapter is about how not to come on too strong, I want to show you two before and after screens from Weave, shown on the next page. The original screen had too much text, particularly the instructional copy for the sign-up process. What do all those words say? Essentially, you need to "make a passphrase." Notice

*The opposite of limited choice. How many different options do you see in this online pizza order form?*

*A before (left) and after (right) version of the Weave account setup process.*

how much simpler the conversational redesign is: the user interface mimics a conversation. The site says, "To get in, you need to make up a passphrase." You can go ahead and type your passphrase, or if you don't know what a passphrase is, you can ask, "What is a passphrase?" Clicking that link reveals a bit more text that says, "Oh, thought you might ask. A passphrase is something Weave uses to keep your data safe." Now that you understand, you can type your passphrase. There's a conversational interaction happening between you and the system. Notice how this is similar to the inline contextual action we talked about earlier. Are there places in your application where you could simplify things by introducing a more conversational interaction?

## FUN DISTRACTIONS

You don't necessarily have to remove content to be less intense.

The investment site Kapitall has done something rather interesting with its Investor DNA

quiz. To determine what kind of investor you might be (and tailor their investment advice), they present you with a series of questions like, "How long do you hold stocks?" or "Which quote best describes your approach to investing?"

To be honest, I don't know how far I would have made it through this process. I'm not exactly a typical investor, but Kapitall isn't intended for the typical investor—it's geared precisely toward people who aren't heavy investors. Accordingly, they've made even the task of completing this survey a playful experience. First off, notice in the figure on the next page how they present two possible options: instead of overwhelming me with eight radio button options, the screen is designed more like a kiosk or touchscreen interaction with eight big, clickable buttons (similar to the iLike example in Chapter 1). Here's where things get more interesting. The first question was fairly straightforward: "How long do you hold stocks?" I click on the next page and the second question they ask me is, "What kind of music do you enjoy most?"

"Huh? What does this have to do with investing?" I wondered. But I was intrigued and I clicked on the type of music I enjoy most. Then the survey asked me another very direct investing question, followed by "Pick your favorite movie." Then another investment question. And so on. The questions alternated between very direct (boring) investment questions and questions that were much more fun and personal.

What's going on here?

One explanation is that they have some really smart algorithms that can actually factor in personality traits based on personal entertainment preferences. Under this scenario, they are learning vital investment information through indirect questions. This is possible. Another (more likely) possibility is that these are dummy questions, thrown in to keep you *engaged* throughout the process. Maybe there are only four real investment questions, but by adding these "just for fun" questions, do more people actually complete the form? Either way, it's an example worth sharing, and another use of subtle details that kept me seduced.

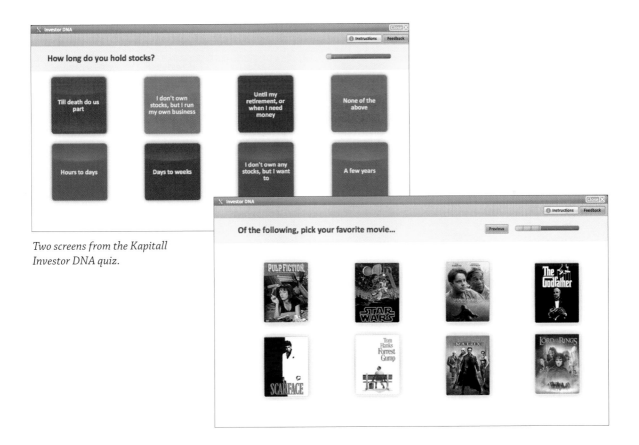

*Two screens from the Kapitall Investor DNA quiz.*

## CREATING THE ILLUSION OF LESS BY HIDING INFORMATION

Have you ever seen a form like the one below on the bottom left?

A bit overwhelming, right? This is from Highrise, the Customer Relationship Management tool from 37signals.

Fortunately, this is not how Highrise asks for customer information!

In fact, the only way you'd ever see this screen is if you were to open up every available field. The image to its right shows how the screen is actually presented.

If you're adding a contact, there are basically two things everyone in the world is going to add—first name and last name. Then, there's a bunch of other stuff you could potentially add, like phone number, e-mail address, Twitter name, Skype ID, mailing address—whatever is needed or available.

Understanding this experience, 37signals exposes only the fields that users are certain to need. Everything else is hidden behind a mouse click. If you want to add a phone number, for example, you click on the phone number and it then exposes the form field. If you want to add a Web site, it exposes the field. In the case of a physical address, it exposes the set of fields related to an address. Hiding these form fields by default is a subtle design decision. But in doing so, the designers have also hidden the complexity. The interface seems very simple to use, without reducing the range of available contact options someone might need to choose from.

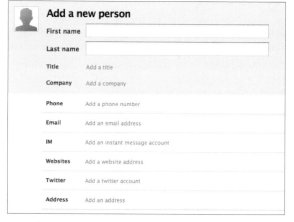

*The Add a new person screen from Highrise, showing the default state (above) and all possible fields exposed (left).*

# IS THIS REALLY NECESSARY?

One of the questions I like to ask clients when I see unnecessarily long forms is this:

*If every additional form field lowered response rates by 10 percent, what would you cut?*

(Yes, your math is spot on. If there have to be ten form fields, you have 0 percent conversion.)

This isn't a scientific question. It's a focus question. While I've spoken with plenty of researchers who'd agree that every additional question correlates to lower conversion rates, this question is simply a tool to help clients focus on what's essential. Too often, we think in the reverse: what can we ask of people? But do you really need to ask for gender or date of birth? Do you care that much about someone's hometown? You may have legitimate reasons for asking for so much information, if you're a bank, for example. But in my experience, businesses typically assume they need a lot more information than is often necessary. This question helps trim the fat from bloated user interface forms.

## HACKING THE VISUAL SYSTEM TO MAKE THINGS SIMPLER

Let's say you have four fields you need completed: first name, last name, e-mail, and phone. In the database, these are four distinct tables. Compare the two designs below:

### Your Contact Information

First Name:

Last Name:

Email:

Phone:

### Your Contact Information

Name:

First Name        Last Name

Contact:

Email

Phone

In this example, we've gone from asking four questions to just two, or so it seems. The inline form labels work in this example as it's very obvious what I'm asking for (be careful of inline labels with less common or familiar requests). First Name and Last Name are visually represented as one request instead of two. And e-mail and phone, while still separate fields, are associated with only one form label, Contact. Nothing has changed on the back end; there are still four

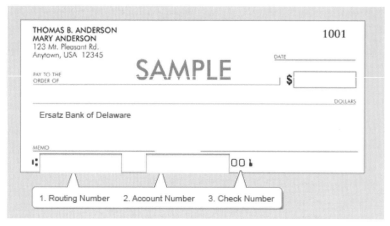

THOMAS B. ANDERSON
MARY ANDERSON
123 Mt. Pleasant Rd.
Anytown, USA 12345

1001

SAMPLE

DATE

PAY TO THE
ORDER OF

$

DOLLARS

Ersatz Bank of Delaware

MEMO

1. Routing Number     2. Account Number     3. Check Number

*An image of a check is used to help people locate the needed information.*

fields being collected. This is really just playing with perceptions and how you present information, to make your request less overwhelming.

Also note the subtle addition of icons to visually reinforce what is requested. Effective visuals, from icons to infographics, can help people make sense of information much more quickly and with less potential for errors. The icons here primarily reinforce the inline form label; let's look at something a bit more complex.

Have you ever been asked to provide your bank's routing number and your checking account number? If you're like most people, you probably had to pull out your checkbook to confirm what these were. Check out the example above.

We see an image of a check, and the input fields have been aligned with the corresponding information on the check. The image helps

people understand where to find the information that's being asked for and reduces potential errors.

## LESS TO THINK ABOUT

While we're on the subject of currency, let's look at collecting credit card information to demonstrate how even a familiar interaction can be improved with a good eye for detail.

Let's start with the typical credit card checkout process:

Look familiar? Here's an after version that I recommend to clients:

While this layout defaults to credit cards, you can choose other forms of payment.

You never have to select the type of credit card. The available credit card options are shown visually (more iconic information), but selection isn't required. Since each credit card begins with a unique number, we can identify the credit card type based on the first few numbers typed. Then, as you're typing your credit card number, you get visual confirmation: the credit card you're using is highlighted and the other options dim.

Finally, here's a nice bit of convenience. American Express, MasterCard, and VISA all handle CVC numbers a bit differently (some are on the front of the card, some are on the back). This is a point of confusion, which leads people to click on the Help question mark icon for a reminder of where to find this number. Since you can anticipate this question, why not have a tooltip with this reminder pop up when the customer gives focus to the CVC field? Better yet, take it a step further and tailor the tooltip to the credit card type.

If you're a start-up with a low volume of traffic, aside from being easier to use, you may not see the immediate benefits of these minor changes. However, it's exactly these kinds of subtle details I've seen make measurable differences when A/B tested with sites that have significant traffic.

# WHAT IS BEHAVIORAL ECONOMICS?

Many of the ideas in this section come from the field of "behavioral economics," which explores ways that social, cognitive, and emotional factors influence economic decisions. Traditional economic theory is based on the idea that people make rational decisions; however, a number of studies, dating back to the early 1950s, demonstrate that we often make inconsistent and irrational decisions. As an example, consider how you might respond to the following scenarios:

Scenario A:
*You live around the corner from an electronics store that carries the new computer speakers you've been looking at for $100. You also learn that a discounter, located ten miles from your house, has a special on the same speakers for half price: $50. Do you drive the ten miles?*

Scenario B:
*You live near an electronics store that carries the new computer you've wanted for $2000. Ten miles from your house, another store is carrying the same computer for $1950... a savings of $50. Do you drive the ten miles?*

The question posed in each scenario is essentially the same: Do you drive ten miles to save 50 dollars? Most people respond "yes" to the first question, but "no" to the second. All that's changed is how the question is presented, which demonstrates an idea central to behavioral economics: the way a scenario is worded influences the decision of the respondent.

While some people may make rational decisions, it's more likely we make decisions based on things such as:

- available information (also known as *bounded rationality*)
- heuristics and biases (mental shortcuts to help us make safe decisions quickly)
- how a question is presented (also know as a *frame*)

If you've ever heard about studies where researchers secretly changed the labels on wine bottles, or explored what happens when you add higher priced options—those are popular examples from behavioral economics. The studies are varied, and explore such things as how we react to multiple choices, the influence of others, near-term vs. long-term decisions, how we rely too much on one piece of information (*anchor*), ways to exploit gaps in perception and attention, the changing state of memory, and related topics.

Many of the conclusions from all these different studies can be summarized as follows:

- We are not very good at making long-term decisions.
- We are better at understanding relative rather than absolute values.
- Emotion or affect influences our behaviors.
- We are very bad at predicting what will make us happy, and we are even bad at describing what made us happy in the first place.

Some of these studies are described here in detail. For more information, I'd recommend starting with a book like *Predictably Irrational* by Dan Ariely, or *Nudge* by Richard Thaler & Cass Sunstein.

# CHAPTER 15

# Attracting Attention

LET'S TALK ABOUT WAYS to attract attention by creating *contrast*. Contrast occurs when two elements are different. If all the girls at a dance are wearing dark evening gowns, it's the girl who shows up in a bright red dress who stands out. Contrast is *relative* to the surrounding elements. On the basketball court, players don't seem that tall standing next to each other. But if you meet one of these players on the street, the height difference is obvious.

For years, designers have used visual contrast to capture attention and guide our eyes through a page. For a great example of this, check out this homepage for Blinksale, below.

Your eyes are grabbed first by the screenshot, as it's the point of highest contrast. Next, your gaze probably falls on the big yellow "Sign up for a free trial" button. This is by design. For this page to be successful from a business perspective, people need to click on that button. Consequently, this is the primary action—any other links from this page are minimized through scale and color. All of the surrounding content is there to help you feel comfortable with clicking that button.

But does making a button stand out really affect behavior?

*Where is your eye drawn to in this homepage?*

Consider these A/B testing results shared by health site CareLogger: changing the color of the button on the homepage from green to red improved sign-ups by 31 percent!

One quick comment on this example. While there's certainly substantial color theory about red being a much stronger color than all the others, the takeaway from this study isn't "change all green buttons to red" or "red outperforms green." The takeaway is that a high-contrast button outperforms a lower-contrast button. With CareLogger's before screen, everything about the design is a "cool" color scheme (blues and greens, light grays). Consequently, the green button blends in with the surrounding elements. When you introduce the color red, and it's the only warm thing on the page, it's the thing that catches your eye. However, if the surrounding color scheme had been maroon and red, a green button would be the high-contrast element.

These are common examples of contrast. But, if we're thinking about the psychology of contrast, and how something enters our consciousness, contrast isn't limited to graphic design.

## CONTRAST AND CHARACTERS

While it's easy to think about contrast in terms of shape, color, size, and other graphic elements, we tend to forget that letters and numbers themselves can create contrast and get people's attention. For proof, scan the page at the top right from Craigslist.

Do any particular lines stand out? Users have hacked the available characters to catch people's attention. This also happens in much more subtle ways.

| Nov 29 - home repairs @ a fair price - (fort worth) <<*household servi* |
| Nov 29 - ☛ ☛ ☛Tile~Crown~Paints~All Remodeling - (REFRENCE |
| Nov 29 - ** Mobile welding, Cutting, Arc gouging, Fabricating, Re |
| Nov 29 - Offering Cleanup Services, Junk Hauling, Debris Remova |
| Nov 29 - TEXAS HOME REPAIR AND HANDYMAN SERVICE |
| Nov 29 - Hauling, Moving, Cleanup Services Offered - (Fort Worth, T |
| Nov 29 - ***TRASH/JUNK/DEBRIS** CLEAN UP**HAULING |
| Nov 29 - HOME IMPROVEMENTS! - (PLANO AND SURROUNDING |
| Nov 29 - ■ ■▄Portable welding, fab, welder▄ ▄■ - (ALL DFW- |
| Nov 29 - We Speak Your Language-Landscaping,Painting,Flooring. |
| Nov 29 - Tony's Lawn Service & Mulch - (Plano/Frisco/Richardson/Mcki |

*Notice how people use different characters to draw attention to their listings on Craigslist.*

While researching subtle user interface changes, I came across an interesting article from Ryan Jenkins, an expert in paid search. Jenkins shares some tips for writing effective display URLs for Google AdWords.*

Beginning with a rather straightforward URL, http://www.bennetcarsales.com, Jenkins walks through several iterations that would be more likely to have a higher clickthrough rate. I've summarized tips from that article in the sidebar on the following page.

While Jenkins never specifically mentions contrast, that is precisely reason the these recommendations are effective. By introducing mixed cases, and chopping off meaningless text like http or www, you made the information more scannable, and more likely to be recognized by the conscious brain. You're playing with contrast and shaping what captures attention, even if on a small scale.

---

*The Optimizer's Guide to Google AdWords: Display URL Strategy," a guest post at blog.performable.com.

# CONTRAST AND GOOGLE ADWORDS

Typical display URL option.

> Affordable Toyota Corolla
> Quality Toyotas at Great Prices
> No High-pressure Salesmen
> http://www.bennettcarsales.com

With the http:// removed

> Affordable Toyota Corolla
> Quality Toyotas at Great Prices
> No High-pressure Salesmen
> www.bennettcarsales.com

Capitalized letters make the URL easier to read

> Affordable Toyota Corolla
> Quality Toyotas at Great Prices
> No High-pressure Salesmen
> www.BennettCarSales.com

www is removed. (.com indicates this is an Internet address)

> Affordable Toyota Corolla
> Quality Toyotas at Great Prices
> No High-pressure Salesmen
> BennettCarSales.com

Add the keyword "Corolla"

> Affordable Toyota Corolla
> Quality Toyotas at Great Prices
> No High-pressure Salesmen
> BennettCarSales.com/Corolla

*From Ryan Jenkins article at blog.performable.com, ads get progressively more desirable as you move down.*

## SHH!
## WE'RE HOPING NO ONE NOTICES

Here's another example of contrast. Remember the store I mentioned that wanted to discourage people from placing phone orders on hold? Here you see the original comp and the one that was recommended:

> Would you like to
> • pay online
> • pay over the phone
> • or place this order on hold

*versus*

> Pay online or over the phone?
>
> You can also place these items on hold and pay for them when you pick them up.

The information is still there, but we're trying to encourage people to take one of these top two actions—pay online or over the phone. Even the phrasing of these options implies that you have just two choices. No one is being prevented from placing something on hold, simply nudged toward a preferable option.

37signals does a similar thing on its plans and pricing page for their product Basecamp (see the image on the next page). I seemed to remember that the site used to have a free plan—they still do. Can you find it? The free plan is still available, but it's presented in a quiet whisper, in the hope that no one will notice. This is deliberately hidden because it's a

Pricing page for 37signals' Basecamp. Can you spot the free plan?

behavior the company would like to discourage. A post written by 37signals commented that if they could go back and undo the free accounts, they would.

Both of these examples use size to create contrast (and effectively hide options).

## DID YOU SEE THAT?

Contrast can also occur over time through animation. In an example from StumbleUpon, the button has a subtle gloss highlight that loops about every ten seconds. The designers added this subtle animation to catch our attention. It's a very subtle use of *temporal* contrast. A more overt use of temporal contrast is seen on many news sites, where a small box slides out as you scroll nearer to the end of an article.

Temporal contrast can also happen over much longer periods of time. If you get a daily e-mail with essentially the same subject line, you'll eventually become blind to this, as we do with certain ad slots on a page. You can use contrast to draw attention by varying the *frequency* at which the e-mail is sent, thereby ensuring it doesn't become noise.

Jetsetter has added a very subtle and elegant touch to its login page. As with most login pages, you see two boxes: one for members to log in and one for nonmembers to sign up. To reinforce that only *one* of these options applies to you, the box and associated elements that are not needed fade back into the page. Hovering over one box brings it into focus and dims the other box. The result is that you only concentrate visually (and cognitively) on one set of questions.

# CHAPTER 16

# The Path of Least Resistance

LET'S BE HONEST, most of us are pretty lazy. Given a choice between action and inaction, we choose the latter—we do nothing. Don't believe me? Have you ever signed up for a "free three-month subscription" to a magazine of your choice? If so, then you probably know how that story plays out: like most people, you probably neglected to cancel within the grace period. As another example, consider how students tend to sit in the same seat, even when there's no seating chart. Or think about how one television show bleeds into another, chances are much higher we'll stay on that station (something television networks exploit to their advantage).

Given two choices, we tend to choose the one that doesn't require anything of us. This behavior is described as the *status-quo bias*, a term coined by William Samuelson and Richard Zeckhauser (1988). We tend not to change an established behavior (unless the incentive to change is compelling).

## DEFAULT OPTIONS

Unfortunately, status-quo bias in the form of default options has been abused in the marketplace. Think of the "Yes, you can share my information with third parties" checkboxes we neglect to uncheck, only to realize it later when we start receiving unwanted e-mails. Or think of those free trial subscriptions we forget to cancel. There's a reason these tactics are so widespread:

*Inaction* is easier than *action*.

While inertia can prevent us from taking the action when we probably should, it's also possible to use this intertia—by adjusting the defaults—for *positive* change. Consider the chart at the top of the next page. Each bar represents a country and the gold or blue color of the bar represents where organ donation is either opt-in or opt-out. Without reading the labels, care to guess which color represents which?

The first four countries, Denmark, the UK, the Netherlands, and Germany, all offer explicit opt-in programs (gold). You can see that in these countries a very low percentage of residents have opted-in to this program. Contrast

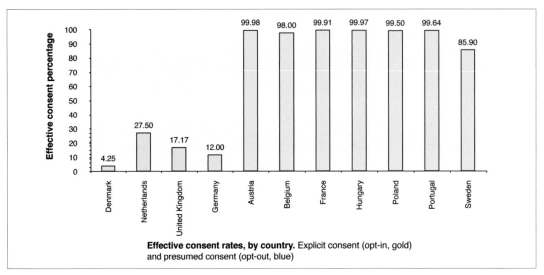

**Effective consent rates, by country.** Explicit consent (opt-in, gold) and presumed consent (opt-out, blue)

Source: Johnson, E. & Goldstein, D. (2003, November 21). Medicine: Do Defaults Save Lives? *Science Magazine, 302 (5649), 1338-1339.*

this with countries where a national donor program is presented as an opt-out option (blue). Almost everyone sticks with this default option. In both cases, the *decision* to enroll in the program is left to the individual. The difference is that you're either enrolled automatically (and you have to opt out) or you're not enrolled (and must opt in). You can see the huge difference. We're lazy. We tend to go with the defaults. Fortunately, in this case the default can be used for something good—encouraging people to become organ donors.

## THE POWER OF SUGGESTION

Status-quo bias isn't limited to playing with the default state of checkbox items. Suggesting a specific option (or options) is a very effective way to guide people, especially in uncertain situations.

If you've ever asked your co-workers where they want to go for lunch, you know the conversation that follows. There'll be 15 minutes of "we could go here" or "we could do this." Contrast this with someone who stands up and says, "Hey, I'm going to Joe's for lunch. Join me?" This latter situation is much more direct. The decision has shifted from "Where can we all eat and be happy?" to "Do I want to eat at this place or not?" (Most people tend to go along with the suggested option.)

Let's consider ways that we can offer suggestions in our Web apps.

*Tip for freelancers/anyone. When setting meeting times, don't ask when they're free. Choose a time, then ask if that's OK. Saves back/forth.*

—TWEET FROM @BOKARDO (JOSHUA PORTER)

### Ocado and its suggested defaults

Ocado, an online grocery and delivery service in the UK, uses suggested defaults in a brilliant way. While you can choose from a list of available delivery times, Ocado suggests a specific time when it is most economical (and green) to deliver to your neighborhood: "A van will already be in your area, booking it will help save fuel." While there is no price savings to the customer associated with picking the green option, the site is going one step beyond most booking sites by *sharing* a time that would make most sense logistically. If even a small percentage of

customers opt for this suggestion, the company benefits in an area where many customers aren't likely to have a strong preference. Rory Sutherland, who shared this observation, suggested that the airline industry could benefit from a similar strategy by recommending which flight a passenger might choose.

### The power of suggestion on Twitter

One of Twitter's ongoing challenges has been moving the casually interested visitor to an active—engaged—user of the service. In a previous iteration of its registration process,

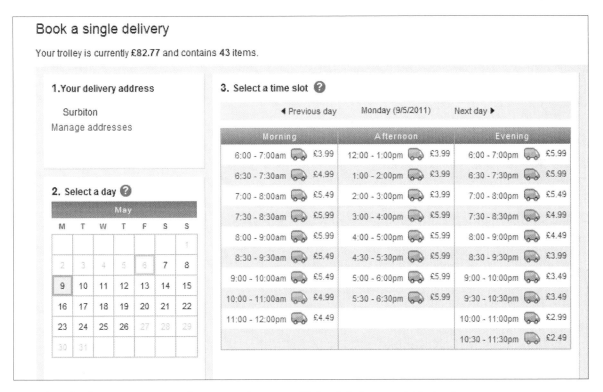

*Notice how Ocado encourages you to select a time when a van will already be in your neighborhood.*

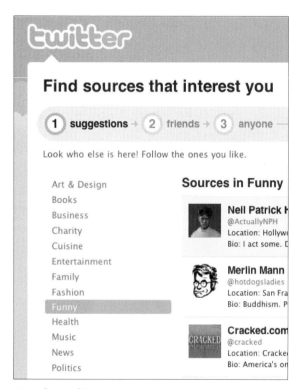

*The redesigned Twitter signup page.*

Twitter did offer some suggested options, such as, "Tell us what you're doing in the box above" and "Find some friends to follow." Users were even presented with a list of celebrities they could follow. However, this was an area for much improvement. New registrants were not becoming active users themselves.

In a redesign of this registration process (see screen above), the Twitter product team opted to suggest various accounts to follow within all sorts of categories. According to Twitter employee Josh Elman, "Rather than suggesting a random set of 20 users for a new user to follow, now we let users browse into the areas they are interested in and choose who they want to follow from these lists." In effect, the site lets you say "I'm interested in *family*" or "I'm interested in *food*" and then follow people within that category.

But, did these specific suggested options make a difference? In a 2010 presentation, Marc Trammell, a researcher with Twitter, announced that this change had increased completions 29 percent and participation afterward has been significantly higher. New users can quickly find and start following more personally relevant people, which in turn leads to more participation.

## CONVENIENCE AND PERSONALIZED RECOMMENDATIONS

Shown below is section from Wells Fargo's online bill pay system. For the longest time, if you wanted to *add* a payee (someone to pay money to), you had to go through a rather cumbersome process of inputting different identifying information, so that the business could

**Add a Popular Payee**

Select a link to add one of these popular payees and make a

▸ AT&T BILL (SBC - AR, KS, MO, OK, TX)

▸ AT&T MOBILITY

▸ AT&T U-VERSE

▸ ATMOS ENERGY

▸ BAC HOME LOANS SERVICING

▸ BANK OF AMERICA CREDIT CARD

▸ BEST BUY

*Wells Fargo suggests likley payees you might be adding.*

be found. Fortunately, over time the bank has built up a list of companies that are frequently added. Now if you go to add a popular payee, such as an electric company, there's a good chance you'll find that company presented in a list for you. This leverages *recognition over recall*, discussed in Chapter 1. It's also incredibly convenient and personalized to me.

### Now or later?

Speaking of convenience—what about more intelligent defaults? In Ketchup, a tool for taking better meeting notes, notice how the time defaults to the present:

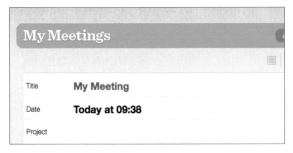

*"Add a meeting" in Ketchup defaults to present time.*

While anyone can click in the date area and reveal specific date and time options, defaulting to the current time supports a behavior I saw in my research: half of the time, people planned a meeting in advance. The other half of the time though, people remembered to open up our tool just as a meeting was about to begin. In this context, you'd want the "Create a Meeting" process to be as simple and streamlined as possible—the tool should never hold up the meetings it was designed to support. It's less common for people to override the default and

schedule a meeting at some point in the future. And in these cases, you have a bit more time to customize a few extra drop-down options.

### Subtle cues

Here's a subtle example of how a system might encourage more *effective* writing. Let's say this is an education app and you want to encourage people to write well-formed tasks for their students. Most well-written commands begin with a verb: *write, recall, create, present, argue, evaluate*, and so on. So, you might have your form label written in such a way that it encourages people to begin with a verb:

> **By the end of the year, Gabriel will be able to...**
>
> [                                    ]

However, even with this subtle nudge, I've seen plenty of situations where people break grammar, creating more problems later on. For example:

> **By the end of the year, Gabriel will be able to...**
>
> persuasive essay

In this case "persuasive essay" is not a goal or task, or rather it hasn't been stated as such. Perhaps "write a persuasive essay" is what the teacher had in mind. Here's a neat way to elicit that well-formed goal: what if, as you were typing that goal, you received instant feedback from the system that said "Oops! 'persuasive' is not a verb!" This is relatively easy to do—simply check the first word against a list of verbs. If the

| By the end of the year, Gabriel will be able to... |
|---|
| persuasive essay |
| *Oops! "persuasive" is not a verb!* |

word is not a verb, offer a bit of coaching. Suggest that the user look again at their text (and explain why beginning with a verb is a good thing when writing goals). This is a very small example of a *feedback loop*, where the system gives immediate feedback on some action taken.

(We'll discuss this in the next section on gaming, as feedback loops are a critical part of how games motivate people to continue playing.)

### *More information, please!*
Let's zoom out a bit and consider a *set* of form fields, perhaps a conference submission or a customer survey. At one point, you might have asked, "How can we get people to complete the requested information or add more written information in a text field?" The customer feedback app Get Satisfaction (screen below) has

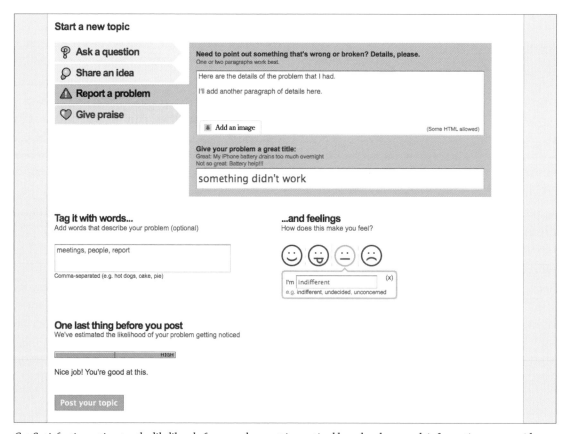

*Get Satisfaction estimates the likelihood of your probem getting noticed based on how much information you provide.*

an elegant way to nudge people into providing more information. With Get Satisfaction, you can share ideas, questions, problems, or praise for a site or service you're using.

Here's the neat part: They estimate the likelihood of your post getting noticed based on how many fields you complete and how much text you type in each field. This strength meter is a real-time feedback loop.

Let's take the example of reporting a problem. If I say, "Page didn't load when I clicked the Submit button" (or something equally vague), there's a *low* likelihood that my feedback will be noticed.

If I include more information, like additional details and some tags, then the strength meter goes up. If I add my feelings about it, the strength meter climbs higher still. So, it's giving me that feedback and letting me know "Hey, we think you should add more information here."

While we're on the subject of convenient, personalized details, let's look at a brilliant rating system developed at Steepster, an e-commerce site specializing in teas. As with many other sites on the Web, you can rate the items you've purchased. This was initially a simple thumbs up/down system, which resulted in 90 percent of their teas having a positive review—not very

useful for separating out "a really great tea from the best tea you've ever had."

One problem with rating systems is that our opinions are mutable, not absolute. Many people love to rate movies. If you use a service like Netflix, you've no doubt rated a bunch of movies. But, have you ever looked over all of your ratings next to each other and wondered, "Why did I rate that movie higher than that one? That doesn't seem right." Our internal frame of reference changes over time. We don't make absolute judgments.

In the case of something like different flavors of tea, you're rating a lot of products that are all pretty decent. You're *more* likely to make inconsistent votes.

So what's the solution?

Steepster, a tea site, explored a five-star rating system, a series of four smiley faces, and a 100-point scale, before arriving at the design shown below.

You have the familiar smiley faces. You also have a slider that affords a high degree of fidelity in your ratings. This combination should appeal to tea fanatics as well as new tea drinkers. But, the genius of this design is in the little tick marks you see. These are other teas you've rated; hovering over each tick mark reveals the

*Rating a tea at Steepster. As you hover over a tick mark, your previous ratings appear so you can make relative comparisons to your previously rated teas.*

name of that tea. So, as you begin to rate the new Earl Grey Creme tea you've just tried, you can also make a *relative* judgment, "Is this better or worse than this other tea I had?"

## AFRAID TO LET GO

We've talked about sticking with defaults, or continuing with what we already do. But why do we have a *status-quo bias*? Why do we prefer to leave things as they are?

There are the obvious candidates: Fear of the unknown. Laziness. Safety ("Hey, this seems to be what most people choose"). A sense of identity. Habit.

One of the more interesting findings about our inertia has to do with *ownership bias* and *loss aversion*. We hate to lose stuff. Even if there is more to be had, we hate letting go of what we already have. This can be seen with investors who hold on to stocks long after they should (rationally) have let them go. (Loss aversion explains this "sunk cost" effect.) But, personal investment is not required for us to develop an attachment to something. Consider some studies conducted by Amos Tversky and Daniel Kahneman.

In an experiment that has been repeated dozens of times, students in a class are asked to put a value on a coffee mug branded with their university's logo. Here's the catch: half of the students are given the mug, and then asked how much they would *sell* it for. The other half (those students not given mugs), are asked how much they would *pay* for a mug. Does ownership make a difference? In nearly all cases, the students with the mugs demand a value roughly twice that of what the students with no mugs are willing to pay. Once you have a mug, you don't want to give it up. But if you don't yet have one, there isn't an urgent need to purchase one. There isn't an *absolute* value we place on things.

In a similar study, half of the students are given coffee mugs (same as before). But in this variation of the experiment, the other half of the students are given large chocolate bars. Does ownership make a difference in their valuation? In a pretest, the students value these objects about the same. However, after taking possession, only one in ten was willing to switch their coffee mug for a chocolate bar or vice versa.

### Please correct our assumption

So, how might loss aversion or ownership bias apply to a Web context? One simple way is to place people in a position of ownership.

Signing up with BuySellAds.com presents you with this assertion:

# Hiya, Brandon!

I am indifferent with BuySellAds.com. CHANGE

Rather than ask you what you think of their service, they assume you are indifferent (unless you state otherwise). But "indifferent" is quite different from no stated opinion. Having your name (and identity) attached to such a statement is likely to encourage you to take some action to correct the situation.

# BRIGHTER PLANET COMBINES SUBTLE DETAILS TO INCREASE ENGAGEMENT

Brighter Planet—a service designed to help you become greener by lowering your energy consumption, recycling more, and the like—takes this same idea of defaults linked to your identity, but on a grander scale. But, to help you out, Brighter Planet first needs to assess your overall carbon footprint. To do this, they need personal information from you—lots of personal information. For the service to be useful, you have to answer dozens of questions in multiple categories, like residence, travel, and so on.

Fortunately, they made some subtle design decisions that make this experience… seductive!

First, you're given a default carbon footprint–*before* you've provided any information! How is that possible? Brighter Planet preloads answers based on national averages: average square feet most people occupy, average number of kids and pets, and so on. Naturally, we feel the urge to replace those defaults with our own, real data.

Next, as you start to add your own data, you notice the carbon footprint score changing—no page reloads or refreshes—simply entering the actual square feet of the house or apartment you live in changes your score. This is an example of a very tight feedback loop, something we'll discuss in Section Four, "The Game of Seduction."

As you "correct" the default information with your own, your also get to see how you compare to the national average.

Then, you might pause and notice that you've already answered at least ten questions. Why? Remember how we discussed not confronting people with a bunch of fields that need to be filled in? As you complete this form, there is only ever one form field exposed at a time. The moment you click enter, or tab to the next question, the input fields (or radio buttons and drop-downs) are replaced with your answer and the next question is opened up. It is very easy to answer several questions with no difficulty (and a brilliant way to make filling out a difficult–and long–form quite simple).

### "Mayorship" and loss aversion

A much more powerful example of loss aversion comes in the form of "mayorship" with Foursquare, a mobile check-in service where you can alert friends to your current location.

When you check in, not only are your friends alerted of your whereabouts, you also earn points and badges. The points haven't meant much—you might get listed on a weekly leaderboard. The badges are a bit more fun. You get a Newbie badge for your first check-in, and graduate to Adventurer, Explorer, and Superstar badges as you check-in at more places. There are also badges for checking in at specific times (Bender, for checking in after 7:00 p.m.) or places (Jetsetter, for checking in from diverse locations), or for certain activities (Photogenic, for sharing photos from the places you visit).

But Foursquare's secret sauce has to be the notion of mayorship.

You're going along, checking in at your favorite bookstore for the fifth time this month, when you get alerted that you've become the mayor of BookPeople. Foursquare mayorships are awarded to people with the most check-ins at a venue over the last 60 days. Mayorship doesn't mean much, initially. You might get a free beverage or 50 percent off your bill. The real fun kicks in when you steal the title of Mayor from someone else. And if it's a friend, assuming you're both competitive, some fun can ensue from the struggle to reclaim mayorship.

Mayorship also doesn't mean much until it is threatened. This is something I learned first-hand (see my story, involving pizza, on the next page).

It's worth adding that loss aversion isn't limited to things we've personally earned or created. Behavioral economist Dan Ariely conducted a study where students were asked to put a price on a basketball ticket they had *won*. At Duke University, tickets to these national games are hard to come by. To be fair, the university conducts a lottery to determine who gets tickets. Seeing this as an opportunity to investigate the idea of ownership, Ariely and his team set about calling those students who had won tickets to the game, asking them, "How much will you

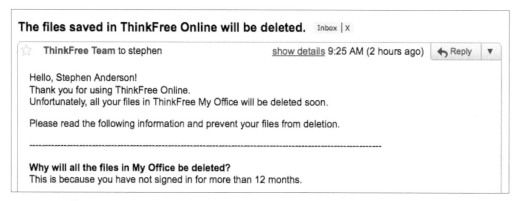

*Want to avoid losing your files? You must login to your account.*

# A STORY OF LOSS AND IRRATIONAL BEHAVIOR

Let me tell you about Chicago Street Pizza. I live in Texas, in a north Dallas suburb. I also enjoy good food. A while back, I got the craving for Chicago-style pizza. Not just any pizza claiming to be "Chicago style," it had to be the real deal—thick as a brick, sauce on top, the kind of pizza that's more like a pie than its flatbread cousins. After considerable searching, I finally found a place that makes pizza just like I remembered from my trips to Chicago. In fact, after chatting with the owner, I learned she was from Chicago and returns there every few months just to make sure her dough recipe hasn't changed. Of course I let my friends know about this place—in person, on Twitter, via Facebook. When you make a find like this, you naturally want to support the business by telling others. And, because of my check-ins there, I was the mayor (on FourSquare, at least) of Chicago Street Pizza. This went on for some time, until one day I received a rather alarming notice: "Michelle N. has just replaced you as Mayor of Chicago St. Pizza!"

Who the heck was Michelle N. and how did she just become mayor of my place! I had never really cared about mayorships before (at the time it wasn't particularly hard to become a mayor), but this was different. The place I had discovered and told others about, the place where I was the mayor, had been claimed by someone else. The nerve! I did what any rational person who has been threatened would do—I took my family to Chicago Street Pizza for dinner that night!

As silly as this may seem, I've spoken to dozens of people who all shared similar stories. People will go out of their way to stop by a bar to reclaim their mayorship status in Foursquare. While this isn't true of everyone, it's a good example of how things are valued much more once our ownership of them is threatened or removed.

Hey there -

Sorry for the bad news, but Michelle N. has just replaced you as mayor of Chicago St. Pizza!

http://foursquare.com/venue/78977

Don't take it too hard - a few more checkins and you could be back on top...

- foursquare

**Congrats! You just stole the title of Mayor of Chicago St. Pizza from Michelle N.**

sell it to me for?" On average, the people who had won tickets wanted at least $1,400 dollars for them. The researchers also called those students who had not received tickets and asked them how much they would be willing to pay for a ticket. These people wouldn't pay more than $170 for a ticket on average. What was going on? The more the team probed, they discovered something interesting. People who owned tickets talked about and viewed the tickets from an owner's viewpoint. They had already incorporated going to the game in their personal narrative. The ticket transcended a purely financial transaction. There was now a *story* attached to these tickets: owners spoke about the game as "an experience I will always remember" or something to tell their grandchildren about. In Ariely's words, "When we have buyers and sellers, we have two different people, from two different perspectives, each viewing the transaction not as the same thing that they give and get but focusing more on what they tend to give up in the transaction."

What have you "given" to your users? What can be claimed? What can be lost?

### Abuse of loss aversion

It's worth noting that loss aversion and ownership bias can create a frustrating, even if effective, experience. For example, I've encountered surveys that promised a payoff in the end. It should have been a simple exchange: I'd answer a dozen questions and the site would provide some interesting assessment of me. Only, there was a catch. After answering the last question, instead of giving me the promised payoff, the site required me to provide an e-mail address to find out the results of the test. This is a *bait-and-switch* technique. It might work in this case, especially if I've taken the time to answer the questions, but it is a frustrating experience, akin to a hostage situation: "You want the answer? Give us your e-mail address." While conversion and response rates are certainly a metric to watch, so is customer satisfaction and the likelihood that people will refer you to others. As with everything described in this section, you have to take a broader look at the relationship you're building with a person, not just a single metric.

### Fear of loss affects decisions

Loss aversion also shows up in a much more subtle way, in the choices we make. In numerous studies, when things are *framed* in terms of loss, people are much less likely to choose that option. For example, would you rather get a $5 discount, or avoid a $5 surcharge? Rationally, these two options are the same, but the idea of "losing" an extra $5 bothers people a lot more.

This leads us into the next chapter, one focused on the power of language.

# CHAPTER 17

# The Influence of Words

AS WE NEAR THE END of our discussion on the subtle art of seduction, we'll turn our attention to how your choice of words can influence behavior.

## FRAMING

Let's begin with the idea of "framing" a choice. I'm going to ask you a difficult question:

> An epidemic breaks out that's likely to kill 600 people if left untreated.
>
> Treatment strategy A will save 200 people.
>
> Treatment strategy B has a one-third chance of saving 600 people and a two-thirds chance of saving nobody.

Which one do you choose? When asked this question, 72 percent of people choose option A, the one that will save 200 people.

Now, I'm going to present you with a slightly different question:

> An epidemic breaks out that's likely to kill 600 people if left untreated.
>
> Under treatment strategy A, it is known that 400 people will die.
>
> Under treatment strategy B, there is a one-third probability that nobody will die, and a two-thirds probability that 600 people will die.

Which one do you choose? When asked *this* question, 78 percent of people choose option B.

Look carefully at each of the options. In both questions, options A and B were exactly the same. Yet, the majority of people chose the *opposite* answer when the language changed just slightly. The only difference is how the question was presented. The second scenario frames things in terms of a loss, which, as we just discussed, people would rather avoid. According to the researchers, "The way a scenario is worded influences the decision of the respondent." This is the basic idea behind framing, which states that *the way in which issues and data are stated can alter our judgment and affect decisions.*

This notion of "framing" is a hot topic in politics, where choosing the right frame can influence popular opinion and legislation. For example, the *War on Terror* was a strong frame—who's going to be against that? If you're against the War on Terror, what does that mean you're for? Contrast this frame with the abortion debate: two positions—*pro-life* and *pro-choice*—are competing with each other. Neither has succeeded in framing the issue.

Framing isn't limited to issues though. Consider this sign (see below, left) from a local sandwich shop.

I can pay $2.50 more for one deal, or $3.50 more for another deal. Wait a second! Look at how they've framed the purchase. They're trying to frame my purchase in terms of an *additional* cost versus a total cost. Thinking in numbers like $2 and $3 is more likely to lead to

a purchase. If it were presented in terms of the total amount, something closer to $10, I might not want to choose a combo.

One particularly powerful frame that almost worked on me was in a commercial for a Kenmore Elite washer and dryer. The voice-over went something like this: "How much can you get out of the Kenmore Elite washer? How about enough water and energy savings to pay for the dryer?" The cost of this purchase was framed in terms of how much it will save. Hey, it'll pay for itself in a year or two!

The hosted blogging site Posterous has tried to use framing in a recent campaign aimed at Tumblr users (see below, right).

In a rather overt message, Posterous is trying to establish itself as the more mature option that more serious users eventually graduate to. Notice the language that is used to characterize

**Hey Tumblr users: Want comments? Need privacy? Graduate to Posterous**

Tumblr is a pretty cool service. They offer easy set up, loads of funky themes and super-simple reblogging.

But blogging on Tumblr is sort of like being in high school. But you know deep-down that you can't be in high school forever. Eventually, you have to move on.

It's the same with blogging. After you get your feet wet, you need comments and the ability to moderate them.* You need to add different media types to each post. Your sharing needs are more complex, and your site needs to grow with you.

Face it. You need to leave Tumblr behind and graduate to Posterous.

**WHICH COMBO**

**+ $2.50**
Includes 20oz Fountain Drink & Chips or a Just-Out-Of-The-Oven Cookie™

**+ $3.50**
Includes Small Milkshake & Chips or a Just-Out-Of-The-Oven Cookie™

**GRAB A GREAT DEAL**

*(Left) Sandwhich shop framing their combo in terms of additional cost (versus total cost); (Right) Posterous trying to frame Tumblr as the less mature option.*

Tumblr: "pretty cool," "funky," "super simple," a place where you can "get your feet wet." Sounds like the option you should leave behind, right? That's what Posterous is hoping for.

## ANCHORING

This leads us to another rather curious mind hack, one exploited by salespeople, magicians, and others: *anchoring*. When making decisions, we rely too heavily—or anchor—on one trait or piece of information. This is because most of our judgments are not *absolute* (based on all available information in the world), but rather *relative*, typically to the initial anchor being set. If a consultant says her average hourly rate is $20, then you determine value based on how that number goes up or down in negotiations. If that same consultant opens with an hourly rate of $2,000 an hour, our judgments are based on the changes in that number.

Sales people frequently use this in negotiations by starting off with a high opening cost, and then giving you a good deal that's below the original price. In any store, if you see an original listing price next to the sale price, that store is leveraging anchors to create the perception of a great deal. High-end restaurants sometimes do this on their menus. By drawing your attention to a dish that costs $130, the $30–$40 menu items seem cheap by comparison. The restaurant could care less if they ever sell the expensive menu item—they're trying to make the other items seem more reasonable.

Here's where things get interesting. Our brains will anchor on completely irrelevant information! In numerous studies, people have been asked to write down a random number, typically the last few digits of their social security number. They are then asked to make some judgment: the population of a city, the price of a wine, an historical date. Whether or not they're aware of it, participants key off of these numbers, however irrelevant they may be.

In one study by Dan Ariely, students were asked to write the last two digits of their social security number. With this number in front of them, Ariely asked if they would pay this amount for items whose value they did not know (wine, chocolate, and computer equipment). They were then asked to submit a bid for these items. The results? Those audience members with higher two-digit numbers placed bids that were "between 60 percent and 120 percent more" than those students with the lower social security numbers. We're great at setting relative values, but terrible at placing an absolute value on something. An obvious example of this comes in the form of charities that set a range of options from which to choose. If the options are something like $5, $10, $25, and $50, we're going to donate much less than if the options start at $50 and go up to $5,000. These anchors give us a cue from which we can adjust our assessment.

Anchoring goes beyond numeric data, however. In another study, college students were asked two questions: "How happy are you?" and "How often are you dating?" Asked in this order, there was little to no correlation between the two questions. However, when the sequence was reversed, students apparently saw a correlation between the two questions. "Hmm. I haven't had a date in a while. I suppose I am unhappy." We are still learning about the cognitive processes that underlie our judgments and behavior, but studies like these point to the mental associations that our brains make between things—even irrelevant things—that are brought into short-term memory.

What's the point of all this? Be very careful with the keywords, numbers, and even the sequence of questions you place in your content—our brains are looking for things from which to anchor our judgments.

## LET'S GET PERSONAL

Speaking of things our brains look for, here's a quick bit of advice I picked up from Kathy Sierra, wildly successful author and lecturer:

*"Never underestimate the power of using 'you' in your writing!"*

Why does Sierra advocate an informal, conversational writing style? Because this is what the brain looks for to see if it should be engaged. We may think we want to pay attention to a lecture, but when the speaker (or writer) speaks directly to "you," the brain thinks we are now engaged in a conversation.

I've tried making this shift in many of my communications (you've no doubt noticed the conversational voice throughout this book). I feel it draws you into the text and allows for a story to develop. I'm speaking to *you* about a particular subject.

Speaking directly to a person can be particularly useful if action is required. For example, I could send out an e-mail stating, "All employees need to turn in their TPS reports by 5:00 p.m." or I could say, "You need to turn in your TPS report by 5:00 p.m. today." The latter phrasing is more direct and urgent.

### *"You should follow me on Twitter here"*

In 2009, blogger Dustin Curtis, curious about the effects of forceful language, ran a little experiment. At the bottom of his Web site, he has a call to action that invites people to follow him on Twitter. He wanted to see if he could "increase the clickthrough rate even more by altering the way [this phrase] was worded."

He began with a *statement*: "I'm on Twitter," and found that this produced a 4.70 percent clickthrough rate.

Then he switched to a *command*: "Follow me on Twitter," which produced a 7.31 percent clickthrough rate.

Then he tried a stronger personal command: "You should follow me on Twitter," which produced a 10.09 percent clickthrough rate.

Finally, he added the literal callout "here," for a final phrase of "You should follow me on Twitter here." The result was a remarkable 12.81 percent clickthrough rate.

From the first phrase to the last, that's nearly three times as many people clicking through—due to a simple variation in phrasing.

### Effective e-mail headlines

On a purely anecdotal note, some of the most effective e-mail subject lines I have received came from Marc Cenedella, Founder and CEO of TheLadders.com, a site for potential job hunters. See if you wouldn't feel the urge to open some of these e-mails:

Fresh Ammo for Your Job Hunt

I Have 3 Things To Tell You

It's Time Your Resume Retired

Recession-Busting Career Secrets

I Took Your Advice!

Seeking VP, Anything

Bye-Bye!

Should You Trade Some Salary for a Top Title?

I Didn't Hire You for a Reason

Leonardo da Vinci's Resume

How Do Other People Ace Their Interviews?

I Thought My Resume Was OK, until I Saw What Everybody Else Is Doing

Compare these to the daily job listings e-mails sent out by another company:

Saved search results - 2/5/2011

Saved search results - 2/6/2011

Saved search results - 2/7/2011

Saved search results - 2/8/2011

Based on these e-mail headlines, I decided to do a bit of personal analysis. Combing through a backlog of archived e-mails, I culled those with the most compelling subject lines. Was there a pattern to the different language used that resulted in a higher clickthrough? After looking at a variety of subject lines and doing a bit of research online, I arrived at this list of headlines that work (assuming there's a payoff):

- PERSONAL/RELEVANT INFORMATION: *"Your Recent Purchase of..." "Since You're Now a Proud Homeowner"*
- PROVOCATIVE QUESTIONS: *"Are You Making These Investment Mistakes?" "Have You..." "Did You Remember to..."*
- HOW TO...
- REASON: *"Why You Should..." "Nine Reasons Why..."*
- TESTIMONIALS: *"How I Did...," "I Had..."*
- *COMMANDS:* "Stop..." "Become..." "Don't..." "End..."
- POWERFUL WORDS: *"Free..." "You..." "Your..."*
- HELPFUL INFORMATION: *"10 Investment Tips"*
- ANNOUNCEMENTS: *"New Financing Offers"*
- Finally, I'd look at top headlines from any site that aggregates top stories from around the Web (one of my personal favorites is PopUrls.com)

Note, this list is not unique. Plenty of copywriters have identified similar lists of persuasive headlines. I include this as a reference list of tactical ways to engage your readers, whether the final context is e-mail or otherwise.

## CLEAR LANGUAGE

Obsessing over every word isn't always required. Just being clear and direct can change behavior.

We've seen this many times over with simple changes to button labels: changing "Submit" to "Place Order." Or, instead of a simple "Upgrade" button label you can be more specific with something like "Upgrade to the Shiny Gold Platinum Program." One of my personal favorites is to dynamically generate the language used in a button label. For example, instead of a simple "Place Order" button for shopping online, why not a "Place Order for $24.57" button. In this case, the button serves double duty as a means to submit data and as a confirmation message. The results of pressing that button are very clear.

Here's a different example of being clear and direct from Facebook product design manager Julie Zhuo.

Looking over usage data, Zhuo and her team found that 85 percent of people who uploaded a photo were only uploading one. However, the team also found that "a lot of people wanted to upload *albums* but just didn't know how." People were uploading multiple photos, just one at a time.

The solution was a bit of education. The team added a tooltip that explained how to hold down shift and select multiple photos to upload. The result? The number of people uploading just one photo at a time dropped from 85 percent to 40 percent!*

Plenty more could be said about the use of language in interface design. We could look at the two-thousand-year-old field of rhetoric, or explore linguistics or speech act theory or Neuro-Linguistic Programming (NLP). There is also much to be learned from poets, speechwriters, lawyers, and other professionals for whom choosing the exact right language is critical. I'll sum up what I've highlighted here in three short phrases:

Be short and to the point. Be conversational. Be aware of what is suggested by your choice of words.

*"Note to the single men out there: 'Lemme get your number' is a lot less effective than 'Can I call you sometime?'"*

—Tweet by @whitneyhess

---

*"Podcast of Julie Zhuo's talk on How Facebook Uses Data" at www.zurb.com, December 2010

# CHAPTER 18

# An Eye for Details

WE COULD GO ON with more small details devoted to the subtle art of seduction. However, I'd like to end this section with *an approach you can use* to identify all kinds of subtle user interface details and nuances that might be worth deeper consideration.

## STEP ONE: ROLE-PLAY THE INTERACTION

Interface designers commonly talk about "conversational interfaces," but have you actually had a conversation with an interface? Yes, we've all sat in front of a screen and had internal dialogues. Or we may have seen our share of think-alouds in a usability session, where participants are asked to share their every thought during an interaction. Here, however, I mean literal conversation with between a person and the interface.

Okay, it's a person role-playing the interface. But it is dramatic how this two-way conversation is so much more powerful than the one-sided commentary we are used to hearing. Because it is actually an interaction, it more closely mimics the experience and is more revealing. It's very effective in helping clients to see—literally—the problems with their existing user interface. And it's a fun activity!

"Bringing the Browser to Life!" is described in detail on the following pages. It provides a structure for this role-playing, and helps you envision the conversation and capture what is learned through the process.

The conversation reveals where unnecessary details may be cluttering the experience, as well as where user interface decisions need to be rethought. You could be evaluating an existing interface and/or generating ideas for a new one.

I started doing this exercise a few years ago and continue to be impressed by the kinds of insights it can provide. It works especially well with clients who know nothing about interface design, but also provides surprises to the most seasoned teams of design professionals. Somehow being able to experience a page as a conversation helps people recognize all the difficulties and frustrations of interacting with a browser.

# BRINGING THE BROWSER TO LIFE!

For this exercise, you'll need three things:

- A willing participant
- A screenshot of the interface being evaluated (this works best with forms pages)
- A browser window prop (this is key to the whole exercise—don't skip this detail!)

I typically assemble a browser window from of a sheet of gray foamboard. Cut out an opening, being careful to leave double the width in the top border (where the URL and title bars go). I use white electrical tape to create the title and search bars and then a black marker to accent the details. Round price tags (like you use in a garage sale) can be used for the close, minimize, and maximize browser buttons.

On a projector, display the form to be evaluated for all to see. Ask for a volunteer to role-play the interface, with these instructions:

*I'm going to try to complete this form. Of course there will be a conversation between the two of us. I'm going to say everything that is on my mind, and you will respond, as if we're having a real conversation. However, your dialog is limited to the form labels (and any subtext or microcopy) in the current user interface.*

Assuming the interface in question is quite bad, you can encourage the volunteer to be dramatic and a bit annoyed by your think-alouds.

Then, begin the fun part of having a dialog with the screen. To show how this plays out, I've provided a sample dialog (I'll let you imagine the user interface).

During the process you are likely to discover subtle details that could be improved (like replacing a specific date with a date range). In the example here, a lot of frustration could be avoided by first asking

what kind of event the reservation is for (which would limit the questions that follow).

To leave things on a positive note and uncover some ideas for correctly designing the user interface, you should follow up this first exercise with one in which you have a real conversation with the person pretending to be the interface. By this point, they know enough about the situation that they can improvise and have a more realistic conversation. I advise groups to have a notetaker for this portion, as some good UI ideas are likely to come up.

*Context: I'm trying to get more information about reserving a room at a hotel for an all-day conference in Amsterdam.*

**ME:** I'd like get an idea of what you charge to rent a room for a day. About 30 people. Breakfast, lunch and afternoon snack also needed.
**PH:** You need to fill out an RFP.

**ME:** A what? I just need an idea of what you might charge.
**PH:** You need to fill out this RFP.

**ME:** But I just want an estimate—I don't want to put you through too much effort. My questions are really quite staightforward…

**PH:** Fill out this RFP.

**ME:** That's a lot of information…
**PH:** And you must complete every field.

**ME:** Geez. Okay…
"Contact Person" You mean my name, right?
**PH:** Contact Person.

**ME:** So why not say "Your name"?
**PH:** Contact Person.

**ME:** How many people are filling this out on behalf of someone else—seriously. Okay…
Email. Makes sense. You'll need that to contact me (though you could have said as much).
**ME:** Phone?! Are you seriously going to call me?
**PH:** Phone.

**ME:** I'm in the U.S. What will you need to call me about that can't happen over email?
**PH:** PHONE!

**ME:** Okay, okay.
Now, wait a second. Since this will be international for you, do I need to add the +1?
**PH:** Phone.

**ME:** Yeah, I get that. But how will you know I'm in the States?
**PH:** Phone.

**ME:** Okay, I'm guessing you'll need that info from me, even though you're not being very helpful here…
**PH:** Company.

**ME:** Will I be bringing any company? Yeah, I get you. I have a company name. But, this isn't for a company. Look, I really just need a quote. Do you really need my company info for this?
**PH:** COMPANY!

**ME:** Okay…
"Event name"—here we go…
Umm, if I write the title of the workshop, you might get the wrong idea…
**PH:** Event name.

**ME:** It's called "Seductive Interactions Workshop" but you might get the wrong idea…
**PH:** Event name.

**ME:** This is really for you records, right? You just need something to refer to this… (why isn't "your workshop" enough?!).
**PH:** EVENT NAME!

**ME:** Okay, I'll be safe. Let's just call this "Design Workshop" (I don't think that will raise any eyebrows.)
**PH:** Type of Event: Training, Meeting, Conference, Customer Promotion, Family Event, Other.

**ME:** It's a workshop.
**PH:** Type of Event: Training, Meeting, Conference, Customer Promotion, Family Event, Other.

**ME:** It could be a conference. No, it's more like training.
**PH:** Type of Event: Training, Meeting, Conference, Customer Promotion, Family Event, Other.

**ME:** Maybe I should put Other—I'm guessing you need this info for… What exactly?
**PH:** Just choose a type of event from the list I've given you and stop being difficult.

**ME:** <Shrug> Other.
**PH:** When do you arrive? When do you leave?

**ME:** It's a one-day conference.
**PH:** When do you arrive? When do you leave?

**ME:** It's a one-day event. Can I put in the same arrival and departure date. That's stupid.
**PH:** When do you arrive? When do you leave?

**ME:** Oh, to Amsterdam? What does this have to do with getting a quote for the day? I may or may not be staying at your hotel. I just need a quote for a single day event!
**PH:** When do you arrive? When do you leave?

**ME:** The event is on Tuesday, Nov 9th.
**PH:** I don't know Tuesday. Just the date. Starting with the day.

**ME:** Oh, this is a European thing… ;-)
**PH:** What year?

**ME:** Umm, this year. Do people really plan out events 14 months in advance? Why is last year an option? Can I plan this in the past? <sarcasm>
**PH:** When do you depart?

**ME:** Conference ends on the same day.
**PH:** When do you depart?

**ME:** Ugh.
**PH:** Single Rooms? Double Rooms?

**ME:** What? The number of…? Again, why do you need this? This isn't a conference. People won't be staying at your hotel. Maybe just me. And I'm reconsidering that…
**PH:** Single Rooms? Double Rooms?

**ME:** None!!
**PH:** Date of event.

**ME:** I just gave you that.
**PH:** Date of event.

**ME:** Oh, so I didn't need to tell you when I'm arriving or leaving. Wait a second, I'm confused…

We could go on, but—you get the idea!

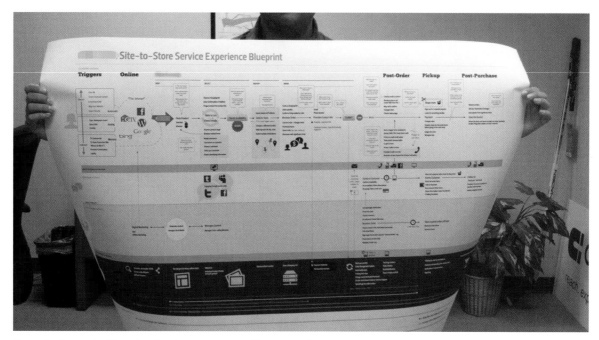

*Example of a service blueprint that documents every discrete step in an experience.*

## STEP TWO: SCRIPT THE NARRATIVE EXPERIENCE

If you've ever created a task flow diagram or service blueprint (like the one shown above), this will be familiar. Document every step of the experience, including tasks and emotions that people feel along the way. By documenting the user's journey in a narrative fashion, we're more likely to see where things break down or where the experience might be improved.

## STEP THREE: BREAK DOWN COMPOUND REQUESTS INTO SIMPLE NEXT STEPS

This is also known as sequencing. If there's a situation where you're asking multiple questions at once, can you ask them in sequence? For example, asking someone to vote is a complex request, with many steps along the way. Start with finding your voter registration card, then move on to identifying your polling place, and so on.

## STEP FOUR: MINIMIZE CHOICES
## (AT EACH MOMENT IN TIME)

Restrict to an absolute minimum the number of choices (and actions) a person has to make.

This step is easy to get wrong and requires us to really put the experience under the microscope. Here's a real world example:

In most restrooms, at least more recent ones, you put your hands under the faucet and the water starts flowing. However, you still have to push down the soap dispenser to get any soap out. Look back at the image. This soap dispenser had a sensor exactly like the water does, so I didn't have to touch anything to dispense the soap. All I had to do was move my hands under the dispenser and back to the water to wash them. Whoever designed this dispenser turned a two-step process (push on valve, collect soap) into a one-step process (place hands under soap dispenser).

This may be a silly example, but it demonstrates how even the simplest of tasks can be made simpler.

Shown below is another example, a user interface where we face the same kind of decision when asking for contact information. We had to decide *when* to ask for contact information. We could ask for all of it at the moment someone put something on hold (left) or ask for it in stages using a confirmation page (right).

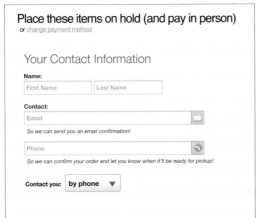

*The initial interface is shown on the left. On the right the choices are separated, first you complete the fields and subsequently, on a confirmation screen, you are asked the next question.*

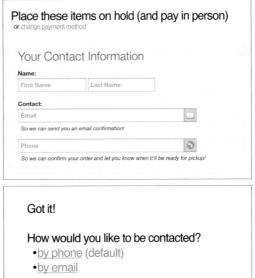

Ask yourself whether this is something that can be done later on and how critical it is. Again, look at every field and ask is this critical *at this moment*? What I recommended was to move that to the confirmation message and then ask, "How would you like to be contacted: phone or e-mail?" We've broken up the conversation—you only ever have to make one choice at a given moment. Because the user might forget to click something in a confirmation message, the default here is phone, which is likely to be the way the business prefers to contact people.

### STEP FIVE: LOOK FOR MICROMOMENTS

In the role-playing exercise, you no doubt witnessed moments of apprehension or genuine concern. Responding to these moments doesn't necessarily translate into a literal back-and-forth conversation or adding a step in the process. Sometimes the dialogue can happen on a single form page. It's things like the microcopy below a form field that support a back-and-forth conversation.

### STEP SIX: CHOOSE CLICKS OVER CHARACTERS

Any time you can have people keep their finger on the mouse and click on one of the available options (versus having to switch to the keyboard), you'll likely see a higher uptake. Take, for example, the difference between iLike and most sites that ask you to list your favorite bands, separated by commas. iLike never did that. They simply asked me to click on bands I like and it was a much more fun, much more engaging process.

# CONNECTING BEHAVIORAL GOALS WITH BUSINESS GOALS

You may be thinking something along the lines of: "My company is would never do anything fun like what you're describing. How do you get businesses to invest in some of these ideas?"

Let me share a brilliant question I picked up from Joshua Porter in his book *Designing for the Social Web*.

What do people have to do in order for your business to be successful?

What I love about this question is that it connects business goals to behavioral goals. In one simple question you ask "What will success look like for the business?" and "What are the behaviors that support these goals?"

Businesses work toward goals such as adoption, retention, and increased sales, but in this case, we're best off when our goals can be stated in behavioral terms. These behavioral goals represent changes in the way people act—changes that can be observed or measured. This includes changes in cognition or emotion, too.

While a business goal might be to "increase the number of paid subscribers," the associated behavioral goals might be to "get more people to click on the register button" and "help people understand our pricing plan options." You may find that one business goal often fans out to multiple behavioral goals. Defining these behavioral and business goals ahead of time, before a project starts, does several things for us.

1. Links design work directly to business outcomes.
2. Too often, there's a disconnect between business stakeholders and the work done by designers. This question creates a link between these groups, and the accountability that goes along with it. We can trace the effects of our design decisions back to measurable business goals.
3. Brings focus, and ideas.
4. Knowing what behaviors to design for at a page by page level creates focus, and leads to better ideas. As you walk through a designed experience, you can ask at every moment, what is the desired behavior at this moment or on this page and does this design support that goal in some way? I've found that there's a correlation between detailed behavioral goals and creative, effective ideas.
5. Opens the door for creative ideas
6. By agreeing to specific behavioral goals up front, before any design work begins, you have objective measures against which you can evaluate the proposed designs. This frees you up to explore ideas, even crazy ones, so long as they prove effective. CEO hates pink buttons? If you can produce the results that show more people clicked on pink buttons compared to other colors, then the decision becomes objective—do we go with the option that more people click on, or not? By defining behaviors to design and test for, the conversation shifts away from whims and personal preferences to measurable results.

Here's how this might play out:

Let's start with a business goal. For this example, let's pretend, hypothetically, that we work for YouTube and the goal is to improve the quality of the video content uploaded to our site. You can imagine some stakeholders sitting behind close doors who've decided that as a brand, they'd like people to associate YouTube more with new HD offerings and films, as opposed to the "talking head" web cam videos

*continued on next page*

continued from previous page

Business Goals ⟶ Behavioral Goals
(which should align w/ User Goals)

Psychology

they've become associated with. Again, hypothetical situation.

The first thing we'd need to do is translate this business goal into a behavioral goal. "improve the quality of the video content uploaded to our site" is not a behavior you can design for—it's an outcome of some changes in behavior. Something like "encourage people to be more selective about what they upload" is a good behavioral goal. This is something designers can work with.

Next question: "How do we encourage this behavior?" This is where the fun starts, by exploring what we know about human behavior—how we make choices, what gets our attention, what we recall later. Basically, the things described throughout this book!

Let's pull a few of these ideas at random and see how they might help in our scenario.

*Scarcity*—We infer value in something that has limited availability or is promoted as being scarce.

What if we limited uploads to just a few per week—everyone is allowed to upload three videos, but no more. Might this give people pause to think

twice about what they're uploading?

*Limited Access*—We naturally desire things that are perceived as exclusive or belonging to a select few.

What if those users who uploaded HD or highly rated content were given access to more editing features?

*Authority*—We want to follow the lead and advice of a legitimate authority.

What if we sent out short video tips from noted directors?

*Shaping*—To teach something new, start with the simplest form of the behavior; reinforce increasingly accurate approximations of the behavior.

What if we started of with very small, generic challenges that would apply to most people uploading videos. Try using dramatic lighting… This week, try a dramatic angle… Use this filter… Practice the "rule of thirds." No one is expected to become a film director, but easy techniques like this would raise the bar on quality of videos uploaded.

You get the idea.

## ASSIGNMENT

Are you humans involved in your project? If so, then stop. You have an assignment:

1. What are you working on, right now? (The name of a project)
2. What are some of the business goals associated with this project?
3. Once you've written down a few business goals, translate these into behavioral goals.
4. Now, let the fun begin! What do you know about human behavior? What have you learned from this book that you might apply? Again, the theme of this book is "How can we apply what we know about human behavior to interaction design?" It's time to put that knowledge to the test.
5. Have fun!

As a handy reference tool, I created a deck of cards (Mental Notes) to help bring these ideas from psychology out of textbooks and research papers and into our projects. find out more at www.getmentalnotes.com

# The Game of Seduction

A first date leads into a second, and so begins the dating process; a thrilling mix of blissful highs, anxious moments, and difficult choices. How much do we reveal? How does the other person feel? Am I coming on too strong? Should I play hard to get?

We celebrate anniversaries—two weeks, two months. We pore over letters written to each other. We seek out new ways to show affection. And we reflect on moments and mementos from time shared together.

And in the process, we learn about that person: their needs, desires, and interests.

Up to this point in the book, we've focused on the *initial* ways to connect with people, through aesthetics, play, and subtlety. But what if you want more than a one-time conversion? How do you continue to delight someone and lay the groundwork for a longer-term relationship? How do we move people from *falling* in love to *staying* in love with our applications? How do you continue delighting people?

Naturally, games are a good place to start, given the ongoing devotion games inspire. Consider the social game FarmVille, which peaked at 80 million active users—all acquired in a matter of months. Or the check-in service Foursquare, which has warmed up people to the idea of sharing their location in return for points and badges. In the tech community Stack Overflow, members earn points and privileges through defined activities. These kinds of services hint at the addictive power of games, but there's much more to a good game than meets the eye.

A game first has to be fun and engaging—without the points and badges that get so much attention; a simple reward schedule—however addictive—leads to frustration if people don't enjoy the activity being reinforced. In contrast, good games bring joy to people's lives.

Why is it possible to spend hours transfixed on a screen with no awareness of the passing time? Why do people enjoy games? And can we create the same emotions with things that are not games?

As with the previous chapters, we'll focus on the psychology that motivates these passionate behaviors, and explore what it is that keeps people coming back for more.

# CHAPTER 19

# Real World Games

WHEN I FIRST GAVE A TALK on seductive interactions, several people commented that it was the best talk on "game design" they had heard.

Huh? I was genuinely baffled.

Here I was, pulling together all these ideas from psychology, persuasion, neuroscience, and other fields and it came off as a lecture on game mechanics? What's even more interesting is that I am not a gamer. I do have a Wii and an Xbox at home (the Xbox was a gift), and I've got my share of casual games on the iPhone, but I don't have much time for these pleasures.

So how is it that I gave a talk on game mechanics without knowing it?

## GAMES ARE FIRST AND FOREMOST ABOUT FUN

What people naturally think of when we talk about games is the fun and joy of playing them. In fact, a lot of what makes a game fun is the *play* within the game. Much of what we discussed in Section 2, "Playful Seduction," is central to many games. We bravely explore new worlds (curiosity). We look for patterns (pattern recognition). We are delighted by pleasant surprises (delighters). We create representations of ourselves (self-expression). From this perspective, we've already started talking about making a game by making something playful. But, games are different from play. Whereas play can happen spontaneously and without any declared purpose, games have rules, objectives, and other characteristics that set them apart. And it's these dynamics that lead to emotions like conflict, anxiety, flow, or delight.

Given the sustained interest that people give to a good game, it should come as no surprise that businesses have begun looking to gaming as a way to create customer loyalty or build interest in their service. This trend of adding things like points and badges to make sites more gamelike is widespread. The news site The Huffington Post now awards badges to frequent

# WHY ARE WE ADDING GAME MECHANICS TO REAL THINGS?

At its core the idea is something like this...

A thing → Add game mechanics → That thing now has a new layer of fun it didn't have before → People are more likely to engage with that thing

*This slide from Matthew Guy's presentation "Reality Invaders" pretty much sums up "gamification."*

contributors. The site I'm using to write this, 750words.com, tracks my writing habits and places me in a competition of sorts with others. Even the music site thesixtyone.com has added the idea of quests and points to the act of music listening. These experiments are no doubt inspired by the success of gaming elements on sites like Foursquare and Stack Overflow. The reasoning behind adding these simple mechanics goes something like this:

*A thing*

*Add some game mechanics*

*The thing now has a new layer of fun it didn't have before*

*People are more likely to engage with that thing*

Every business owner wants growth, repeat visits, and active users. Games seem like an easy way to encourage and further these goals. And they might work, for a time, with some people.

But adding points and badges to an everyday behavior won't make something a game, at least not a game worth playing for very long, and certainly not one that leads to joy and delight. Game designers spend months or years testing all kinds of elements to get the exact, right mix that will challenge and delight players. To understand why games can be so addictive, we have to look past the visible trappings associated with most games (points, badges, levels, and so on). There is far more to creating a good game than simply adding external reinforcers to an everyday behavior.

# WHAT MAKES SOMETHING A GAME?

I'm extremely interested in why it is that games are such powerful motivators. Why is it I get anxious waiting for my turn in Settlers of Catan? Why do I get so much joy out of rolling up stuff in Katamari? Or why do I care about not lowering my average score in Drop 7?

I like to approach games as a detached but curious bystander. While I'll get sucked into a good game as easily as the next person, it's also fun to analyze "why" the games we love are so addictive.

So, what are the common elements shared by most games? Before I offer up an answer, let's do a little exercise.

## STEP 1

We're going to identify as many different kinds of games as we can.

The goal here is to list specific games, without repeating multiple games of the same type. For example, Go Fish and Texas Hold 'Em are both group card games. Just list one of those and move on to a different type of game. In this case solitaire would be different as it's a solo game, or you could go for something quite different, like World of Warcraft. I'll jumpstart your list with some of the games I might include:

| | |
|---|---|
| *Tetris* | *Hopscotch* |
| *Monopoly* | *Bingo* |
| *Tic-tac-toe* | *Bejeweled* |
| *SimCity* | *Halo* |
| *Drinking games* | *Flight Simulator* |
| *Crossword puzzles* | *Poker* |
| *World of Warcraft* | |

So, go on. Add at least ten more games to this list. Done? Now on to the next part.

## STEP 2

Review your list of games. Look for the things that makes each of these a game. What are the common characteristics shared by most games? For example, there's often a scarcity of resources (limited lives or time), and some element of chance and skill. Perhaps a prize for successful behavior. Go on, add all of your observations!

Once you've done this, look over your list. Do you start to see some recurring themes or patterns? Are there common characteristics shared by most games? Can you sort and group some of your observations?

I've done this very exercise in multiple workshops and, while the language may vary, the resulting list is remarkably similar from group to group. After some sorting and aggregating, I've found that most items tend to fit into one of these categories:

Play & Challenges
Conflicts & Choices
Feedback Loops
Goals & Rewards
Imaginary World

This thinking forms the basis for my "Elements of Game Design" model.

Note: I consider "social" to be an influencing actor rather than
a core element. "Players" may be present in the conflicts. Also,
feedback loops may be linked to status, identity, reputation, and
other dynamics linked to social behaviors.

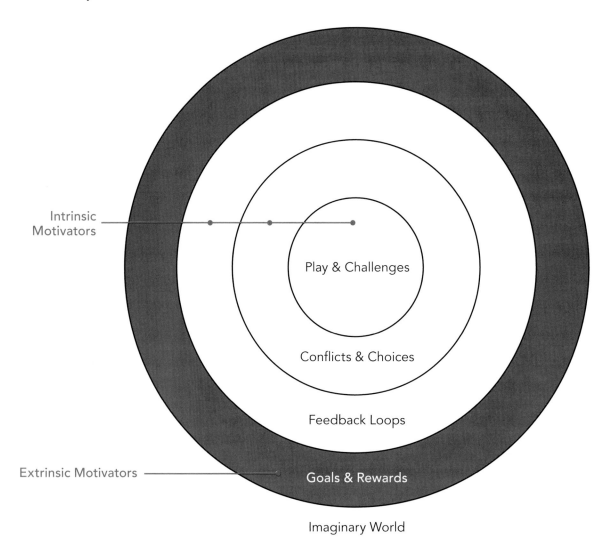

*This Elements of Game Design model provides the conceptual basis for much of our discussion in this section.*

## THE ELEMENTS OF GAME DESIGN

At their core, games are about play. But, what makes them games is the introduction of a *challenge* (or a series of small extrinsic challenges presented in the form of *goals*). Win the most points. Stay alive. Solve the riddle. Avoid being tagged.

Succeeding at this challenge is complicated by artificial *conflicts* and *choices*. These are imposed by a set of rules that all players (or the player) agree to. Conflicts may come in the form of scarce resources, competition, or choices and calculations we have to make during the course of the game. Other players may help or hamper our efforts.

Along the way, there will be all kinds of *feedback loops* to let us know how we're doing. These can be in real time or at periodic intervals. That strategy didn't work so well. I wonder what will happen if I pair these cards? Dang, I lost a life.

Sometimes these feedback loops lead to or come in the form of extrinsic motivators such as *goals* and *rewards*. Get to the next level. Earn a badge. Try this path next.

Finally, all of this takes place in an *imaginary world* that we choose to enter.

Fortunately, these observations seem consistent with the analysis of folks who are much more steeped in game design. Consider this commonly accepted definition of what makes something a game:

*A game is a system in which players engage in an artificial conflict, defined by rules, that results in a quantifiable outcome.*

—KATIE SALEN AND
  ERIC ZIMMERMAN

What I like about my model is that it takes a broad view. My interest is not in designing formal games, but in understanding those elements of a game that motivate and sustain interest. In truth, we create many different kinds of games for ourselves on a daily basis, whether or not we recognize them as such.

A friend of mine who lives in New York City described how he likes to predict which individual subway car will have the least number of people. He's taken the subway enough times to make some predictions (based on patterns) as to where to stand and wait. Conflict and choice comes in the form of choosing which place to wait, based on past experiences at different times of the day. And when the train does pull in, he gets immediate feedback on his predictions. This is a game he has constructed to make taking the subway a bit more interesting. I'm sure you've created any number of games as well. On a recent road trip, I found myself setting goals as to when I would reach different destinations. The act of breaking down a rather long road trip into smaller, measurable segments made the journey more enjoyable. Combine distance, time, and possibly some risk with regard to top speed, and I was essentially placing a game layer on top of my reality.

For more examples of game elements in everyday life, let's look back at my list and replace "game" with "Education," "Investing," or "Corporate America" (see the table below).

All but goals and rewards are naturally occurring parts of intrinsic motivation. We create challenges, which are complicated by reality, and we get feedback along the way. It's when we introduce the extrinsic motivators in the form of goals and rewards that these real-world games begin to resemble the games of our pastimes. This distinction between intrinsic and extrinsic motivation is perhaps the most important discussion for any "gaming the real world project." We'll look at this distinction in more detail soon. With the next chapter, I start by examining the center of any gamelike activity: appropriate challenges.

| | EDUCATION | INVESTING | CORPORATE BUSINESS |
|---|---|---|---|
| Play & Challenges | Learn to speak French; flirt with the French girl | Make lots of money | Become the CEO |
| Conflicts & Choices | Memorizing vocabulary words; choosing how much time to spend studying | Time pressure; how much to invest; which stocks to buy | Competition from coworkers; choosing who to align yourself with; taking a stand versus staying under the radar |
| Feedback Loops | Successfully ordering a menu item (en français) | Stock goes up or down | Promotions; quarterly performance reviews; successful product launches |
| Goals & Rewards | Get an A; pass the quiz | Cashing out with a sizeable sum of money; 30 percent annual growth | A new title; more employees under your direction |

*Games exist all around us, whether or not we define them as such.*

CHAPTER 20

# A Challenge Worth Pursuing

REMEMBER THE INFORMATION GAPS we talked about in Chapter 11 ("Are You Mysterious?"). It turns out that curiosity drives us to do a lot more than just sign up for something or rate a movie. In many ways, curiosity, and its cousin *appropriate challenges*, are vital to human progress. Curiosity leads to challenges. What happens if we do that? Can we go there? Am I capable of doing this? We accept challenges because we are curious about our own abilities or some new subject. (We also accept challenges because we are threatened, but that's another discussion!)

Whether it's kids daring each other to stick their tongues to a frozen pole or a mission "to boldly go where no one has gone before," this exploration of the unknown and our own abilities pushes us into new places. And we rise to the occasion (or return to try again another day). A well-known human motivation psychologist sums it up like this:

*Human beings have an inherent tendency to seek out novelty and challenges, to extend and exercise their capacities, to explore, and to learn.*

—EDWARD DECI

If we return to our dating analogy, the dating process is itself a series of personal disclosures and intimacy challenges. It's the mystery, intrigue, and allure of the other person that often makes him or her so interesting. And so challenging to figure out!

But, to really understand appropriate challenges, and how they differ from goals, let's return to school. Observing how different teachers approach their subjects and classrooms offers a clear look at what makes something a challenge.

## BACK TO THE CLASSROOM

When I was a teacher, I noticed at least three different attitudes towards teaching. Each parallels a different approach to motivating the people using our software. We'll discuss two just ahead and, don't lose hope, the third will appear in good time.

The **first teaching attitude** goes something like this:

*"This stuff is boring. I'll do my best to teach it. But, you'll have to work and apply yourself to get something out of this class."*

This mindset holds that the subject being taught—be it biology, grammar, or English lit—may be important to learn, but isn't really all that interesting for most folks. So do your work and study—it's what you have to do.

Let's call this the "apply yourself" attitude. You have to do all the work. You are responsible for developing the study and learning techniques needed to help you pass the class. While textbooks and handouts make it fairly easy to run a classroom like this, it certainly steals a lot of joy from the classroom. The act of learning becomes something of a chore.

This is typical of most of the software that has come out in recent decades. If you can't figure it out, read the manual. It's up to you to figure out how to make things work. And if motivation is an issue, tough. You'll just have to apply yourself and make the best of it. This is the state of most sites that that stop at merely being useful and usable. This attitude holds that just working is enough for all users.

The **second teaching attitude** goes something like this:

*"This stuff isn't all that interesting. But, I've added some activities to the content that will make this a lot more fun for everyone."*

In these classrooms, teachers might open with a fun exercise or a playful activity before moving onto the meatier stuff. I've seen this in everything from crossword puzzles for reading comprehension to playing a fun board game as a reward for getting through an assignment. This is common in most classrooms. These teachers recognize that education is part entertainment and you have to make things fun for the students. While well intended, there's a subtle but dangerous perspective that underscores this attitude, one that says, "No, this subject isn't all that interesting, but we'll make the best of it." There is no inherent joy in the subject being taught. This approach is about sugarcoating the pill to make it go down easier. Accordingly, let's call this the "sugarcoating attitude."

This sugarcoating is the current state of "gamification." Well-meaning businesses are led to believe that adding a layer of fun to an otherwise dull activity will increase user engagement. This may be true for a brief period of time, but it

doesn't last. The motivation is for the fun layer, not the activity itself. A former teacher himself, Alfie Kohn says, "Do rewards motivate people? Absolutely. They motivate people to get rewards." The more you have to use rewards as incentives to motivate people, the more people lose interest in the thing you're trying to reinforce.

Author and speaker Daniel Pink has explored this complex world of incentives and motivation in his 2009 book *Drive: The Surprising Truth About What Motivates Us*. Drawing on four decades of research on human motivation, Pink systematically dismantles many of our notions about what motivates people at work, school, and home. He draws a sharp distinction between intrinsic and extrinsic motivation. In brief, extrinsic motivators—*rewards*—may work in situations where there is a routine, robotic activity, such as stuffing envelopes. But, creative challenges are ultimately killed by these same kinds of rewards. As most of the challenges of the twenty-first century are ill-defined and creative in nature, Pink argues for developing intrinsic motivation. Specifically,

he discusses the three elements of true motivation: autonomy, mastery, and purpose. As this section is as much about motivation as it is about games, I'd recommend adding this book to your reading list.

For the purpose of this chapter though, let's simplify my Elements of Game Design model from Chapter 19 with this equation.

*(Play + Challenges) + (Rewards + Goals) = Game*

The problem with many of the current attempts to "gamify" real life and business applications is that the formula above has been replaced with something more like this:

*(Play + Challenges) + (Rewards + Goals) = Game*

But rewards and goals (without challenges and play) do not make something a game. Or at least not one that's very fun to play.

So, what does make something a good game? We've already answered this in the opening pages, but let's do another exercise, similar to the one we did in the last chapter.

For this exercise, you'll need an index card.

On one side of an index card, write the name of a game that you're familiar with. This can be a board game you enjoy, a playground activity, an arcade or console game, a party game—any kind of game—but preferably a simple one rather than a complex one. (This exercise won't work if you write down something like World of Warcraft!) In case nothing comes to mind, there's a list of popular games on the next page—just pick one.

Now, think about that game. I want you to peel back the layers and focus on the mechanics and dynamics that make that game fun and addictive.

For example, the social game FarmVille works because of three things:

- *Appointment mechanic*—you must return at an appointed time to harvest your crop
- *Self-expression*—you decide how to plant your garden
- *Social gifting*—you get ahead in the game by inviting more players

Or, take Pictionary. What makes it a fun game?

- *Limited duration*—60 seconds to guess what's being drawn
- *Group competition*—groups compete against each other
- *Teamwork*—you must work together (in your team) to win the game
- *Self-expression*—whoever's turn it is must decide how to render their image
- *Pattern recognition*—the team must guess what's being drawn

Got some ideas? Flip over your card, and list the things that make this game work as a game, make it fun and addictive. It's not important that you know the proper name for some dynamic, only that you can spot it and write it down in a way that is meaningful to you.

That's the first part of this exercise. The sole purpose of this step is to abstract your selected game to some set of principles that make it engaging. Just repeating this part of the exercise will help you to see the patterns underlying many different kinds of games. Are there other players involved or do you play against yourself? Do players compete or cooperate? Do you take turns? What about teams? Are there constraints like time or scarce resources? Is there an element of chance? How much skill or strategy is required? There's much more to games than points and badges!

Now for the challenging part: applying this to an existing application.

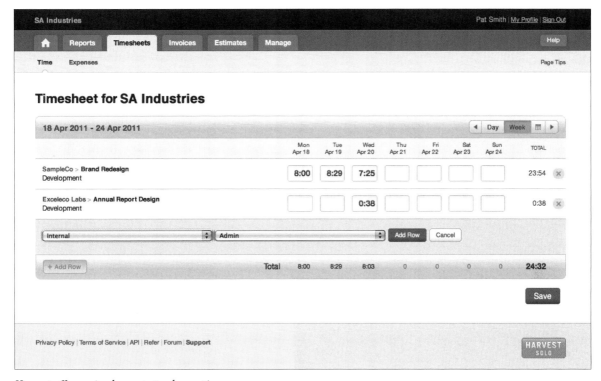

*Harvest offers a simple way to track your time.*

To do this, let's make a better time-tracking application. I happen to love Harvest for tracking time—it's one of the simplest, easiest tools to use (see screen above). However, as easy as it is to use, there's a behavioral problem: how do you motivate people to regularly and accurately track their time? Making something easy to use and motivating people to use something are two different challenges. While I love the idea of tracking my time, I often fail to do so. My *motivation* is high, but for some reason I can't seem to follow through on a regular basis.

Could you persuade people to track their time by making time tracking more like a game? Look at your card. What would you get if we made a time-tracking application with the characteristics you wrote down? Adding points and badges isn't the route to go. But see if a better idea results from your mashup.

### Time tracking meets FarmVille?

A time tracking and FarmVille application might reward you for returning to input your time at regular intervals. Failing to come back at the scheduled time would result in fewer points to spend on your virtual garden. This might help people track their time on a daily basis, rather than a few times during the week.

**Saturday, December 6**      Now - 11:11 AM

| | 08 • • • 09 • • • 10 • • • 11 • • • 12 • • • 01 • • • 02 • • • 03 • • • | Daily Total | Daily Goal |
|---|---|---|---|
| **Read** | | 1 hour | > 45 min. |
| **Watch TV** | | 45 min. | < 1 hour |
| **Exercise** | | 30 min. | 30 min. |
| **Work for Spacely Sprockets** | | 3 hours | - |
| **Personal Dream Project** | | 30 min. | > 1 hour, 30 min. |
| **Volunteer at the SPCA** | | 30 min. | - |
| Practice cello    Add   Cancel | | 6 hours, 15 min. | |

*BubbleTimer lets you track time in 15 minute increments.*

### Time tracking meets bubble wrap?

What about time tracking and bubble wrap? Maybe this is a mobile app where you track time in 15-minute increments. Imagine a big sheet of virtual bubbles, with each row of bubbles representing a different client or type of activity. You could "pop" off your time. You could also layer in some variable rewards to make this more rewarding.

You see the point. This is a good exercise for generating ideas, and evaluating the underlying dynamics that make up good game design.

Here are some examples of the *kinds* of ideas this exercise might lead you to come up with:

The music site theonesixty.com offers music quests to its listeners. The Earworm quest, for example, has you listen to the same song three times in a row. The Guide quest has you listen to seven songs in the popular section on the home page.

In 2010, the software company CoffeeCup hid dozens of "Easter eggs" totaling more than

*theonesixty.com offers listeners music quests.*

$20,000 in prizes across its site, with the goal of encouraging exploration. According to Vice President of Operations J. Cornelius, "People commented they learned a lot about us from browsing the site. Like they didn't know we had product X or Y, that we've been around for 15 years, or that our support/community was so strong." The Easter eggs also led to "a boost in traffic and sales."

And last, here's a rather intriguing registration page I came across:

**The record for filling out this form is 15.6 seconds...go!**

Name — First / Last
Business Name
Primary Email
Timezone — (UTC –6) Central Time (US & Canada)
Password
Confirm Password
Postal Code
Country — United States

Your 30-day trial lasts until midnight on February 19, 2011.

By clicking 'Create Account' you agree to the Terms of Service and Privacy policies.    **Create Account »**

These are certainly all fun ideas. In the case of music, that activity is probably fun for most people already—no problems there.

However, for more mundane activities, there's a good chance you have something resembling the sugarcoating attitude, the one that wraps something in fun, gaming elements. You might have added punching bubbles or tending to a virtual garden to try to bring fun to an otherwise dull activity. However clever your idea, if it's not integral to the activity itself then it is sugarcoating.

In my workshops, we come up with a lot of *creative* ideas. However, one of the first filters I challenge participants with is this: Did you have to *add* something to the application to make it fun? Or did you find the *fun already* in the application?

## A REAL CHALLENGE

This leads us into our **third teaching attitude**, which goes something like this:

*"This stuff is really quite interesting! I'm going to show you why this is important. But first, I've got a challenge for you."*

Teachers with this attitude present even the most boring subject in an enlightening way, engaging students with stories, challenges, and other delights. And learning is a by-product of all this fun. This is a challenging task, to frame a topic in such a way that students are engaged. But when you succeed, you've created the kind of interest that is rare and powerful.

In the book *Made to Stick*, Chip and Dan Heath describe a study in which different groups of elementary students were taught the same material. In the first group, teachers presented the material in such a way as to foster consensus. In the second, teachers took a different approach, presenting the material in a way that was "designed to produce disagreements about the right answer." As the Heath brothers recount:

*"Students who achieved easy consensus were less interested in the topic, studied less, and were less likely to visit the library to get additional information. The most telling difference though was revealed when teachers showed a special film about the discussion topic—during recess! Only 18 percent of the consensus students missed recess to see the film, but 45 percent of the students from the disagreement group stayed for the film."*

# EASY IS OVERRATED—MAKE IT CHALLENGING

This notion of interesting and appropriate challenges is also central to Mihaly Csíkszentmihályi's idea of "flow." Flow is defined as "the state in which people are so involved in an activity that nothing else seems to matter; the experience itself is so enjoyable that people will do it even at great cost, for the sheer sake of doing it." This is discussed in *Flow: The Psychology of Optimal Experience*, 1990, by Mihaly Csikszentmihályi.

The secret to creating a state of flow is creating an appropriate challenge. Make something too challenging and people give up; too easy and they'll get bored. Video games excel at creating flow, by offering progressively more difficult challenges.

In a 1996 interview with *Wired* magazine, Csíkszentmihályi offered this critique of Web design:

*Goals.* "Site designers assume that the visitor already knows what to choose. That's not true. People enter hoping to be led somewhere, hoping for a payoff."

*Feedback.* "Most Web sites don't very much care what you do. It would be much better if they said, 'You've made some interesting choices.'"

*Challenge.* "A flow experience has got to be challenging. Anything that is not up to par is going to be irritating or ignored."

*Progression.* "You need clear goals that fit into a hierarchy, with little goals that build toward more meaningful, higher-level goals."

*Flow results when the challenge is equal to your ability; If something is too easy, boredom results. Too challenging, and people become overwhelmed.*

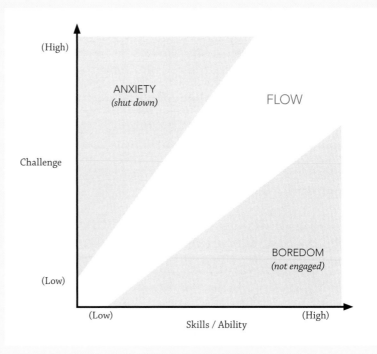

Elementary kids chose an educational film over recess? There is joy to be found in all kinds of activities, but it depends entirely on *how* we approach things (or how that task is presented to us). Igniting curiosity or presenting someone with an interesting challenge is a powerful way to create engagement.

What does all of this have to do with gaming and interaction design?

Game mechanics reinforce an already fun challenge. Game mechanics can be added, but only to something that people already enjoy. Simple mechanics like points, levels, and badges merely reinforce, encourage, and shape the play that is already, in and of itself, enjoyable. The problem with gamification is when these mechanics are used to stimulate interest in something that people don't already care about.

We may confuse caring for an activity with caring for the rewards. But this is short-lived. The task is to find the challenge that is already in the core activity. Find the game that's already in your design. We create games all the time in our personal lives. Why not in our designs? If engaging users is an important part of our job, we should be looking to surface the games and motivations already inherent in the activities we're designing for. As with good teachers who find and share the joy in their subject, there is something fun to be found in all kinds of subjects and applications.

Let's return to our time-tracking example. What's the game that's *already* there, waiting to be surfaced?

I had to repeat the game mashup exercise several times before I spotted one possible idea, a game that already exists in time tracking, but hasn't yet surfaced. I was playing a puzzle game where the primary motivator (for me) was *status*. I was competing against my *own best average*. Every new game threatened to raise or lower my average score. I wondered, what might a time tracking game based on status look like?

## A QUICK NOTE ON STATUS

Status is often confused with reputation. While status may indicate your standing relative to others, it can also indicate your standing relative to your own personal best.

*[Flow is] being completely involved in an activity for its own sake. The ego falls away. Time flies. Every action, movement, and thought follows inevitably from the previous one, like playing jazz. Your whole being is involved, and you're using your skills to the utmost.*

—MIHALY CSÍKSZENTMIHÁLYI

Arcade games are a great example of your standing relative to others as well as to your personal best.

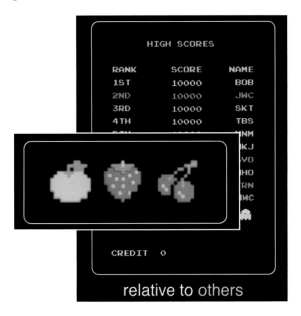

relative to others

You can earn status by climbing your way into the leaderboard. But I doubt this was a reality for very many of us. Instead, the reason many of us kept on playing these games was to beat our personal best. If you've ever been prodded along in a game to beat your "best streak"—that's status.

The check-in app Gowalla uses status in a very subtle way. In weekly e-mails, in addition to news and other interesting details, Gowalla lets you know how you did in the last week (see the screens at the top of the next column).

Three fewer check-ins than last week is a subtle form of the "best streak." You are being asked to compete against yourself. (We'll talk more about these kinds of feedback loops in a moment).

**The Numbers**

The skinny on how much you went out this week with Gowalla.

Check-ins
**5** ↑ 3 more than last week
Unique Spots
**3** ↑ 1 more than last week
New Photos
**0** No change since last week
Friends
**177** No change since last week

**The Numbers**

The skinny on how much you went out this week with Gowalla.

Check-ins
**4** ↓ 3 fewer than last week
Unique Spots
**4** ↓ 2 fewer than last week
New Photos
**0** No change since last week
Friends
**178** No change since last week

So, how might status lead to a better time-tracking app?

When I started peeling back the layers of why we should care about time tracking in the first place, I came upon an interesting insight: time tracking is the other *half* of the estimation process. We track time to see how well we estimated.

Peel back the layers on why someone should track their time and the answer is about *balance*. If you want a good work-life balance, your have to get better at accurately estimating the time a particular task might take: e-mails, lunches, wireframes, catching up on Facebook. How do you make accurate estimates? You track the time it's taken you to do the same or similar tasks in the past. Time tracking and task estimation are two sides of the same coin.

So based on this insight, what was the game I came up with?

Imagine a game that combines weekly (or daily) time estimation with time tracking. We all know the value of planning our days. Time tracking is the other half, a way to *reflect* on our planning.

**FRIDAY, MAY 16TH, 2011**

ESTIMATED:

9
RESEARCH
8
WRITING
7
EMAIL
6
5
CLIENT 2
4
3
2
MEETING
1
CLIENT 1
0

ACTUAL:

EMAIL

CLIENT 2

MEETING

CLIENT 1

**79%**
ACCURACY RATING

*A rough concept for a time-tracking game based on status.*

In this sense, time tracking moves from a chore to an estimation game—with the goal of seeing how accurately you estimated your time. Time tracking becomes analogous to checking your answers on a test—you naturally want to find out how you did.

Contrast this with the time-tracking-meets-FarmVille-or-bubble-wrap ideas mentioned earlier. While it might be fun for a little while to decorate a page every time I report my time, I doubt this concept would *sustain* interest for very long. You need an idea based on the person using the application; you need to find that thing that people naturally want to get better at. It's not about adding a fun layer but about finding the core challenge and presenting it in a fun way.

## CHALLENGES VS. GOALS

By now, you've no doubt sensed a difference between challenges and goals. The two are easily confused, but are worlds apart when it comes to sustaining interest. There's a big difference between "getting an A in French class" and "learning to speak French." One is a goal, the other a challenge. Goals are intended to help you along the way, but only challenges lead to mastery.

So how do you find the challenge?

Unfortunately, there's no magic formula for surfacing the inherent challenge in every project because every project is different. Status worked in my time-tracking example. But, you'll need to find what works in your case. What I've tried to share here is the process of

# PLAYING WITH SPREADSHEETS (NO, SERIOUSLY!)

Here's how my attitude toward spreadsheets was changed forever.

I'm an analytical person, but the thought of profit and loss sheets, budget forecasts, and five-year projections puts me to sleep pretty quickly. Or rather, it used to.

In a workshop I attended years ago, the instructor changed my perceptions of business spreadsheets, and in a simple way. As a designer, it's common to sketch ideas and explore options on sheets of paper. Designers are known to carry notebooks to jot down these mental doodles. We are creatives after all, right? Spreadsheets, however, invoke an entirely different perception: because we're working with numbers, spreadsheets are clearly in the realm of accuracy and rigorous analysis.

Or are they?

I learned that many kinds of spreadsheets are just as much about play as doodling on a blank sheet of paper. Set up a few variables and assumptions. Make some guesses as to how things *might* do. Let the macros do their thing and you can paint several different pictures of your financial performance, or predicted success. In fact, most spreadsheets that attempt to predict the future typically only have a few hard numbers to play with. Everything else is speculative. Analysts play with numbers just as creatives play with shapes. But both are playing.

In this workshop on business models, we set up a five-year forecast and, based on the same present-day data, painted three *entirely different* futures, from the absolute worst to "we could own the market."

We were *playing* with numbers.

Since then, I've never been afraid to question a spreadsheet and run my own numbers, especially if that "analysis" is being held up as a roadblock to some new idea. It's actually kind of fun to play with spreadsheets.

*Fun from games arises out of mastery. It arises out of comprehension. It is the act of solving puzzles that makes games fun... with games, learning is the drug.*

—Raph Koster

play and discovery I went through to find the real challenge. Ask yourself whether the challenge was there all along or if you had to add it to your application. That's a good question for separating out real challenges from added rewards and goals.

One exercise I can offer to find the challenge already in your app or service is known as the "5 Whys" or "Laddering." This is a qualitative research technique used to get at core motivations. Basically, you ask a question; whatever is answered back you turn into another question. Repeating this several times will—if people are being honest—lead to some pretty profound insights.

In my example, the first question was "Why do I want to track my time?" Since I don't bill by the hour, that wasn't my answer. Rather, it was "To know how long I'm taking." Why did I want to know how long I'm taking? So I can "learn where I'm underestimating my time." Why? So I "can get better at estimating my time." Why? So I can "have a more balanced life." (Working late really isn't all that fun after a while!) By asking myself these questions, I was able to find the core challenge already in time tracking—getting better at estimating my time. This exercise helped reveal that time-tracking is only half of the game, the other half being time estimation.

## CLOSING

If you're going to make a service more gamelike, think about the dynamics that make gameplay interesting. Don't borrow superficial details from a game, but start by understanding what makes a good game fun to play. Then, look for these dynamics in your service. When you do this, the challenge and accompanying reward isn't like an artificial sweetener added to the content. Pleasure is found in the challenge that was there along.

*Does your service have something that is inherently interesting? Or more to the point, have you found the way to frame your service in a way that is engaging in and of itself?*

By creating a challenge, you can sustain some of the delight. Let's continue now with some of the things that make the challenge more intere

# Making Things Difficult

GAMES ARE INEFFICIENT. There are quicker paths to the top corner of Candyland—just ignore the winding path. Throw in some extra gear, and first-person shooter games like Halo or Call of Duty could be completed much more quickly. If the goal of Hopscotch is to reach a particular point, just get rid of the squares—that'd be easier, right? And what about Poker? If we just had everyone keep their cards face up on the table, it'd be a lot easier to know what to play or bet.

But it is precisely these kinds of conflicts that make a game fun and allow the game designer to shape the path on which players travel. Take away these artificial constraints and the game ceases to be a game. Conflicts and choices, however inefficient and artificial, are necessary to a good game.

In this chapter, we'll look at a few of the ways we can make someone more effective at a task (or make that task more thrilling) by introducing a few simple constraints into our designs. And we'll focus primarily on the granddaddy of all constraints: *scarcity*.

## PLAYING HARD TO GET

People infer special value in something that has limited availability. This is true in dating, commerce, gaming, and other fields. Everything from gold and diamonds to "limited edition" candy bars to baseball cards prove this point. Games create a thrill by making something scarce. Imagine Monopoly with unlimited cash or any arcade game with unlimited lives. Yes, there's certainly a pressure that's coupled with scarcity. But it's the kind of pressure that creates an appropriate level of anxiety, which can actually make things more fun, playful, and exciting.

But what about Web applications? In most cases, we're not dealing with physical goods, but rather with digital content that can be copied or throttled as needed with little to no costs. Where everything is digital and scarcity should be a quaint notion, does this same idea hold true? And can we use this to influence behaviors, or to get people to do more than just purchase something?

## USING SCARCITY IN COMMERCE

The most obvious application of scarcity is in retail and e-commerce. A retailer may have only a few shirts left in your size. A car dealership may have only one car on the lot with the features you want. Collectible items fetch a lot more money in aftermarket auctions. These same sales tactics apply to online shopping as well: a travel site might advertise "only three tickets left at this price," or an artist only has "six copies of this print remaining."

> **Roundtrip:** from **$338.00** + $39.80 taxes &
> 📇 3 tickets left at this price! See details
>
> **3:40 pm** Depart Dallas (DFW)                    Th

This idea has also been used in domain name landgrabs. There is a very real scarcity of domain names on the Web. But custom URLs, such as stephen.somereallycoolnewsite.com can also leverage this scarcity to encourage sign-ups.

But scarcity can be used for more than simply encouraging purchasing behaviors; because people value things that are scarce (the reason we feel pressured to purchase something), this same principle can be applied in other creative ways.

## USING SCARCITY TO INCREASE QUALITY

Foodspotting is a site where people share photos of their favorite dishes. Rather than reviewing a restaurant, you can share pictures of your meal. You like the pad woon sen at that Thai place? Let people know by taking a picture of it the next time you eat there. Foodspotters,

*Can you spot the implied scarcity in Jango's home page?*

as Foodspotting users are called, love sharing these photos. In fact, before there was Foodspotting, there were groups on Flickr where people shared interesting food photos.

So how is Foodspotting using scarcity?

If you're making the effort to photograph your dinner, you probably at least enjoy that dish. But what about your favorite dishes—the ones you rave about to your friends? For these, all Foodspotters get "noms," special ribbons reserved for those dishes you've tried and loved best. But there's a catch. As Foodspotting states, "You only get five noms to start with and must earn the right to nom more foods after that!"

By limiting noms, Foodspotting encourages people to be more selective about which foods deserve special recognition. The site claims, "The blue ribbon (the 'nom') means more because it's hard to get." People won't give every dish a nomination lest they have no remaining noms to give to a dish that really is exceptional.

This idea could be applied in other, more familiar contexts. Imagine YouTube limiting each person to a handful of five-star ratings per month. Or what if Facebook limited the number of "likes" a user can use per day? While this isn't the behavior Facebook wants to encourage, introducing a limited supply would change how people use the "like" button.

Here's another way designers are using scarcity to encourage quality.

Remember show and tell from elementary school? Dribbble is a new site where designers, developers, and other creative pros can share sneak peeks (or "shots") of their current work. Just as Foodspotting encourages people to be selective about their noms, Dribbble encourages people to be selective about what they share by limiting how many shots users can share each month.

Dribbble's founders don't hide their use of scarcity to encourage high quality submissions:

*"In case it isn't obvious, the reason we throttle shots is to encourage players to post with care—we hope scarcity induces quality. (So far, so good.) We'll be introducing other ways to accrue shots for meritorious behavior, but we want everyone to know that you'll always have a base of 24 shots to work with each month."*

So far, the high quality of the submissions that have accumulated on Dribbble is impressive. This is partly attributable to the caliber of the designers who were among the first to contribute to the site, but also to conscious planning by the site's founders. Through scarcity and other intentional design decisions, they hope that people will post with care and maintain the high quality of shared images.

## USING SCARCITY TO ENCOURAGE PARTICIPATION

There's another twist on scarcity, one that may seem contrary to everything stated so far. This twist is one of creating artificial limits—specifically, character limits. By enforcing a scarcity of characters, you can actually encourage participation. (This is different from creating desire as with the examples above.) Twitter is the perfect example of this.

The technical limits of mobile text messaging were the original constraint behind Twitter's 140-character limit. But it is precisely this character limit that has driven a new form of written expression. Prior to Twitter, there were blogging tools such as Blogger, WordPress, and Six Apart. Anyone could certainly have written short, one- or two-sentence blog posts. But we didn't. I would never have written a blog post about eating my last piece of Leonidas chocolate, but I can certainly tweet about that. It's this character limit that allows people to be more casual about what they write—after all, it's only 140 characters! It's okay to say less, speak informally, or make typos in such brief messages; this isn't a research paper, after all. The context lowers the bar on what can be "published" on the Web. It's liberating to have none of the expectations inherent in other forms of written communication.

To be clear, this is a very different kind of scarcity than if you were allowed, say, only one tweet per week. If this were the case, we might see much more thoughtful 140-character exclamations. But the character limit has made it much easier to post (and, in doing so, lowered expectations). Tweets are unlimited, more like words in a conversation. Why unlimited? It comes back to because a tweet can't exceed 140 characters. By making this number so low, Twitter is essentially saying, "It's easy, what's stopping you?" Scarcity encourages participation by making it that much easier to join in.

Rypple uses this same insight to make feedback and coaching easy. With Rypple, users can request peer reviews to help them get better at their jobs. If you want candid feedback on that presentation you just gave or your management skills, Rypple creates a safe environment to solicit and give such critiques (see the screen at the top of the following page). Co-founder Daniel Debow observed, "The most senior people tend to send very brief e-mails." While people would like to give feedback to others, there isn't always time to do so. By limiting comments to 400 characters, the "cost [in terms of time] to the reviewer is much lower, especially in contrast to long surveys and other corporate tools."

This number, along with other variables, has been iteratively tested over the past year. Rypple wants to encourage people to respond, and to do this the team has tested limits as low as 120 characters. However, they also want to leave enough room for constructive feedback, so the team has tested much higher limits. Allowing 400 characters seems to strike the best balance between increasing the number of responses while still allowing for substantive feedback. Debow adds, "When you encourage and design for brevity, you also encourage people to focus their feedback."

This idea of using scarcity to increase participation isn't limited to characters. What if

*Rypple limits comments to 400 characters to encourage participation but still allow enough room for quality feedback.*

e-mail in-boxes could only hold 15 mail items at a time? Would that encourage us to clean out our in-boxes? Or what if a sign-up form allowed users to list only three of their favorite movies? Would that limit be less intimidating than a big, empty text box?

## WHY SCARCITY WORKS

One explanation of why scarcity works so well on us has to with decision making. It's easier to go along with the crowd and buy the thing that is scarce. Why? According to persuasion expert Robert Cialdini in his 1998 book *Influence: The Psychology of Persuasion*, things "that are difficult to possess are typically better than those that are easy to possess." People use this defining attribute—*limited availability*—to aid in their decision-making processes. If a bakery is running low on one kind of pastry but has plenty of the alternatives, that might be a good indication of what is popular (and what's to be avoided!). Scarcity is often a shortcut to the best choice.

This helps explain scarcity as a selling tactic, and possibly why character limits might help people choose a restrictive format over an open-ended one that offers no constraints. And with Foodspotting and Dribbble we saw one other effect of scarcity: it can improve quality.

Another way of looking at scarcity has to do with freedom—or rather loss of freedom. If something is scarce, it may be unavailable in the near future. And that idea doesn't sit too well with people—it violates our sense of control over a situation. Psychologist Jack Brehm wrote about psychological reactance, or the ways people fight against restrictions on their freedom. Brehm explains why teenagers who are only mildly interested in each other will continue dating to protest their parents disapproval, or why people rush to protest government restrictions on their rights, even when the issue means very little to them personally. Scarcity of something is essentially a threat to freedom of choice. But this threat isn't necessarily a bad thing; it can be a useful means of encouraging desirable user behaviors.

## OTHER FORMS OF SCARCITY: LIMITED DURATION

In all of the examples above, there is a limited availability of something. But what if the thing that is scarce is time? This is an element used by games such as Pictionary or Tetris. Players have a fixed amount of time in which to reach the end or recognize the pattern. While it may seem odd to add this pressure to business applications, there are some good precedents. Think about limited-time trial offers, in which you have 30 days to sample some new software. Or consider the persuasive role of deadlines—knowing something is due at a specific time encourages us to take actions we might not otherwise take. Interested in being more productive? Francesco Cirillo's Pomodoro Technique encourages people to work in 25-minute bursts (see sidebar, top right).

In these cases, limiting the time encourages focus. Given a choice between action and inaction, a limited time to respond increases the likelihood that people *will* participate.

## YOU HAVE 25 MINUTES... GO!

The basic unit of work in the Pomodoro Technique™ can be split into five simple steps:

1. Choose a task to be accomplished.

2. Set the Pomodoro to 25 minutes (the Pomodoro is the timer).

3. Work on the task until the Pomodoro rings, then put a check on your sheet of paper.

4. Take a short break (5 minutes is OK).

5. Take a longer break every four Pomodoros.

In addition to setting time limits, you can also create windows of time when certain actions can be taken. (FarmVille makes use of this *appointment dynamic*, where players schedule a time to return and harvest their crops). You can make rewards available at specific times or have options that disappear if no action is taken within a specific period of time. As with scarcity, limited duration exploits our sense of freedom: we need to be in control. Not taking action now means losing freedom to take action later.

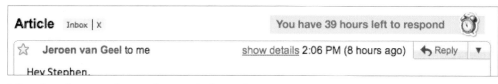

*What if emails came with a time limit in which to reply?*

I've observed another kind of limited duration, in the form of *periodic events*. These are things that only take place at specific times—holidays, rituals, meetings. My kids are routinely excited by some big event happening in the online world of Club Penguin. There are parties that occur on specific days, and narratives that develop over time. "Being there" is an important part of the play experience. If you don't show up on the appointed day, you might miss out!

## LIMITED ACCESS

Another kind of constraint comes in the form of *access* to a group or tools. We naturally desire things that are perceived as exclusive or belonging to a select few.

This was proven in the early days of Gmail, when this new e-mail system was only available to those who had been invited or had invitations to share. This "private beta" tactic, now used by most start-ups, has since been played out, but the underlying desire for things that are withheld from us is timeless. In games and in real life, we talk about the privileges that come with different ranks or as a result of belonging to certain social groups. Think of the backroom card games available only to a select few, or the opening of a new nightclub that everyone's talking about. The catch? You need an invitation. "Secret organizations" such as the Freemasons hold a certain allure due to secrets shared only among members.

Games routinely use levels to create exclusivity and reward proficiency. While this idea of limiting access is a common element in online communities for kids, we rarely see this same tactic used in communities for business people or socially active adults. Here's an exception:

In 2007, I worked for a company that built its own internal knowledge-sharing application later offered as a white-labeled version (called cubeless) to other companies. Think of this tool as a combination of a question-and-answer site with a heavy social component.

Most of what you see in cubeless is pretty typical, until you go to add a second photo to your profile page. At this moment you are confronted with a message:

"Karma? What's that?" you wonder. It turns out that certain things are withheld from users until they've earned privileges. So while the first photo was free, all photos after that cost karma points. You can also join up to three groups for free, but every group after that costs you karma points.

This, of course, begs the question, "How do I earn more karma points?" While there are answers *describing* how to earn karma, you're really only left with this impression: Be a good online citizen. Participate. Answer questions. Connect people asking questions with people you know who can answer them. Vote answers up. By not spelling out the formula for earning points, players are discouraged from gaming the system. The goal is not to earn karma points but to ask and answer questions.

This probably sounds counterintuitive. Encouraging behaviors by withholding features? We're accustomed to sites like Facebook where the goal is for users to share photos, status updates, and other personal data. Most sites prostitute themselves before us: "Please use our features." However, by holding back, desire and participation only increase more. Unlike Facebook or Myspace, cubeless wasn't concerned with photos. The system could afford to withhold *secondary* features naturally desired in a community (photos, ability to join groups) to drive the *primary* behavior of knowledge sharing.

Did it work? According to the cubeless Web site, here are the rather stunning results (bear in mind this is for a 5,000 person company):

- 60 to 70 percent of employees actively use the system each month
- 60 percent of questions asked are answered within one hour of posting; 90 percent are answered within 24 hours
- Average of 30 page views per employee user visit
- Each question posted to the community receives an average of nine answers

Stack Overflow is another community site that has succeeded by limiting access to features based on participation within the community.

As players in the Stack Overflow community earn points, they also unlock access to new features and tools not available to everyone (see below).

**What is reputation?**

Reputation is completely optional. Normal use of Stack Overflow — that is, asking and answe[r] require any reputation whatsoever.

If you'd like to help us run Stack Overflow, you'll need to earn some reputation first. Reputatio[n] community trusts you . Reputation is never given, it is earned by convincing fellow users that [...]

The primary way to gain reputation is by posting good questions and useful answers. Your p[...] cause you to gain (or, in rare cases, lose) reputation:

| | |
|---|---|
| answer is voted up | +10 |
| question is voted up | +5 |
| answer is accepted | +15 (+2 to acceptor) |
| post is voted down | -2 (-1 to voter) |

A maximum of 30 votes can be cast per user per day, and you can earn a maximum of **200** r[...] and bounty awards are immune to this limit). Please note that votes for posts marked "comm[...]

The other way to gain reputation is by suggesting edits to existing posts as a new registered [...] accepted, you will earn **+2** reputation. You can only earn a maximum of **+1000** total reputatio[n]

Amass enough reputation points and Stack Overflow will grant you additional privileges:

| | |
|---|---|
| 15 | Vote up |
| 15 | Flag for moderator attention |
| 50 | Leave comments† |
| 100 | Edit community wiki posts |
| 125 | Vote down (costs 1 rep) |
| 200 | Reduced advertising |
| 250 | Vote to close, reopen, or migrate your questions |
| 500 | Retag questions |
| 1000 | Show total up and down vote counts |
| 1500 | Create new tags |
| 2000 | Edit other people's posts, vote to approve or reject suggested edits |
| 3000 | Vote to close, reopen, or migrate any questions |
| 5000 | Vote to approve or reject suggested tag wiki edits |
| 10000 | Vote to delete closed questions, access to moderation tools |
| 15000 | Protect questions to prevent answers by new users |
| 20000 | Vote to delete negatively voted answers and stronger question deletion votes |

† you can always comment on your questions and answers, and any answers to questions you've asked, even with [...]

At the high end of this reputation spectrum there is little difference between users with high r[...] intentional. We don't run Stack Overflow. The community does.

*Stack Overflow offers additional privileges as you earn reputation points.*

## CHOICE AND CALCULATIONS

The ultimate effect of all these constraints is that people are forced to make choices:

*Do I do this now, or later?*

*How should I go about doing this task?*

*Who should I involve?*

*What should I focus on first?*

In the previous section on subtle details, we discussed the positive effects of limiting how many choices you present people with. But what if your choice involves a calculation?

In RPG (role-playing) games, there may be a limit on what your character can carry. Do you carry the heavy armor, which is good for defense, but quite burdensome? Or do you carry an assortment of weapons to help you attack and defend yourself? You're asked to calculate which option will ultimately help you realize the larger goals of the game.

What if your e-mail app or time-tracking tool only lets you select three resources to aid in the task? Or, what if you could only select three features to test out? Would this increase your focus on all features before selecting?

Old Navy ran a promotion where visitors were challenged to find different coupons spread across the site (see screens below). Like the CoffeeCup example mentioned in the previous chapter, this hunt for coupons encouraged exploration and interaction with the different clothing and merchandise sold by Old Navy. Here was the difficult choice: once you found a coupon, you could hold on to that one (and stop looking) or pass on that one in hopes that you might find an even better coupon. At this point, you had to make a choice: to pass or hold. Sounds a bit like some card games.

There's plenty more that could be said about choice and conflicts, but truthfully, this is a relatively new area outside of formal games. In the gaming world, characters are forced to

*Old Navy made a game out of hunting for coupons hidden across their site.*

# BOOKS ON GAME DESIGN

*A Theory of Fun for Game Design*
by Raph Koster

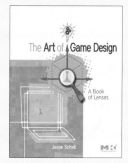

*The Art of Game Design: A Book of Lenses*
by Jesse Schell

*Fundamentals of Game Design, 2nd Edition*
by Ernest Adams

make calculations and decisions all the time. In fact, much of the tension in games comes from setting up opposition between your long-term and short-term goals. For example, the big goal in Donkey Kong might be to save the princess. However, you're presented with a short-term goal: go after the mushroom. This will give you more strength and points, but also puts your life in jeopardy. This immediate reward may jeopardize your success at the larger goal. Do you put yourself at risk? Or play it safe and focus only on the long-term goal?

Obviously, most of the software apps and Web sites we use haven't yet reached this level of sophistication or emotional involvement. The field of behavioral economics has studied the factors that affect a decision. Game designers have explored ways to present players with different challenges.

For more on choices and conflicts, I'd recommend reading some of the books on game design listed in the sidebar to the left.

CHAPTER 22

# How Are We Doing?

SUPPOSE YOUR BOSS ASSIGNS YOU a special project, say, researching possible lunar locations for future growth and expansion. Whatever the topic is, you do your due diligence. You pull together your findings, package them up in a PDF, and send them off to your boss. And you hear nothing. Silence. A week goes by with no response. When you've all but forgotten about this little project, you get an e-mail response from your boss: "Thanks. This is what I needed."

How might this affect your performance on future requests from this boss?

Let's replay that scenario, with a few changes.

You pull together your findings, package them up in a PDF, and send them off to your boss. And you get a reply within the hour. "Thank you! I'll check this out in more detail this afternoon." The afternoon rolls by and that quick e-mail response is followed by a thorough review of your recommendations. "What about the dark side of the moon? Have you considered weather conditions? How much will it cost?" Your boss raises some good questions and challenges you to think about some things you hadn't considered.

Chances are your response in this second situation (and with similar requests in the future)

will be quite different from the first, quite deflating, situation.

The difference in each of these stories is the *feedback loop*. In the first instance, the feedback loop was very poor (almost nonexistent) and likely to have a negative influence on future requests. But in the second scenario, we find a good, tight feedback loop. Right away, while the task is still fresh and relevant, you get to find out how you did. Not only is there a response, the response is critical and helps you improve at your job.

Feedback loops are evident in all areas of our lives, from e-mail exchanges like the one described above to report cards to firing ranges. We like to know that our actions are influencing the world in some way, that our actions cause a

reaction—cause and effect. From infants grasping at objects to finally earning a diploma, we are engaged by situations in which we see our actions modify subsequent results.

The clearest example of a feedback loop is found on many local streets:

I suspect that many of us respond in much the same way. We're probably going just a few (ahem) miles over the posted limit. Seeing our actual speed (the feedback) makes us aware of this difference and we slow down (the loop).

The same things can be observed in first-person shooter games. If we fire at a target and miss because we're a little too far to the right, what do we do? We move a bit to the left and fire again in hopes of hitting the target this time.

These adjustments to external feedback are examples of a very tight feedback loop. But feedback loops come in a variety of forms with different delays. A report card might be an example of a very *long* feedback loop. Fortunately, we get much tighter feedback loops along the way, in the form of quizzes, tests, grades on papers, and progress reports.

The kind of feedback loops I want to focus on here are related to individual performance; those things that when held up to a person affect future behavior (people love statistics about themselves). Much of what we'll look at might fit under the label of *personal informatics*, the tracking of personal data for reflection and correction.

One very minor, but powerful, example of this kind of feedback loop is a decision by the founders of Twitter to display follower count, the number of people following, and the number of times listed. Of course, the moment this information was displayed, people began focusing on these metrics. For many, this created a race to acquire the most followers. Right or wrong, the mere act of displaying this metric created a goal for many people: acquire the most followers.

| 428 | 4,461 | 560 |
|-----|-------|-----|
| following | followers | listed |

This leads to a cautionary note:

*Attaching a measure to anything turns it into a game.*

We can debate the pros and cons of people focusing on acquiring more followers. (I'm sure there are good business reasons to motivate people to acquire followers.) I just want to point out the influence of choosing to display certain metrics.

## UNINTENDED SIDE EFFECTS OF HYPERMILING

For the first time in my life, I'm conscientiously tracking my gas mileage. I'm really curious to see if my diesel car can attain the advertised 56 mpg, or at least something in the 40ish range. Thanks to a couple of mobile apps, I can track any number of automotive details. This is also the first car I've owned that displays real-time mpg feedback—I can see an estimated mpg while I'm driving (see below). As a result, I'm learning to adjust my street driving (slower starts, coasting at times) to improve overall

gas mileage. Of course, this real-time feedback is simply a guess, based on averages and other data, and this number fluctuates every few seconds between 4 mpg and 200 mpg—you can't really know your average miles per gallon until you fill up your gas tank. But, this real-time estimation has opened the door to some interesting games.

The first game was born out of curiosity. At some point, the estimated mpg changes to dashed lines (if you're coasting on the highway, what's the point of saying you're getting 623 miles to the gallon). Partly prodded on by my son, we wanted to see what exactly is the highest number displayed before the dashed lines show up. We assumed it was 199, but this hadn't been confirmed. Well, it took nearly a month, but eventually, my average mpg (for all of two seconds), was exactly 199, before changing to dashed lines. Goal accomplished.

Of course, once you accomplish a goal, that particular game is over. So we had to invent a new, rather mischievous, hypermiling game. This one was a tad different, focused on how low we could get the average mpg! This game involves giving the engine far more gas than is necessary when pulling out of a neighborhood. I've got my average down as low as 3.6 mpg.

The point? Anytime you attach a measure to something, you've laid the groundwork for people to create all kinds of games, good *and* bad.

Another, curious example of personal feedback loops can be observed at most Target stores. If you look at the clerk's checkout screen immediately after you pay, you'll see this screen:

Your last 10 scores? What kind of game are Target employees playing? The "GRGGGGRGGG" scores represent how quickly you checked that person through the line. G is for green, good. R is for red, bad. And Y (not shown) is for yellow, meh. This kind of metric could easily be abused by managers to unfairly evaluate an individual's performance. However, the clerk I spoke to commented that they had formed teams and different teams were recognized at the end each week based on overall group performance. The goal of this game is efficiency and these feedback loops let employees know how they're doing.

So how are feedback loops being used by Web apps and services to influence individual behaviors? Consider these examples:

Rypple helps individuals improve themselves professionally through peer feedback. Klout helps people realize the effect and reach of their tweets. Dopplr lets us track our travels (and our carbon footprint). iPhone apps like trackyourhappiness.org produce a happiness report

based on simple self-reporting. According to Hunch, I'm an optimist (based on answers to hundreds of microquestions). The dating site OKCupid offers users all kinds of personal reports, from which profile to use to observations on a person's personality.

*All the endless questions a person answers also produce "personality" reports on the type of person you are. So, even if you're not seeing anyone on the site you want to date, you keep coming back for more because you get to learn more about yourself and your tastes. Pretty ingenious if you ask me, and I've been through the gamut of almost every online dating site out there.*

*–A comment on OKCupid*

But what about business applications like e-mail, time-tracking, or business intelligence applications? Is there a place in this buttoned-up world for these same kinds of personal feedback loops?

## A LITTLE PERSPECTIVE

If we step back from software and Web apps, the idea of tracking performance is nothing new. I mentioned e-mail communications and driving. But feedback loops are everywhere. Baseball cards reveal every numeric detail of a player's performance. Schools grade students' performance. And many people routinely track their diets and workouts. Even in an agricultural society, having a good or bad harvest is the ultimate comment on how well a farmer did that season. The only difference now is that technology is making it easier to *passively* monitor personal details we couldn't monitor just a few decades ago.

Where games like Pac-Man rewarded us with fruits, more intricate games like Guitar Hero quantify our every action: percentage of correct notes, longest streak, breakdown of success by parts of a song—the list goes on! Through this report, you quickly learn—or confirm—which sections you need to work more on, and you can find out just how close you are to being a rock deity. But those are games, right?

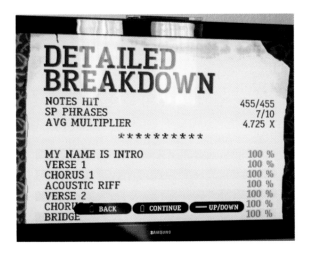

## SERIOUS GAMES
What we're really talking about is setting up systems whereby individuals can see in a tangible way, reflect on, and learn from their past behaviors. Think about what Mint has done for personal finances, or Nike+ for workouts.

From report cards to Pac-Man, we're talking about the same thing: *feedback loops that affect future performance.*

Through personal informatics or competitive scoreboards, when someone (or something) holds up a mirror to our behaviors, we gain information to help us improve in that area. I think it's something as simple as Twitter's follower count (and now list count) that has brought this "How am I doing?" concept top of mind for many people. I mentioned hypermiling earlier. And we're seeing new devices to help us monitor energy usage in the home. But why aren't these same kinds of feedback loops more common in everything from invoicing tools to e-mail apps? Why doesn't e-mail have a scoreboard? This may seem far-fetched, but we're talking about individuals and we respond to the same psychological nudges, whether we're working or playing.

## MAKING A GAME OUT OF E-MAIL
"Okay," you're saying, "interesting ideas but how do we apply these 'nudges' to a more serious subject?"

To test my hypothesis that "serious" applications can be turned into a game by adding feedback loops, let's walk through a process I might go through to transform e-mail. Starting with the stated goal of "in-box zero," let's design a system that might help us become better e-mail players. Let's create the Game of E-mail.

### 1. Identify specific behavior patterns to encourage or discourage
What behaviors do you want to change? Is there a behavior you want to see more often? Maybe it's a bad habit you'd like to eliminate? For some

applications, identifying this can be a challenge. Fortunately with our example, thousands of bloggers and self-help gurus have already identified both good and bad e-mail habits and translated these into helpful tips like these:

- Never open an e-mail twice.
- Read e-mails in the order they were received.
- Answer briefly.
- Respond in a timely manner.
- Only check e-mail twice a day (or once an hour).

We'll build on these tips for our little e-mail game.

## 2. Translate desired behavior patterns into data that can be passively tracked and measured

Once you've identified (and prioritized) specific behaviors to influence, let's see if these can translate into specific data that can be passively monitored by the system. Sometimes, translating an idea is straightforward: with something like "respond in a timely manner," we can start a timer from either the moment an e-mail is received or opened for the first time. Be careful though; depending on your context, even a simple translation like this may need to factor in things like business days or adjusting what "timely manner" means to various people.

The biggest challenge you'll find is with tracking *qualitative* behaviors. For example, if I wanted to know how clearly I'm communicating in my e-mails, that is much more difficult to measure compared to simply tracking

if or when I responded to a message. That said, tracking qualitative achievement is possible when we introduce a social layer, something I'll talk about below.

## 3. Attach points to these behaviors

Now that we've identified the behaviors we want to encourage, and determined how to track those behaviors, let's recognize them. We're going to award and deduct points for the behaviors listed above; points earned will form the basis of our scoring system.

Using "never open an e-mail twice" as an example, a good system would encourage you to:

- Read and delete.
- Read and respond.
- Read and file.
- Discard without reading.

So, we offer helpful text to remind people of these four options (think of this message as training wheels that eventually go away) and then we award points based on behavior:

- Plus 10 points for taking action when you open an e-mail.
- 0 points for opening an e-mail a second time.
- Minus 5 points for opening an e-mail a third time.

If we were to create a similar point scale for the other behaviors we identified, you end up with a total number of possible points and actual points earned. So, for a specific e-mail exchange, you might get something like the image shown on the next page.

**Meh. For this email, you only got 25 out of 40 possible points.**

### 4. Translate points into a periodic score and other useful information

While tracking performance per e-mail exchange is kind of interesting the first few times, the novelty wears off quickly. Think about ways you can introduce cycles into the system—an end-of-month report is a great idea to see how we're doing overall. By slicing the data in different ways, we could also learn what our average response time is to specific individuals. Or maybe we might learn what time of day (or night) is best to respond to e-mails. The possible types of reports are limited only by what you can imagine: just don't lose sight of what is interesting and worthwhile to people.

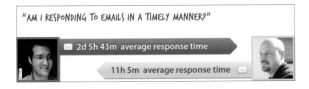
"AM I RESPONDING TO EMAILS IN A TIMELY MANNER?"
2d 5h 43m average response time
11h 5m average response time

### 5. Display the score in a fun way

Far too often, we have interesting data, but it's not displayed in a way that is compelling. In this discussion of numbers and data, it's easy to lose sight of the fact that we are emotional beings; there's a growing body of research exploring how our affect (emotion) governs everything from decision making to memory. Make the time to look at what you are revealing and determine if there is a more compelling or emotional way to present that information. Dopplr chose to represent each user's personal velocity (distance traveled in a year) not as a number, but as an animal that moves at approximately the same speed. What if a credit score was shown as a hot air balloon, or a measure of collaboration as a beehive? Get creative with how you represent the data—our brains will thank you for it with extra attention.

6.47 km/h is
Stephen's Personal Velocity
Which is about the same as a duck.

### 6. Create rules to translate data into helpful information

While cumulative scores and fun representations are somewhat useful, think about how you can turn specific activity patterns into helpful tips. This can be a tedious process of defining rules and correlating messages, but the resulting personalized tips can be quite helpful:

*Ouch! You only responded to 38 percent of your e-mails in a timely fashion. This may be due to your lengthy (average 17.4 sentences) replies. For next month, focus on shorter responses in a shorter timeframe.*

Where data and scores hint at a story of your performance, offering helpful text makes the story explicit—sometimes painfully so!

I've heard of one experiment by Byron Reeves and Clifford Nass that had a word processing program praise subjects for correctly spelling difficult words. The plug-in would passively monitor the unique words that you had trouble spelling correctly. When you correctly spelled a word that you had trouble with in the past, the tool would compliment you for doing so.

### 7. Set challenges

Competing with yourself is a very powerful motivator—if you provide something to compete against. This can be a best winning streak, a top score, the allure of the next level of mastery—the possibilities are endless. This is due to the idea of "status," discussed earlier.

A boring game is one that doesn't offer ever-increasing challenges. While mastery of e-mail may be a challenge for some, up the ante for those who are at 100 percent. Decrease the time allowed to respond to incoming e-mails or introduce new barriers, for instance, or say

you can no longer check e-mails as frequently as you did.

One interesting note here: while many games are built on a system that encourages you to "level up" as you increase experience (think karate belts and most video games), this assumes a beginner level. In business contexts I've found the analogy of a "credit score" to be more often the case; that is, you want to maintain the highest level possible, which you may or may not have been at when the "game" began.

### 8. Add social cues

While competing against your own best score is a powerful motivator, social cues are much more powerful: How do I compare to my peers? What's an "avalanche" for other people: 30 e-mails, or 500 e-mails? How does their situation compare to mine and are they any better?

Imagine disclosing your "e-mail ninja" score with others (and likewise). While there has been some heated debate about the use and abuse of leaderboards, we do like to know how we're performing relative to other friends who are also playing the game. In a somewhat quantified

CONGRATULATIONS! YOU'VE EARNED THE "EMAIL NINJA" BADGE.

way (or maybe something more playful, like Dopplr's personal velocity), you could discover those folks who, like you, seem to have their act together. Maybe a privilege of the game is earning the status to share a tip or two with others in your Game of E-mail network.

### 9. Have fun and make it interesting

This is a catch-all for the other fun things we've discussed throughout this book. Think about pleasant surprises, or ways to create scarcity. (For example, at seriosity.com Attent with Serios has introduced scarcity by creating a virtual economy where you earn and spend points to increase the importance of an outbound e-mail.) You could use curiosity to motivate people. What information could you tease people with? What about earning privileges, such as new features or customization opportunities that tap into our desire for self-expression. What about exchanging virtual gifts? What about injecting some humorous language?

## CLOSING

We could go on specifying the details of the Game of E-mail. But you get the idea. We're introducing feedback loops that tell you—in objective terms—how you're performing not just at periodic intervals, but along the way with tight feedback loops so you can adjust and change course.

The rules are up to us. The game can be personal or social. We can layer on tons of other game mechanics (challenges, levels, variable rewards, prizes, and what have you). But underneath it all, there's a system offering you reflection on your behaviors.

Could business applications benefit from this kind of thinking? Would these numbers change anything? It's a nudge in the right direction.

BACK AGAIN SO SOON?

IT'S ONLY BEEN

# 3 MINUTES

SINCE YOU LAST CHECKED YOUR EMAIL!

## (GO AWAY!!)

# WHAT ABOUT INCENTIVES AND LOYALTY PROGRAMS?

In a sense, the points and badges aspect of gamification bears more resemblance to loyalty programs than to games. And loyalty programs are, for the most part, fairly successful at encouraging repeat business. I tend to book flights with airlines that I've accumulated frequent flyer miles with, and the same goes for hotel purchases and credit cards. But when is this a bad thing?

In loyalty programs, the equation is fairly straightforward: spend this much, get this much. It's a *transaction*. Where these kinds of incentives break down is with more qualitative tasks.

I was designing a Web site for a client with a strong background in radio. They had been quite successful with their incentives programs for radio and assumed the same would apply to motivating user behaviors online. They proposed awarding points for things like commenting on a blog post or liking something.

This is dangerous territory and likely to yield less than stellar results. We know from various studies that what drives online behavior is not economic capital, but *social* capital.

The reasons people comment, share, like, and do all manner of social actions has to do with status, identity, reputation, and a host of other naturally occurring, intrinsic motivators. Things like open source software and Wikipedia exist because of people's intrinsic motivation. Mixing in external rewards and incentives is a surefire way to smother this passion or lead to unwanted results.

As you read earlier, "Rewards motivate people for more rewards." If every comment is suddenly worth a few extra loyalty points, you really don't care about the *content* of your comments anymore—you can start writing garbage and lots of it because you're focused on the points (especially if they're redeemable).

Yes, incentives work, but for very specific types of behavior. And they do shift the focus from the task to the reward being offered. For more on this, please see Daniel Pink's book *Drive*.

# CHAPTER 23

# What's the Prize?

LET'S TURN, FINALLY, to extrinsic motivators, the most obvious indicators that something is a game.

In the previous chapters, we focused on core, intrinsic motivations that are an innate part of human existence. I emphasized the importance of starting with *challenges* that lead to mastery. Games excel at breaking down these daunting challenges into manageable milestones, or small goals, that move us closer to realizing the larger goal we hope to accomplish. The game layer makes things fun and quantifiable in some way. I can show off my badges, point to a report card, or show you my collection. These are tangible signifiers of the choices I've made, the challenges I've conquered, and the feedback I've received. Just remember, these things are only *meaningful* if they represent some part of my identity, or the identity I'm trying to create for myself. Points and badges, collections, leaderboards—these things work when they reinforce something I'm aspiring to. When they are used to *create* interest where there is no intrinsic motivation, the effects will be short-lived.

With that out of the way, what are the external things we can use to encourage and recognize different behaviors? Let's begin with a few of the most obvious and common game mechanics:

## Points

These are the base currency of most games. Different activities will earn varying amounts of points. Points can be identified as points, or something similar like "coins" or "crystals." Points can lead to new levels or be spent to purchase items that may help you in the game. We talked briefly about calculating points in the previous chapter. Whether or not your "game" uses points, you will likely need to track something like points in order to make different calculations.

## Levels

Game play often advances through different levels of increasing difficulty. This allows players to quickly advance to a level that is appropriately challenging and then work their way up from there. Levels correlate with the appropriate challenges and the idea of "flow" (see p. 162).

### Scoreboards

Scoreboards will show you how you're doing on any number of criteria. Number of shots fired. Hit accuracy. Total distance travelled. Best streak. Whatever things you want to quantify and show back to the player. Outside of formal games, you might think of a report card as a kind of scoreboard.

### Leaderboards

Leaderboards show your ranking relative to other players. Leaderboards feed into our need to compete with others. This can be useful in the beginning, to grow a new service, but leaderboards can quickly demotivate the majority of players who have no hope of seeing their name ranked among the top players. Many sites eliminate or fragment leaderboards as they scale. For example, Foursquare has discussed creating dozens of different leaderboards based on things like regions, types of places checked into, and other facets.

### Achievements

Players will often acquire things in their journey. These things can be purely for recognition of something accomplished or may help

the player in their quest. Going new distances, reaching new speeds, or uncovering a stone may unlock an achievement. These achievements might be helpful like a temporary boost in strength or they may fit together to complete a puzzle.

### Badges

Badges are formal ways to recognize player accomplishments. Part of their appeal is the meaning they have within a social group. Badges and trophies of all kinds predate formal game design. Think of the Boy Scouts and merit badges or tribal villagers who adorn themselves with bones from a particularly challenging kill.

### Assignments

Assignments are structured ways to shape gameplay and provide players with immediate, short-term goals. Assignments can be anything from "deliver this message" (World of Warcraft) to "photograph your favorite pizza place" (Gowalla).

## WHY DO GAME MECHANICS WORK?

Most of these game mechanics are self-explanatory, and can be applied in a variety of fresh and interesting ways. What I find most interesting is why these things work in the first place. Why, from a human psychology perspective, do these mechanics motivate many of us?

Bunchball, a company that focused on bringing gameplay into real-world activities, created a rather nice matrix that identifies the psychological principles that these game mechanics tap into (see top of following page).

| | Reward | Status | Achievement | Self Expression | Competition | Altruism |
|---|---|---|---|---|---|---|
| Points | ● | ● | ● | | ● | |
| Levels | | ● | ● | | ● | |
| Challenges | ● | ● | ● | | ● | |
| Virtual Goods | ● | ● | | ● | ● | |
| Leaderboards | | ● | ● | | ● | |
| Gifting & Charity | | ● | ● | | ● | ● |

*This matrix from Bunchball shows how game mechanics relate to different principles from psychology.*

These mechanics are familiar if you've played any kind of game. Let's dive into some of the more interesting ideas you can borrow from the world of gaming. Or more accurately, let's look at some of the principles of psychology that are commonly used by game designers.

## PERFORMANCE GOALS

I started off by setting up a sharp divide between performance goals and learning challenges. For the purposes of this book, challenges are the core things you want to accomplish—the outcome of your activity. Performance goals are mini-challenges along the way to help you realize what you want to accomplish. So, "getting an A in French class" is a goal to help you rise to the challenge of "learning to speak French." It's not uncommon to motivate people with goals, but if you can tap into the learning challenge (that leads to mastery), then goals help you along the way.

What surprises me most is how underutilized goals are in common applications, though this is changing. No doubt inspired by things like LinkedIn's Profile Completeness bar, other companies have followed suit. The travel booking site Kayak uses this idea to encourage users to try out different features on their site.

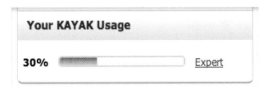

In Ribbon Hero, a gaming plug-in for Microsoft Office, players are challenged to learn features of Word, Excel, and other tools in the Office Suite (see p. 103). While points, balloons, and even competition with friends on Facebook are all bundled with these little challenges, I think there is power in simply challenging someone to do something or to do the same thing in a new way. Applying game mechanics to training programs seems like a natural fit.

***But what about the online tools we use or Web sites?***

Going back to our Game of E-mail example from Chapter 22, what if we were challenged to "respond to five starred e-mails within the hour" or "respond to all e-mails using less than five sentences." How might these goals help us get better at managing an overloaded inbox?

Old Navy and CoffeeCup created a performance goal when they challenged people to find Easter eggs hidden across their site.

Stanford University researcher BJ Fogg speaks quite a bit about behavior change. He has developed a remarkable framework for encouraging behavior change (see Chapter 25). He talks frequently about "baby steps," small goals that help you reach your big goal. If your ultimate goal is to get someone to floss their teeth daily, start with a small goal, say, flossing one tooth, tied to an existing behavior, such as brushing your teeth, that will remind them to do this one little thing.

## ARE YOU OFFERING YOUR USERS ANY PERFORMANCE GOALS?

We talk a lot about badges that people accumulate. Let's look at a closely related topic: set completion.

### Set completion and collecting

Remember the endowed progress effect discussed in Section 3, where a 20 percent head start on the car wash loyalty program encouraged participation? What happens when we fast-forward this kind of activity to the point

when you only need a few stamps to *complete* the card?

As anyone who has ever collected anything can attest, the closer we get to completing a set, the stronger the urge to do it. This is a principle known as *set completion*. With set completion, you have to look at two things: who (or what) defines a set, and the urge to complete that set.

Let's take baseball cards as a practical example. In the beginning, many people might set out to simply collect "baseball cards." At some point, however, you realize that collecting any and all baseball cards is an expensive proposition. So you begin to define a set. Maybe it's all cards for a particular team. Or maybe you refine your collection even more and decide to collect all baseball cards for a particular player. In this case, you have defined your set.

What constitutes a set will vary by individual, as this is often a personal choice, especially in cases where there isn't a formal collection. For example, I like to bring back snow globes from the places I've visited. A set in this case is defined by my travels. Or let's revisit my kids with their Hot Wheels. They may define a set as: blue cars, just trucks, or only Ferraris. There's no end to the Hot Wheels being manufactured,

but my kids have narrowed the range of options they're interested in.

What's interesting to note is how in the last several years toy manufacturers have begun defining sets for consumers. While there are many options to choose from, it's not uncommon to see products marketed as sets. In the case of the Cars vehicles, there are dozens of vehicles to choose from. But, you see things like a "racing set" or "lazy day set" actively promoted in the packaging and accompanying literature. Many other toy companies will actively promote "wave 1" or "series 4." While you may not be able to purchase every item from a vendor (oh my!), you can own all of those within a set. This leads to the *completion* part.

Below is a Simpsons toy that was part of a kid's meal (and ad campaign) at Burger King.

With the meal prizes, you typically get five or six unique items, one with each purchase of a kid's meal. The same is true here, except that the individual items fit together to form a complete whole. In my case, I was missing Bart Simpson. I use this example to emphasize how we feel when a set is incomplete: it'll drive you nuts! This toy is incomplete without Bart Simpson. And here's the interesting part: I didn't care nearly so much when I only owned the first or second character. But now that I have all *but* one, the urge to complete this set is quite strong. It's as if a voice if calling, "You're almost there—don't give up!"

This idea of set completion isn't exclusive to the collector's personality (though, most of us do collect things, even if we don't formally recognize them as such). Remember the studies that George Loewenstein did with curiosity in Chapter 11? According to the information gap theory, you could argue that completing enough of the whole to satisfy curiosity (fill in the gap) is a form of set completion. In fact, in one of the studies on curiosity, Loewenstein did something similar. He'd place subjects in front of a screen. On the screen was a 5x9 grid

*When the set in a collection is nearly complete, the desire to complete it is strongest.*

of blank tiles. Participants were told to click on the squares to familiarize themselves with the mouse (they weren't made aware this was a curiosity study.) For one group, clicking on a blank tile would flip to reveal an animal. Every square was a different picture. With the second group, each tile revealed a *part* of one big picture—the more tiles that were clicked, the more you could make out the animal being represented. As expected, the second group clicked on more squares, in an attempt to "reveal" the complete picture.

So how might this idea apply to an online interaction?

In the case of Gowalla, I mentioned the stickers they give out at variable intervals. What I didn't mentioned was the vault in which you collect these stickers (see below).

Notice that in addition to a count and a listing of all the stickers I've found, I'm also shown the ones I don't have yet. As with most collections, being aware of what I'm missing adds to my compulsion to collect. I do think Gowalla could benefit from defining smaller sets (right now, the only set is "all" stickers); new stickers are added all the time, creating a horse and carrot situation where completion seems always to be within reach but never attainable.

### Set completion and e-mail
Remember when I mentioned how I challenge workshop participants with this question: Did you have to *add* something to the application to make it fun, or did you find the fun already in the application? I often ask this question in the context of set completion. Many of

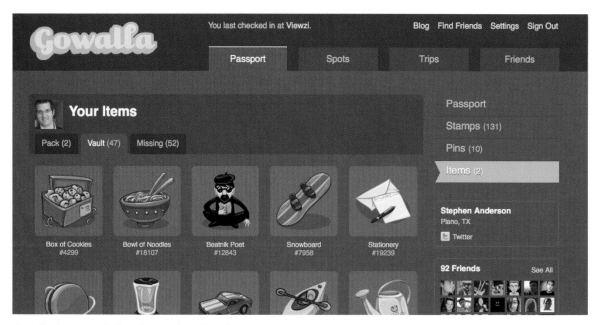

*Gowalla show you which stickers you've collected, and which ones you're missing.*

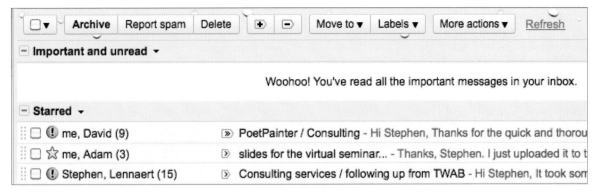

| ☐ ▾ | Archive | Report spam | Delete | ⊕ | ⊖ | Move to ▾ | Labels ▾ | More actions ▾ | Refresh |

**⊟ Important and unread ▾**

Woohoo! You've read all the important messages in your inbox.

**⊟ Starred ▾**

| ⋮ ☐ ❗ me, David (9) | ⊛ PoetPainter / Consulting - Hi Stephen, Thanks for the quick and thorou |
| ⋮ ☐ ☆ me, Adam (3) | ⊛ slides for the virtual seminar... - Thanks, Stephen. I just uploaded it to t |
| ⋮ ☐ ❗ Stephen, Lennaert (15) | ⊛ Consulting services / following up from TWAB - Hi Stephen, It took som |

*Set completion inside of Gmail's Priority Inbox.*

the ideas involve adding a puzzle or points to each e-mail. But, if we look at e-mail for some time, you can see e-mail is waiting for someone to spot and define the set. To many of us, e-mail feels like a game of Tetris, a never-ending stream of blocks coming our way. At least Tetris has levels! Where is the "set" in e-mail? One easy set might be all e-mails received in a 24-hour period. If you couldn't get to inbox zero, at least you could measure your progress in terms of days completed. Another set might be all work e-mails, or all e-mails related to a particular project. Yet another set might be the mailing lists we subscribe to but never read. I felt a bit of the satisfaction that comes from completing a set (or e-mails) when I switched to Gmail's Priority Inbox. Priority Inbox sorts your e-mail into three buckets: important and unread, starred, and read or unimportant (see the screen above). This simple addition of buckets helped me manage my e-mail overload much more effectively. But the biggest joy came from this simple message:

*"Woohoo! You've read all the important messages in your inbox."*

Ah. It is in these moments that I feel a sense of accomplishment. I have completed that set of important e-mails (at least until more arrive).

Set completion can show up in even more subtle ways. The following is an observation I made about Launchpad, the single sign-on page from 37signals. (Launchpad was created to address the problem of separate logins for each of the products from 37signals, as well as multiple accounts for one Web app. I have login credentials for about a dozen Basecamp accounts!) This is the initial login screen:

And this is the Launchpad page:

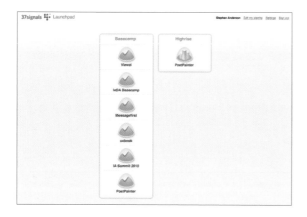

The thing that struck me was the rather odd layout with seemingly *empty* columns. My first thought was that a better layout might have filled this empty space and not forced me to scroll down for a single, long column of accounts. But, there's a clever bit of design going on here. We feel as if something is missing. And the clue is contained in the footer (see the screen at the bottom of this page):

It's only after you add another account that these columns fill in and seem more complete. Without calls to action ("Sign up for this product!"), the design decisions quietly suggest there is more that you are missing and you should complete your "set" of accounts.

## THE FUN LAYER:
## NARRATIVE, STORY, AESTHETICS

No talk of a "fun layer" would be complete without some mention of aesthetics. Aesthetics are a vital part of the emotional connection we feel with games. Without the graphics, story, and audio of a game like Call of Duty, it's really not much different from hundreds of other first-person shooter games. It is precisely this aesthetic layer that engages our senses and takes us into an imaginary world. Imagine the game of Monopoly without the suggestion of hotels, geographic locations, and utility companies. Reduce the game to its underlying math and you remove the magic.

Recognizing this power, Natron Baxter has created an interesting feedback loop that is customizable for just about any business. It's something they call "The Garden." Basically, it's a desktop plug-in (for Mac or PC) that brings some of the joy of gaming to your corporate environment. You're given charge of a virtual garden, complete with flowers, butterflies, and other things you'd expect to be associated with this theme. So how does the garden grow? By tracking your time. Writing on the corporate blog. Closing deals. Basically it can record any metric a business wants to hook up to "The Garden."

Your garden can also begin to wither if you aren't taking the actions you should.

In this sense, the designers behind this application are providing an emotionally engaging face on top of established (and probably lackluster) corporate metrics. In their own words: "Games that tell stories are better designed to elicit authentic curiosity and emotional investment (not just collecting obsession)."

---

**Also from 37signals:** Organize your business with **Backpack**® | Chat with your group with **Campfire**™

*"The Garden" from Natron-Baxter adds a fun way to interact with otherwise boring business metrics.*

## CLOSING

There's plenty more that could be included in this fun layer, but I've mentioned many of these things elsewhere in this book. Pattern recognition, curiosity, self-expression—while presented as *playful* behaviors, there are entire games built on these ideas. Take virtual gifts and pixel-based farms as an example. The games based on these mechanics succeed because they allow for self-expression: people are allowed to reveal their identities in front of their (online) social group.

I recommend that you look back at earlier concepts and think about how they could be applied not just as a way to get someone to *fall* in love, but as a reason to *stay* in love with your application. As with dating, there's always room for things that make us smile. There is always room for more delights.

This leads us to a final, sobering question. Is delight enough?

# CHAPTER 24

# Let's Get Serious

EVEN THE BEST GAMES eventually come to an end. I've dedicated most of this book to exploring the value of delight. I've tried to show example after example of how we can create more valuable and enjoyable services by delighting people. But "delight, unfortunately, doesn't last." That's coming from Raph Koster, and his 2004 book *A Theory of Fun for Game Design*.

This makes sense. All relationships eventually run into rocky terrain. Flowers and chocolates lose their luster. From a biological perspective, the things that used to send dopamine (the chemical that excites us) into our brains, cease to do so. This is why games present you with ever-increasing challenges, until—until what? The game ends. Even World of Warcraft, renowned for its addictive qualities, had to blow up their world and rebuild to create new goals for devoted players. Not that you can't sustain interest and delight people in new and different ways; think of how old married couples continue to surprise each other and bring smiles to each other's face. It's just that more of the same thing loses luster over time.

Developing a long-lasting relationship with your customers requires more than fun and games. You also have to offer something of value, functional or otherwise. This book has been about breaking the ice and keeping people

around long enough to see that value. But, the value has to be there.

I was reminded of this reality when I put forth this question to my peers:

*What are some Web apps/services you've used for more than three years? Why? What motivates you to stick with these services?*

The list of sites and services that came back was amazingly dull, consisting mostly of utilitarian services that do one thing very well. What was even more revealing were the reasons why people stuck with these services:

*It works and they continually update the application.*

*It does a decent job.*

*Very reliable and affordable.*

*Reliability and ease of use.*

*It's not complicated.*

*Management, customization, and layout options.*

*Does one particular thing well.*

*My friends use it.*

*Utility of the application.*

*There isn't another option.*

All things considered, this was a fairly uninspired list of reasons to stick with a service. Imagine if this is how we described the person we're in love with?

While you can't disagree with any of these reasons, I found myself asking, "Where is the love?" Where are the products that excite us even after three years of use? Going back to the dating analogy, I knew there had to be substance behind the romance. But why haven't we also seen delight in the products we use?

The truth is, we do see it in the products we use—the *physical* products. People love their Apple products. I know housewives and hackers alike who love their Roombas. Many of us have an emotional attachment to our cars. There is a sustained engagement created by these products. I just don't think we're quite there yet with the digital services we use. But we're close. To close out this section, I want to share a great framework from industrial design that we can apply to the design of Web apps and services. It is, in my opinion, the single best framework for balancing conversations about delight and excitement with more practical concerns.

## THE KANO MODEL

Invented by Dr. Noriaki Kano in 1984, the Kano model is a balanced way to consider those things that impact customer satisfaction. This model provides a structured way to discuss and evaluate three categories of customer needs common to product and service design:

- Basic needs
- Performance needs
- Exciters or delighters (attraction)

(There's a fourth category that isn't desired for obvious reasons: the indifferent attributes.)

To arrive at these categories, you draw a matrix (see the matrix, next page). Running from top to bottom, we have low to high satisfaction, with a middle zone of "neutral value." Running from left to right we have the product (or service) features that are either not (or poorly) implemented to fully implemented.

1. Drawing a curve from the bottom of the matrix to the middle right represents the *basic needs*. These are the things you must have to even be considered. At best, satisfying basic needs merely minimizes dissatisfaction. Absence of these things (or poor execution) leads to greater dissatisfaction. No one will notice if your product has these, but they will notice if they are missing or implemented poorly. Where most companies fail is in ignoring these basic features as new features are added. The result is systems that no longer satisfy basic needs. To use our dating analogy, this is the expectation that someone brushes their teeth before a date. We don't notice when they do; we do notice when they don't!

2. If you draw a line from the lower left corner to the upper right corner, you end up with the *performance payoffs*. This is the common focus of product development, whereby you increase satisfaction by investing in more features. These are the things customers are likely to ask for. These things will be stated in focus groups and customer surveys. In terms of a relationship, these might be the things you do

together or the requests of your partner, like learning how to cook a certain cuisine or losing a few pounds. There are of course limits to this focus, as we've seen in industries that have been shaken up by competitors that actually offered less—in terms of features—to their customers.

3. Finally, delight enters the picture. This is the wow factor. Drawing a curved line from the left edge to the top of the matrix represents the exciters or *delighters* (attraction). These are things that are not needed, and probably will never be asked for by a customer, but when you deliver them, they bring unexpected value. These are the flowers on a first date (assuming they weren't expected) or surprising the other person with tickets to see their favorite

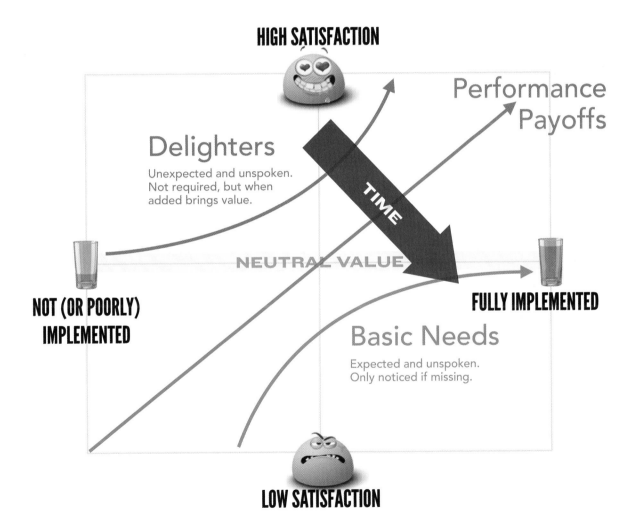

band. Understanding and spotting these "latent needs" comes through observation or genius intuition.

4. Over time, exciters become performance needs, and then basic needs. This explains why receiving a dozen roses isn't quite as exciting as it was the last time, or the time before that. If you bring home flowers every Tuesday, this will quickly become a basic expectation, no longer thrilling and missed only when you forget.

If you think about it, this is a perfect model for staying in love with a person or a product. In one simple model we see a rationale for delighters as well as basic value requirements.

### The Kano model and my love affair with Virgin America

If we look to the airline industry, you'll see the value of delight as well as basic and performance needs. As airlines have cut costs over the years, many have struggled to meet basic needs.

Peanuts are no longer offered. There is less legroom. Some airlines have persistent problems with cancelled flights. On the other hand, you have an airline like Virgin America that excels at delighting its passengers through sarcastic banter and their RED player system. When they provide service between two destinations, they are the clear choice—they are winning hearts and minds. I've flown on Virgin America on a few occasions, and I can say that I was seduced. But as their service is still limited (they only fly to and from a small number of destinations), they don't satisfy basic needs for most of my trips. However, as they expand into new areas, so long as pricing is competitive, I will choose them over other airlines.

Delight isn't enough on it's own—you also have to satisfy basic and (sometimes) performance needs. But, fail to also delight your customers and you leave yourself vulnerable to someone else who will make your customers swoon.

# CHAPTER 25

# Only the Beginning

BY THIS POINT, I suspect you have lots of ideas you can apply to your work. But how do you pull all of these ideas together? What do you prioritize?

The aim of this book has been to *inspire* lots of creative ideas—ideas based on human behavior—that you can apply to your Web sites and applications. I've tried to share examples in both the physical world and in online or mobile contexts, so that the focus is on these timeless patterns of behavior rather than on any particular example.

It would be easy to start throwing some of these ideas at your work to see what sticks. But this might not be the best approach, especially considering that some of these principles work best when used together.

As BJ Fogg advocates, you can think of these ideas as all the different ingredients in the kitchen: paprika, celery, chocolate chips, cheese, salt, brown sugar, tomatoes. You wouldn't grab all of these ingredients and throw them in a bowl. Neither should you grab a handful of these principles and throw them at your project. As in the kitchen, you need a recipe, a way to combine these ideas into something delightful. Unfortunately, there is no magic formula to create this recipe—that's for you to create. This means carefully considering each principle, testing (or tasting) which combinations work well together, and

getting feedback, if only on a concept. It's not unusual to come up with several different recipes, or ways of putting different ideas together.

That said, I do want to offer a couple ways that you can think about structuring these different principles.

## THE RIDER AND THE ELEPHANT

One metaphor introduced by psychologist Jonathan Haidt is that of the elephant and the rider. It's an apt way to think about the brain's *controlled processes* (the rider) and *automatic processes* (the elephant). Picture a rider sitting atop a six-ton elephant. He may know the right way and try to steer the elephant in that direction, but it's a challenging task, and one that's not always successful. Think of how you might make plans, for instance, to get up earlier and begin jogging in the morning, but when the alarm goes off, there's another part of you that

says you should stay in bed and start jogging tomorrow. This is the tension between the rider and the elephant. One part of you is doing the planning and thinking. The other part relies on gut feeling, emotions, and intuition.

In their book *Switch*, Chip and Dan Heath extended this metaphor into a framework for changing behaviors. Specifically, they present three areas to focus on in any change effort:

- Are you *speaking to the rider* by setting clear goals, expectations, and a path to get there? Are you learning from examples where people have been successful?
- Are you *motivating the elephant* through stories and other things that excite and inspire action?
- Are you *shaping the path* to nudge the elephant and rider along in the right direction? Are you making change easy by removing the friction that prevents people from taking action?

I've found this to be a useful metaphor not only for understanding inconsistencies in human behavior (why we desire to lose weight but then give in to the temptation of a chocolate chip cookie), but also as a way to evaluate the proposed combination of ideas. Much of what has been described in this book is about motivating the elephant or shaping the path. But it's important to remember to give the rider reasoned, clear instructions and a way forward. At a minimum, you should be assessing your application to see if it's operating on all three levels. Facts and data are needed, but to motivate you have to arouse people emotionally through stories, play, humor, and other means described in this book. Of course, motivating

people isn't enough—you have to shape the path so that people are nudged to take action.

This leads me into a model designed specifically for behavior change.

## THE BEHAVIOR GRID

Dr. BJ Fogg, Director of Stanford University's Behavior Design Lab, was the first to write about "Persuasive Technology." He devotes at least half of his time to industry projects and innovations, all of which focus on using technology to change behaviors in positive ways. In recent years, he's developed two, brilliant models to help us "think more clearly about behavior change," the Behavior Grid and the Behavior Model.

The first of these, the Fogg Behavior Grid, was created following one of the first persuasive technology conferences in 2006. According to Fogg, "I was frustrated that people were talking about behaviors as though they were all the same thing. Even within a same paper. They would talk about a cessation behavior in the same way they would talk about one time conversion. And I was like, 'No, those are so different.'" It was this imprecision in thinking around behaviors that led Fogg to create the Behavior Grid. Basically, the Behavior Grid identifies 15 different kinds of behaviors; each of which might require a different set of persuasive techniques. For example, "the methods for persuading people to buy a book online (BlueDot Behavior) are different than getting people to quit smoking forever (BlackPath Behavior)." Aside from giving us a structured way to discuss different kinds of behaviors, this model helps us to understand that "each one of these cells has its own psychology."

# FOGG BEHAVIOR GRID

| | GREEN behavior | BLUE behavior | PURPLE behavior | GRAY behavior | BLACK behavior |
|---|---|---|---|---|---|
| | Do **NEW** behavior, one that is unfamiliar | Do **FAMILIAR** behavior | **INCREASE** behavior intensity or duration | **DECREASE** behavior intensity or duration | **STOP** doing a behavior |
| **DOT behavior** is done **ONE-TIME** | **GreenDot** <br> Do **NEW** behavior one time <br><br> *Install solar panels on house* | **BlueDot** <br> Do **FAMILIAR** behavior one time <br><br> *Tell sister about eco-friendly soap* | **PurpleDot** <br> **INCREASE** behavior one time <br><br> *Plant more trees and native plants* | **GrayDot** <br> **DECREASE** behavior one time <br><br> *Buy fewer cases of bottled water today* | **BlackDot** <br> **STOP** doing a behavior one time <br><br> *Turn off space heater for tonight* |
| **SPAN behavior** has a **DURATION**, such as 40 days | **GreenSpan** <br> Do **NEW** behavior for a period of time <br><br> *Try carpooling to work for three weeks* | **BlueSpan** <br> Do **FAMILIAR** behavior for a period of time <br><br> *Bike to work for two months* | **PurpleSpan** <br> **INCREASE** behavior for a period of time <br><br> *Recycle more of household waste for one month* | **GraySpan** <br> **DECREASE** behavior for a period of time <br><br> *Take shorter showers this week* | **BlackSpan** <br> **STOP** a behavior for a period of time <br><br> *Don't water lawn during summer* |
| **PATH behavior** is done **FROM NOW ON**, a lasting change | **GreenPath** <br> Do **NEW** behavior from now on <br><br> *Start growing own vegetables* | **BluePath** <br> Do **FAMILIAR** behavior from now on <br><br> *Turn off lights when leaving room* | **PurplePath** <br> **INCREASE** behavior from now on <br><br> *Buy more local produce* | **GrayPath** <br> **DECREASE** behavior from now on <br><br> *Eat less meat from now on* | **BlackPath** <br> **STOP** a behavior from now on <br><br> *Never litter again* |

©BJ Fogg 2010, used with permission
www.behaviorgrid.org

# BJ FOGG ON THE BEHAVIOR MODEL

The Behavior Model is a way to describe what leads to a behavior. There are three elements that have to come together at the same moment. A person has to have some level of *motivation*. They have to have the *ability* to do the behavior. And then they have to be *triggered* to do the behavior. Those three things have to happen at the same time. If any element is missing then the behavior won't happen.

Motivation and ability are trade offs. Somebody could have low motivation. But, if the behavior is really easy for them to do, if they're triggered, they will do it. Conversely, in the other corner, if it's really hard to do, but they have high motivation, then when the trigger hits, they'll do it.

Of the three elements, motivation is the least important when it comes to behavior change, for most types of behavior change anyway. It's more important to trigger the behavior, and only last do you worry about the motivational piece. If there's a behavior that's not happening that you want to have, focus on triggers first. Make sure it's in their path, next focus on ability, and only last start figuring out how to boost the motivation.

## ON TRIGGERS

Of the model, triggers was the last thing that I really dove into. And it's the coolest of the three. But, they're all interesting.

There are two trigger examples that have been incredibly lucrative for companies. Facebook's e-mail to trigger you to go into Facebook has caused them to become a multi-billion dollar company. You've been tagged in a photo, so-and-so wants to be your friend, somebody commented on your post. In each e-mail, there's a link and a call to action. You can click on the link and it takes you into Facebook. Without those triggers, Facebook would not be the monopoly they are today.

Another trigger example that has made tons of money is sponsored ads that Google puts in your path when you search for something. If you're looking for Elton John tickets or backpacks, in your search results, often at the top and almost always toward the side you'll find what I call hot triggers. These are hot triggers because you take action immediately. You click and you're on your way. Essentially, what Google does is put hot triggers in your path. That was the early financial engine for Google, and it continues to be.

*continues on page 210*

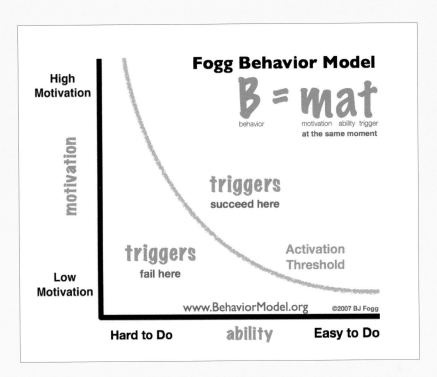

*The Behavior Model charts the user's ability to do the behavior on the horizontal axis by assigning a difficulty level to a behavior from hard (left) to easy (right). The user's motivation is charted on the vertical axis from low to high. The activation threshold is the line below which triggers will fail to cause the user to engage in the behavior.*

*continued from page 208*

But triggers don't have to be links on Web pages or email. It can be your spouse saying, "Will you take out the trash?" A request. It can be in the grocery store when somebody is offers you a sample of an apple. It can be your phone ringing. Triggers have existed for all of history. It's the call to action. It's the prompt, it's the queue.

The nine words I'm most proud of, and the nine words, that should probably be written on my tombstone are: *put hot triggers in the path of motivated people.* That is the secret sauce for causing behavior. These nine words bring together all three elements of my Behavior Model.

## MAPPING TECHNIQUES TO THE FOGG BEHAVIOR GRID

The wrong way to map techniques to the Behavior Grid is to say "here are six techniques or here are 52 techniques or 120, let's put them all into our product because then it will really work."

The metaphor I use is to think about cooking; the techniques are ingredients in the cabinet. The trick is knowing which techniques to use for which recipe. You don't just grab every single ingredient and dump it in the pot. That's going to be awful. You have to know the right ingredients or the right combinations. My contribution is more on the how to think clearly about behavior. Once you know what the target behavior is, you can begin to design for it. I'm really big on patterns. Patterns are like the recipe. So understanding what patterns lead to which types of behaviors, that's the core of my work—not the specific techniques.

## A SENSE OF PURPOSE

In writing this book, I did look at some of the literature on "seducing women" as well as Robert Greene's book *The Art of Seduction*. What struck me in these texts was a common, simple theme: *identity*. Seduction goes beyond any specific tactics or strategies. What many of these pickup artists help people do is develop a sense of identity and self-confidence. The way to pick up women? Start by figuring out who you are and what you stand for.

I think the implications for services and products is obvious: the products we love have a clear sense of purpose. We know what problems they're trying to solve or their approach to solving a problem. We also know what kinds of things they won't spend time on. Take for example 37signals' commitment to a minimalist, get real philosophy. It's evident in their posts, their culture, and their products. They know who they are. Or look at MailChimp. They figured out their personality and have worked hard to ensure that all customer interactions create a consistent impression of their company.

When you have an identity, you know who you *are* and who you *are not*. You know what you stand for. And by figuring this out, you have a story, which is the most powerful way to attract and retain people. People are looking for stories to identify with. Every planned action we take is filtered through our own internal narratives, about who we are and the kind of person we want to be. From this base follows the kinds of people and things we want to associate with. This is evident in everything from the products we buy to religious beliefs. Have you figured out your story?

I had planned a final chapter on stories and identity, but it turns out there's far too much to say in one chapter, especially when you look at the biology explaining how we form stories. I would challenge you with this question: Is there a clear story you can articulate about your service? And if I asked everyone on your team, would they tell me the same story? A hallmark of a great company is that everyone knows the reason for their company's existence.

## ONE THING EVERYONE IS DOING

I'd be negligent to end this book without mentioning one last factor that has had a remarkable influence on behavior. In fact, along with the stories we construct, it's one of the most powerful influences on human behavior.

I'll let you figure out what I'm referring to with this study:

*Your state decides to run an experiment to see what factors might get more people to comply with tax laws. Which of these four approaches do you think might be more effective?*

*The first group of people are sent a fear message, that states that their return will be closely reviewed and a face-to-face audit might be arranged.*

*The second group of people is part of a special group given a much simpler, one-page version of the standard tax filing form.*

*A third group is sent a letter making them aware of the all good things their tax dollars support—education, health care, public parks, and libraries, going so far as to state "when taxpayers do not pay what they owe, the entire community suffers."*

*A final group is told that "most taxpayers file their returns accurately and on time."*

So which approach would work best: a fear letter, an easier-to-use form, a "good for the community" letter, or a letter about social norms?

This experiment was actually run by the state of Minnesota in 1995 (and repeated again in 2007). In both cases, the only approach that had a significant influence on tax compliance was—drumroll, please—the letter that made people aware of social norms (the message saying that most people do pay all of their taxes).

As Richard Thaler and Cass Sunstein state in their book *Nudge*, "Either desirable or undesirable behavior can be increased, at least to some extent, by drawing public attention to what others are doing."

The effect of social norms has been tested in countless studies. One of my favorite studies used social norms to reduce energy usage. An energy company in California wanted to see if they could get people to reduce energy consumption (the behavioral goal). Nearly 300 households in a San Marcos neighborhood were informed about how much energy their household had used over the past several weeks; they were also told the average energy consumption for their neighborhood. As you might expect, those people using more energy than the neighborhood average reduced their energy consumption. However, those people who were under the neighborhood average actually relaxed a bit and began using more energy! Cautionary note here: If you're going to draw attention to the behavior of most people, be careful what you choose to highlight. If most people are turning in their TPS reports late, you might not want to make this public information.

Here's the more interesting part of this research: Half of the households, in addition to information about their energy consumption (and the neighborhood average), received a small emoticon based on their energy use. Customers who were over the neighborhood

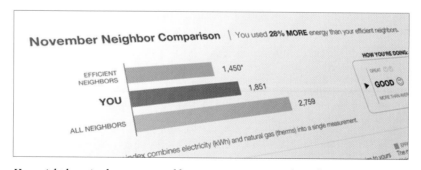

*How might knowing how your monthly energy usage compared to others in your neighborhood change your behaviors?*

average got a frowny face; those who were under the neighborhood average got a smiley face. Did this small addition make a difference? Those people who were using more energy than the neighborhood average reduced their energy usage even more when they saw the unhappy emoticon. And what of those people who were under the average? By adding a smiley face, they actually maintained the below average energy consumption. (Remember talking about achievements a few chapters ago? They're not limited to games.)

It's natural to make decisions based on what other people are doing. We are incredibly social creatures. If you've ever seen a crowd of people watching something in a mall, you probably felt compelled to see what all the commotion was about.

Online, if we're choosing between a presentation that's been viewed 20 times and another that's been viewed 20,000 times, most people will choose the one everyone else seems to be watching. If you look at a service like Digg, it is built entirely on this idea of social proof—the power of groups surfaces the best (or at least most interesting) items on the Web.

But this idea of *social proof*—that in new or unfamiliar situations we follow people we perceive as being similar to ourselves—shows up in other, more subtle ways. Consider testimonials that sing the praises of some site or service. The reason these work is they signal that other people have tried this out and found it to be worthwhile. It's tapping into a drive for safety. If the group is doing it, there's some measure of safety.

If you understand why testimonials work, that they leverage social proof, you can come up with more creative ways to show that lots of people support this idea. One of my favorite examples comes from the fixoutlook.org campaign. Rather than handpick a few testimonials, the entire background for this page is a wall of avatars—everyone who is tweeting about this campaign. The background refreshes every few seconds, so you're literally seeing all of these faces and people who are (presumably) in support of this cause.

In the context of our seduction analogy, I treat the social element as another influencing agent. By including a follower count or allowing people to share things, you add an element of social influence, just like you might use feedback loops or scarcity to encourage a certain behavior. Of course, social interactions are too complex to treat simply as another influencing factor. Fortunately, there are some excellent books devoted to the topic of social design on the Web. One is Christian Crumlish's and Erin Malone's *Designing Social Interfaces*; another is Randy Farmer and Bryce Glass's *Building Web Reputation Systems*. Both of these books are excellent resources for understanding online social systems.

## "SHOW ME THE MONEY!"

After reading my book, it's natural to wonder about the statistics: Will these changes actually make a difference? I've tried to provide actual or anecdotal data wherever possible, but the truth is, I'd be foolish to say, "Yes, this will work for you because it worked over here." Every project is different, serves a different audience, involves a different set of constraints, and has a host of other variables that make predicting success difficult. If there were a simple formula, we'd see many more successful start-ups!

What I can recommend is testing, and lots of it. A/B testing. Multivariate testing. Poring over your analytics. I shared two examples from Facebook, one where showing photos reduced deactivation, and the other where adding a tooltip increased multiple photo uploads. Both of these were design decisions that were data informed. Note that decisions *driven* by data are different from decisions *informed* by data. Data paints only half of the picture: what people are doing. You still need a qualitative picture to understand why people do things. Get both perspectives and you're well positioned to experiment and try new things.

So will any of these ideas work for you? Try some out, and then let me know. While it's fun to gather all these observations and ideas, you'll also want to test them, to prove they're not just crazy ideas. Coming up with new ideas is fun, but ultimately hollow if you never get a chance to try them out in a real project.

What I love about working with start-ups is that you get to try completely new ideas. In many cases, you're starting with a blank slate and you're encouraged to experiment. What I

love about working with larger organizations is that you get to test these ideas. Given the scale at which these large companies operate, it's very easy to make a small change and then observe the results. Many of my opinions have been challenged and refined by this data.

So, try these things out. Set up good test cases. Then share the results.

My friend Joshua Porter wrote *Designing for the Social Web*, an excellent book about psychology and design, before veering into the world of testing and analytics. This progression makes natural sense: our curiosity about human behavior inevitably leads us to another curiosity. We want to validate new ideas or even minor changes. Which of these ideas are working and how effective are they? Joshua's new company, Performable, was created to make Web analytics accessible to marketers who need a complete view of the customer life cycle. Performable's company blog has also done a great service to the user experience community by sharing the results of different A/B tests.

## WHO'S ON YOUR SITE?

In addition to an interest in analytics, the subject of human behavior has led me to an understanding of different personalities and what motivates each type. While we speak of motivation tactics that seem to work in most cases, it's more accurate to say that different people are motivated by different things. It would be nice to follow up these ideas with a classification of different personalities and what motivates each in an online context. In psychology, we've had several frameworks for understanding

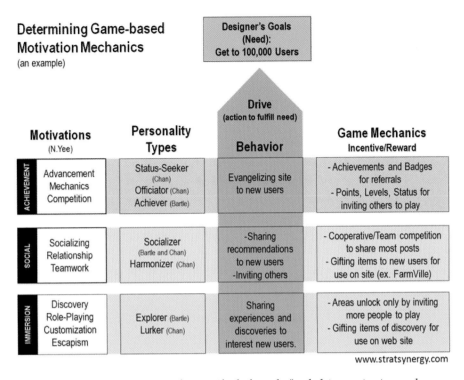

## Determining Game-based Motivation Mechanics
(an example)

| | Motivations (N.Yee) | Personality Types | Behavior | Game Mechanics Incentive/Reward |
|---|---|---|---|---|
| ACHIEVEMENT | Advancement Mechanics Competition | Status-Seeker (Chan) Officiator (Chan) Achiever (Bartle) | Evangelizing site to new users | - Achievements and Badges for referrals<br>- Points, Levels, Status for inviting others to play |
| SOCIAL | Socializing Relationship Teamwork | Socializer (Bartle and Chan) Harmonizer (Chan) | -Sharing recommendations to new users<br>-Inviting others | - Cooperative/Team competition to share most posts<br>- Gifting items to new users for use on site (ex. FarmVille) |
| IMMERSION | Discovery Role-Playing Customization Escapism | Explorer (Bartle) Lurker (Chan) | Sharing experiences and discoveries to interest new users. | - Areas unlock only by inviting more people to play<br>- Gifting items of discovery for use on web site |

Designer's Goals (Need): Get to 100,000 Users

**Drive** (action to fulfill need)

www.stratsynergy.com

*This model by Sharleen Sy is a useful way to think about the "underlying motivations and personality types that make up a gaming community."*

personalities, one of the most popular being the Myers-Briggs Type Indicator personality inventory. But have we arrived at anything resembling this in the design field? Recognizing that people can be attracted to the same game for completely different reasons, a few people have already started developing "player personality types" to design for. See if you fit into one of these three personalities (see the chart above).

While personas are a part of the designer's arsenal, I've wondered if there's a set of universal user archetypes we could arrive at based on need for control, tolerance for ambiguity, tolerance for visual complexity, and other factors. This is a topic I've marked for future exploration.

## FINAL THOUGHTS

Seduction isn't about deception or well-crafted manipulation—it's about giving someone more of what they already want, desire, or need, even when they don't know it yet. Seduction is about building a bridge between two lovers who might otherwise never have known each other. This can be used for nefarious purposes, for instance, leading the user to buy something they don't need, or used instead for the mutual benefit of all involved, as with most of the examples I've tried to share here. But, if you don't have a good value to begin with, fix that before you talk about seducing someone. You're seducing someone as a way to reveal who you are and what you are about—and letting that person know along the way why they should care. If that person will never care, or if the goal of seduction is deception, stop now. Seduction is about people, and the goal should be ongoing love and devotion, not a home run. We don't want regret or remorse, but delight.

My goal in writing this book was to inspire you with lots of interaction design ideas that are relatively new territory for our profession. I also wanted to offer an explanation as to why these ideas have been or might be effective. Like any technical book, the actual examples will soon be outdated (or imitated), but the reasons these ideas worked in the first place won't change. And that's what this book is really about: the psychology behind these ideas—timeless insights into human behavior. If we can start with an understanding of what kinds of things excite and attract us, keep us engaged, and win our hearts and minds, I believe we can create many more delightful, seductive experiences.

I'm looking forward to more experiences that engage me in a meaningful and emotional way.

# Index

3D depth effect, 22
37signals, 110, 117, 195–196
50 Cent music video, 87
750words.com, 150

## A

ability, 208
access limits, 144, 175–176
account creation, 97–99
achievements, 3, 190
action vs. inaction, 119
Adams, Ernest, 178
Adamson, Robert, 17
Adaptive Path, 69
aesthetics, 16
    associations and, 35–39
    attractiveness vs., 43–47
    books on design and, 24
    cognition and, 19–24
    context related to, 45
    dos and don'ts about, 51
    emotions/feelings and, 25–32
    faces or avatars and, 49–50
    "fun layer" related to, 196
    importance of considering, 18,
      34
    MAYA theory of beauty and, 47
    modes of beauty and, 46–47
    perceived usability and, 30–31
    subjective nature of, 45–46
    utility related to, 44
affect
    aesthetics and, 25–32
    positive vs. negative, 60–61
    success influenced by, 18, 60–61
    See also emotions/feelings
airline industry, 202
analytics, 214

anchoring, 133–134
animation, 118
anxiety, 61, 86
Apple products, 36–37
"apply yourself" attitude, 156
appointment dynamic, 174
Ariely, Dan, 72, 114, 128, 130, 133
Art of Game Design: A Book of Lenses,
    The (Schell), 178
Art of Seduction, The (Greene), 211
assignments in games, 190
associations
    aesthetics and, 35–39
    language and, 38–39
    positive and negative, 38
ATM studies, 30–31
attracting attention, 115–118
attractiveness
    aesthetics vs., 43–47
    perceived usability and, 30–31
    subjective nature of, 45–47
authorities, 144
automatic processes, 205
avatars, 49–50, 88

## B

baby steps, 192
Back of the Napkin, The (Roam), 51
badges, 190
bait-and-switch technique, 130
banking information, 112
Barthes, Roland, 37
Basecamp, 117–118
basic needs, 200
beauty
    subjective nature of, 45–47
    three modes of, 46–47
    utility related to, 44
    See also aesthetics

behavior
    playful, 53, 197
    shaping, 102–103
    triggering, 208–210
Behavior Grid, 206–207, 210
Behavior Model, 208–210
behavioral economics, 114
behavioral goals, 143–144
Berlyne, D. E., 84, 85
biases
    decision making based on, 114
    ownership bias, 126, 128, 130
    status-quo bias, 119, 126
Biddulph, Matt, 77
black belt example, 2–3
Blinksale homepage, 115
blog posts, 172
book resources
    on game design, 178
    on visual design, 24
Bouba-Kiki Effect, 38–39
bounded rationality, 114
Bowles, Cennydd,, 46
brain function, 61, 64
Brave, Scott, 61
breadth-first states, 61
Brehm, Jack, 173
Brighter Planet, 127
"Bringing the Browser to Life!"
    exercise, 138–139
BubbleTimer application, 160
bug trackers, 23
Building Web Reputation Systems
    (Farmer & Glass), 213
Bunchball, 190–191
business goals, 143–144
BuySellAds.com, 126

# WATCH
# READ
# CREATE

Unlimited online access to all Peachpit, Adobe Press, Apple Training and New Riders videos and books, as well as content from other leading publishers including: O'Reilly Media, Focal Press, Sams, Que, Total Training, John Wiley & Sons, Course Technology PTR, Class on Demand, VTC and more.

No time commitment or contract required!
Sign up for one month or a year.
All for $19.99 a month

## SIGN UP TODAY
**peachpit.com/creativeedge**

creative
edge